The
Ultimate
ADHD
Parenting
Handbook

The Ultimate ADHD Parenting Handbook

Empowering Your Family to Thrive

Vivian Dunstan

WILEY

First published 2026 by John Wiley & Sons Australia, Ltd

ISBN: 978-1-394-34622-6

A catalogue record for this book is available from the National Library of Australia

Registered Office
John Wiley & Sons Australia, Ltd. Level 4, 600 Bourke Street, Melbourne, VIC 3000, Australia

For details of our global editorial offices, customer services, and more information about Wiley products visit us at www.wiley.com.

Wiley also publishes its books in a variety of electronic formats and by print-on-demand. Some content that appears in standard print versions of this book may not be available in other formats.

Cover design by Wiley
Cover Images: © thawats/Getty Images, © LPETTET/Getty Images
Author photo: © Alicia Dunstan Photography, www.aliciadunstanphotography.com.au
Figure 11.1: Ladder image: © jambronk/Adobe Stock
Set in 10/14 pts and Palatino LT Std by Straive, Chennai, India.
Printed and bound by CPI Group (UK) Ltd, Croydon, CR0 4YY
C9781394346226_090126
The manufacturer's authorized representative according to the EU General Product Safety Regulation is Wiley-VCH GmbH, Boschstr. 12, 69469 Weinheim, Germany, e-mail: Product_Safety@wiley.com.

To the many parents I've had the privilege of walking alongside over the years—your stories, struggles and triumphs have enriched my understanding in ways no training ever could, and you too are part of these pages.

And, to you, the reader: May the weaving of my lived experience and professional knowledge bring you clarity, comfort and hope as you navigate your own journey of raising your child with ADHD.

Contents

About the author

Vivian Dunstan is recognised as one of Australia's leading voices in ADHD parenting. She brings together lived experience, professional expertise and many years of dedicated community leadership to her work with ADHD families. Originally from the UK and now based in NSW, Australia, Vivian is both a parent to a neurodivergent young adult and someone with her own lived experience of ADHD. Her journey inspired her to create the resources and support she wished had existed when she first began navigating ADHD parenting, which is why she writes from one parent to another, offering both empathy and practical insight.

Vivian is the founder of ADHD Support Australia (adhdsupportaustralia .com.au), which began in 2013 as a small local support group and has since grown into one of the country's leading hubs for ADHD knowledge and community. Through nearly 200 expert talks, the organisation has provided education, advocacy and support to thousands of families nationwide.

Alongside her lived experience, Vivian holds a Master of Teaching (Primary) and is an ADDCA-trained ADHD coach. She is also a certified PEERS® Certified Provider and NeuroACT program facilitator, enabling her to deliver internationally recognised, evidence-based programs for teens, young adults and parents. In addition, she has created two flagship offerings: the Parenting Children with ADHD Program, which has supported countless parents with practical, research-backed strategies, and, as a digital health and wellness educator, she created the Digital Parenting Program, designed specifically to help families manage screen time in a balanced, healthy way.

Her expertise and leadership have been recognised across multiple platforms. She has appeared on Channel 7's *Sunrise*, ABC Radio, and in both local and national press; been featured on leading ADHD podcasts, including Dr Hallowell's *Wonderful World of Different*; and spoken at international parenting summits such as Parenting Your ADHD Kid: Create a Calmer Home Environment with Strategies and Confidence to Raise Happy and Healthy Kids.

Vivian's work reflects a rare blend of lived experience and professional expertise, equipping families with tools, strategies and hope to help their children thrive. Above all, she understands the realities of ADHD parenting firsthand and is passionate about helping families feel supported, hopeful and less alone.

Introduction

Welcome to your ADHD parenting journey.

If you're parenting a neurodivergent child or children, or one who has yet to be diagnosed, you'll already know your parenting journey is maybe not what you expected. It's full of joyful moments one minute and challenging and frustrating moments the next. Your journey is a rollercoaster!

You're reading this book, so I'm guessing you're looking to find a better way to upskill, and to gain greater understanding, guidance, reassurance and support with your parenting. Raising a child with ADHD can be a whirlwind and can feel chaotic at times. You wonder, 'Is it me or is it them?' or 'What am I doing wrong?' Whatever your reason for reading this book, you're exactly where you need to be—and you're not alone! This book has been lovingly written by me to support you, your child and your entire family by providing you with the understanding and practical strategies you need to navigate family life with a neurodivergent child.

I initially founded ADHD Support Australia after my daughter received an ADHD diagnosis to find support for both her and our family. This evolved into me wanting to share what I'd learned along the way with others so they could navigate their ADHD parenting journey with more ease. I've been privileged to have supported thousands of families since then, providing the knowledge and strategies they needed to thrive. Since 2013, I've featured world-renowned ADHD experts at monthly talks, facilitated the Parenting Children with ADHD Program, Digital Parenting Program, PEERS® Certified Provider supporting teens and young adults to build social skills and NeuroACT program, provided ADHD coaching and more! All of these experiences, combined with my own personal journey as a woman with ADHD and the mother of a child, teen and now young adult with ADHD and autism, has deeply informed the strategies and perspectives you're about to read in these pages.

My life and professional experiences have culminated in this book and I'm so grateful to share my insights, practical advice and tools I've learned so you can navigate *your* family life with greater ease and grace. Parenting is hard, but with additional challenges, such as ADHD, to grapple with, it can at times seem overwhelming.

No child comes with a manual, and each and every child is unique. As Gabor Maté says, 'No two children have the same environment and the same parents', meaning your experiences, circumstances and environment are different with each of your children.

When we're in the midst of parenting, life can be chaotic, and while we all need to learn from our mistakes in life, sometimes it's preferable to learn from the mistakes of others — especially when it comes to raising our children — because, although we can definitely change course, it's just easier to start on the right path. Learning from someone who has walked a similar path to you, albeit not the same path, will provide you with valuable insights that can save you from making common parenting mistakes.

By reading these pages, you'll be learning from my mistakes (yes, we all make them!) and discovering the strategies I've learned through my lived experience and research. You'll realise how vital it is to understand as much as possible about ADHD and what that means for your child, you and your family. That greater understanding will flow towards a more nurturing home environment where you're able to show greater compassion to your child. You'll be able to manage their challenges with more empathy and patience. You'll find yourself moving towards a more strengths-based approach with your child, recognising your child's unique strengths, celebrating their progress in terms of effort rather than results, and allowing them to establish a growth mindset, where any failures are seen as opportunities for growth.

Remember, ADHD parenting, or any parenting, is about so much more than just managing behaviours and seeking compliance — it's about fostering understanding and collaborating with your child. We ultimately, want our children to build self-esteem, resilience, independence, good social skills, emotional balance and happiness.

You've already taken a significant step in the right direction, and I'm so honoured you've chosen my book to help you transform your parenting journey.

Let's get started together.

About this book

I've written this book so you have a practical and compassionate guide for your ADHD parenting journey. It's divided into five parts, each consisting of clear, easy-to-navigate sections focused on essential aspects of parenting a child with ADHD.

Part I helps you become an expert in your child. It is designed to help you develop an understanding of ADHD; its impacts on your child's brain, emotions and behaviour; and guide you in identifying their strengths and challenges. It also outlines factors that can shape your child's experience of ADHD as a structure for subsequent parts of the book.

Part II provides practical advice on how to work towards a strengths-based, collaborative relationship with your child. It describes your role as a calm, connected, compassionate parent and the importance of prioritising your own self-care to create a balanced environment for your whole family.

Part III explores strategies to establish strong foundations for success for your child by addressing the many factors that shape their experience and impact their ability to navigate life's joys and challenges. It takes a holistic view of physiological and environmental factors — from nutrition and sleep to self-esteem and mindfulness — that can complement traditional approaches.

Part IV applies these principles and approaches to common situations you and your child will navigate, such as school, relationships, the online world and life transitions. Find out how to advocate effectively for your child, build crucial skills and create collaborative relationships with the people in your child's life, including with healthcare professionals.

Part V looks at the bigger picture and considers your ADHD child in the context of the whole family and the broader community. It takes a village, after all! Here, you'll find tips to ensure the sustainability of the changes you make and approaches you take by working together with your child and their broader support network.

How to use this book

Start where it feels right. I know every minute of your time is valuable, so you'll find each chapter can be read on its own. While Part I has important foundational information, the rest of the book is designed to enable you to delve into the section that feels most relevant to your needs right now. Each section has clear summaries, helpful checklists and quick-action steps so you can absorb and implement key information quickly.

Take your time. This is not a checklist exercise nor a race. Take your time with each chapter to think deeply about how to apply these strategies to your family's unique situation or whether there are areas you want to explore further. Begin with one or two strategies, evaluate what works best and gradually add more as your family adapts and grows.

Reflect. Throughout this book, you'll find some reflection prompts to encourage you to journal your thoughts, ideas and goals to engage actively with the principles in the book as well as to track your family's progress. I encourage you to keep a parenting journal where you can jot down your thoughts, insights and observations as you go.

Dive deeper. While I've titled this book 'the ultimate handbook', it's more like 'the ultimate starting point'. ADHD and everything that goes along with it is a fascinatingly complex maze of ideas, emerging science and different approaches you can take. I encourage you to seek out further reading on the topics that interest you or feel most relevant to your child, both through your own research and through our online resource library available at adhdsupportaustralia.com.au. ⊕

⊕ Look for this symbol throughout the book for online resources to help you on your journey.

Revisit as needed. Life isn't linear and neurodiversity definitely isn't! Your child and your parenting will evolve over time. Return to chapters and tools whenever you face new challenges or need reminders of strategies that have worked well for you.

Above all, this book is here to empower you. Yes, the journey of raising a child with ADHD comes with its share of challenges, but it also offers endless opportunities for growth, connection and celebration. Remember, the key is consistency, patience and recognising each small success along the way.

You've got this and I'm here to support you every step of the journey. Take a deep breath, turn the page and know you're exactly where you need to be.

A note on language and neuro-affirming practice

In writing this book, I've done my very best to use language that is respectful, inclusive and affirming of all neurodivergent individuals, including those with ADHD, Autism and related differences. I understand the neurodivergent community holds a variety of perspectives on identity-first vs person-first language. I've tried to honour these preferences while remaining consistent and accessible. I've chosen terms that reflect a strengths-based, compassionate and non-pathologising approach whenever possible. I've used the term 'parent' to encompass biological and adoptive parents as well as those who have a primary or shared responsibility in raising a child.

However, our language and understanding are always evolving, and despite my best efforts, I may not have always got it right. If there is any phrasing that does not feel neuro-affirming, ableist or is not in alignment with your lived experience, please understand this was never my intention. I welcome your feedback and view this book as part of a broader, ongoing conversation about how we support, celebrate and empower neurodivergent children and their families.

Thank you for reading with compassion and curiosity.

Part I

Understanding your child with ADHD

Before you can effectively support your child, you need to truly understand them. Part I of this book lays the foundation by exploring your child's unique brain, behaviours and needs through curiosity and compassion—not deficit. We'll begin by uncovering your child's strengths and the potential often lying beneath their challenges. You'll learn how the ADHD brain works and examine co-occurring conditions, lookalike diagnoses and everyday influences like sleep and stress. My Parenting Hierarchy of Needs, inspired by Maslow's Hierarchy of Needs, will help you prioritise your support. With a deeper understanding of what drives your child's behaviour and what they need to thrive, you can respond with clarity, purpose and connection.

Chapter One

Finding the spark: Understanding your child's strengths

> Every child holds a spark of brilliance — our role isn't to fix what's missing, but to fan the flames of what's already there.

Research and anecdotal evidence suggests Attention Deficit Hyperactivity Disorder (ADHD) is not a 'disorder' and can be a strength. Dr Ned Hallowell reframes ADHD as VAST — *Variable Attention Stimulus Trait* — to highlight that ADHD is not a deficit of attention but a unique way of experiencing an overwhelming flood of stimuli.

Traits often viewed as problematic in structured environments such as school or traditional workplaces, for example, risk-taking, hyperfocus and impulsivity, can play a valuable role in the right setting, especially in creative, entrepreneurial and leadership roles. Many people with ADHD bring energy, creativity and the drive to challenge the status quo.[1]

High-profile entrepreneurs such as Richard Branson (founder/CEO, Virgin Group) and David Neeleman (founder, JetBlue Airways) have openly discussed their ADHD, crediting it with helping them think creatively, take risks and bounce back from failure. Studies report that people with

3

ADHD traits are more likely to start their own business, and the ability to think differently and tolerate uncertainty can provide business leaders and entrepreneurs with a competitive edge.[2]

Many inspiring figures have spoken publicly about having ADHD and how not only does it not limit success but it can be a part of it. When talking to your child about ADHD, let them know people can and do succeed when they have ADHD, and give examples of those sharing their talent or interest to inspire them! Some inspiring role models include:

> Simone Biles, Olympic gold medallist: Simone Biles has discussed her ADHD and how she manages it, especially in high-pressure environments. As the most decorated gymnast in history, her focus and determination has led to extraordinary achievements.

> Michael Phelps, Olympic gold medallist: Michael Phelps has shared how when his ADHD impacted his school experience, he channelled his energy into swimming, becoming the most decorated Olympian in history with 28 medals.

> Michael Jordan, former NBA basketballer: Michael Jordan is considered the greatest basketball player of all time and someone who has made basketball what it is today. Diagnosed with ADHD as a child, he struggled to focus in the classroom, but on the basketball court he learned to channel his energy and focus to his advantage.

> Will.i.am, musician and producer: Will.i.am says his ADHD helps him think outside the box, helping his creativity and focus. He sees ADHD as his 'passion point', something that helps him find inventive solutions, saying one thing about ADHD is '…it's hard to keep your attention and you can't sit still and you're always moving and thinking about a whole bunch of things. But those traits work well for me in studios and in meetings about creative ideas.'[3]

> Jamie Oliver, celebrity chef: Jamie Oliver left school with no qualifications, but after studying at Catering College, he nurtured his passion for healthy cooking. Diagnosed with ADHD and dyslexia as a child, he now advocates for a healthy diet to help ease ADHD symptoms.

This isn't about calling ADHD a superpower, it's about seeing your whole child and helping them harness their traits in ways that empower rather than limit them. Seeing what is possible for people with ADHD can help children feel empowered to build on their strengths and pursue their dreams. It's important to remember that ADHD—despite the challenges it can bring—does not have to be a roadblock. It can be a different path to success, especially when your child is given the right understanding, encouragement and support to work *with* their brain, not against it.

What is neurodiversity?

Neurodiversity celebrates and supports unique ways of thinking, learning and being that are shaped by neurological differences. It recognises that the different ways people experience, process and interact with the world are something to be valued and included, not disorders needing to be 'fixed'.

Neurodiversity simply means that all our brains work in different ways. Just like we celebrate diversity in culture, personality or appearance, neurodiversity reminds us that differences in how people think, learn, feel and process the world are a natural part of being human. Conditions like ADHD, autism or dyslexia aren't flaws to be 'fixed', but unique ways of experiencing and interacting with life. Embracing neurodiversity helps us see the strengths and gifts that come with these differences, while also recognising the challenges. It encourages us to create environments where every kind of mind can flourish.

In the past, neurodivergent individuals were often encouraged to conform to neurotypical standards in environments not designed for their unique ways of thinking and learning. Their differences were described as a long list of difficulties to 'overcome' rather than strengths to be understood and supported. For many people with ADHD, this constant mismatch can take a toll on self-esteem in the early years, which, in turn, can affect confidence, opportunities and, ultimately, their chances of success later in life.

ADHD is a matter of brain wiring. If a neurotypical brain is like an automatic car with motion sensors helping it slow down when needed, an ADHD brain might be a manual with a supercharged engine. Sometimes you struggle to slow down or switch gears at the right time, which can make it harder to follow the road rules and get where you're going safely.

You might feel like your child isn't listening, can't sit still or constantly jumps from one thing to another and mistake these things for laziness, defiance or bad behaviour. But look under the hood and you'll find a different story: the right type of oil and some tender love and care can help your child tap into that roaring enthusiasm for the things they're passionate about.

Grounded in the broader neurodiversity movement, this book advocates for a neuro-affirming parenting approach: the idea that when you understand the neuroscience of ADHD, you're better able to parent with greater empathy, clarity and connection. When you understand your child's brain, you move away from punitive, outdated models of parenting that overlook the neurological drivers of ADHD affecting self-regulation, working memory, time awareness and emotional control.[4]

Understanding ADHD as differences in how the brain handles focus, motivation and self-regulation can help your child figure out how to harness their supercharged engine in the right ways. With effective support, strategies and understanding, your child can thrive, drawing on creativity, energy and unique problem-solving abilities to succeed in their own way.

Do these common myths and misconceptions about ADHD sound familiar? Table 1.1 gives a reality check based on neuroscience.

Table 1.1 *ADHD — Myths vs facts*

Myth	Reality
ADHD is just about being hyper or distracted.	ADHD affects executive function, emotional regulation and impulse control.
ADHD only affects children.	ADHD persists into adulthood, though symptoms may change over time.
People with ADHD are lazy or unmotivated.	ADHD brains process motivation and focus differently, often thriving in areas of strong interest.
ADHD is caused by bad parenting.	ADHD is a brain-based condition with genetic and neurological factors.

The importance of a strengths-based approach

Every child with ADHD is a unique mix of strengths and challenges shaping how they learn, interact and navigate the world. Some of their strengths may lie outside of traditional measures of success or development, but this doesn't make them any less valuable.

Psychologist and leading parenting expert Dr Robert Brooks, together with Dr Sam Goldstein, emphasises the importance of a strengths-based parenting approach for children with ADHD. In their book *Raising Resilient Children: Fostering strength, hope, and optimism in your child* (2002), they explain that children thrive when they feel capable, valued and connected. Rather than focusing primarily on weaknesses or behaviours that need 'fixing', they recommend identifying and nurturing a child's strengths as the foundation for resilience and growth.[5] This might mean emphasising strengths such as creativity, humour, kindness, persistence or a strong sense of fairness—traits that aren't always easily recognisable or positively regarded in structured settings like schools. By highlighting and building on these qualities, you help improve your child's self-esteem and develop their motivation to overcome challenges that arise.

Embedding a strengths-based approach

When parenting a child with ADHD, it can sometimes feel like the challenges are front and centre. A strengths-based approach helps you step back and celebrate who your child is—focusing on their gifts, interests and potential. This doesn't mean ignoring the struggles, it means approaching them in a way that highlights your child's abilities and reframes obstacles as opportunities for growth.

Let go of expectations

Your child's unique blend of gifts, talents and interests may not fit the traditional mould, and that's okay. Letting go of rigid expectations, often based on neurotypical standards of behaviour, and pursuing traditional pathways is one of the most freeing things you can do.

Meet your child where they're at rather than comparing them with their same-age peers. Celebrate their progress without the pressure of conventional milestones. It creates space for more of the good things such as compassion, respect, acceptance and hope, and enables you to advocate for them more confidently.

Identify strengths and interests
Pay attention to what excites and engages your child, whether it's a creative pursuit, physical activity or deep interest in a particular topic. Genuine curiosity about their world can bring deeper connection and empathy, and provide strong foundations for both their growth and your relationship. Encourage growth by providing opportunities aligned with their strengths and use tools and approaches that suit their interests and needs.

Reframe challenges
A strengths-based approach doesn't mean ignoring things your child finds difficult or distressing. It focuses on finding the hidden potential in these challenges, and reframing them so your child sees themselves in a more positive light. For example:

> ➤ While impulsivity and risk-taking can be disruptive or reckless in some settings, in others it can manifest as quick thinking, creativity and a willingness to take action when others hesitate.
> ➤ Hyperfocus (including on niche interests) can be harnessed for deep learning and expertise.
> ➤ The boundless energy frustrating teachers in class can also fuel your child's passion and persistence in other pursuits that capture their interest.
> ➤ Emotional sensitivity, though sometimes overwhelming, can also bring deep empathy and compassion.

As your mindset shifts, blame and frustration give way to empathy and curiosity. You begin asking, 'What's getting in their way?' instead of 'What's wrong with them?' By recognising potential in every aspect of your child, you help them turn obstacles into stepping stones for success.

Practical strategies

Focusing on strengths while addressing challenges helps your child develop resilience, self-awareness and the confidence to navigate their life with ADHD.

➤ Observe when your child is most engaged. Do they thrive in hands-on activities, creative projects or social interactions?
➤ Keep a strengths and challenges journal, noting moments of success and frustration.
➤ Ask your child what they enjoy or struggle with.
➤ Ask others in your child's network (e.g., teachers, therapists, friends and family) for their perspectives.
➤ Tailor their environment using this knowledge; for example, incorporate movement breaks for focus, provide visual schedules for organisation, or explore interest-based learning to enhance motivation.

Try the following quizzes to better understand your child's strengths, interests and needs.

Discovering your child's strength profile

I believe Howard Gardner's idea of multiple intelligences provides a powerful way to understand your child's unique strengths. While not all researchers agree on the science, I find it a helpful framework for parents because it reminds us that there are many ways to be 'smart'. When you combine this with an awareness of your child's learning preferences (e.g., some children learn best by seeing, others by listening, reading/writing or hands-on doing), we begin to see a bigger picture.

Creating a strengths profile for your child helps you celebrate how your child's mind works and guides you in supporting both their learning and confidence.

(continued)

Quiz: Your child's strength profile

For each statement, rate how strongly you agree on a scale of 1 (not at all true) to 5 (very true).

Linguistic/verbal

1. My child enjoys reading, writing or creating stories.

   1   2   3   4   5

2. My child expresses themselves well through words, jokes or conversations.

   1   2   3   4   5

Logical/mathematical

1. My child enjoys problem-solving, puzzles, patterns or strategic thinking.

   1   2   3   4   5

2. My child asks thoughtful 'why' questions and likes to make sense of how things work.

   1   2   3   4   5

Musical/rhythmic

1. My child shows enthusiasm for music, rhythm or singing.

   1   2   3   4   5

2. My child remembers tunes easily or makes up their own songs or beats.

   1   2   3   4   5

Bodily/kinaesthetic

1. My child enjoys and excels at hands-on activities such as building, creating or experimenting.

   1   2   3   4   5

2. My child is highly energetic and thrives in movement-based activities like sports or dance.

   1   2   3   4   5

Interpersonal

1. My child shows empathy and emotional intelligence with people or animals.

   1   2   3   4   5

2. My child is a natural leader and enjoys guiding or helping others.

   1   2   3   4   5

Intrapersonal

1. My child demonstrates deep knowledge and enthusiasm for specific personal interests.

   1   2   3   4   5

2. My child reflects on their feelings, goals or challenges with some awareness.

   1   2   3   4   5

Naturalistic

1. My child shows curiosity about nature, animals, plants or the environment.

   1   2   3   4   5

2. My child feels calm and connected when outdoors.

   1   2   3   4   5

Learning preferences (VARK)

1. My child understands best with pictures, diagrams or visual aids (visual).

   1   2   3   4   5

(continued)

2. My child learns best by listening, singing or discussing ideas (auditory).

   1   2   3   4   5

3. My child prefers written instructions, lists or note-taking (reading/writing).

   1   2   3   4   5

4. My child learns best through touching, building, moving or role-playing (kinaesthetic).

   1   2   3   4   5

How to interpret the quiz

Scores of 4–5 = clear strengths: areas where your child naturally shines.

Scores of 2–3 = emerging strengths: may grow with encouragement or opportunity.

Scores of 1 = less of a preference: not every child enjoys every activity, and that's okay.

Look for patterns — which intelligences scored highest? Which learning preferences stood out? Together, these give you your child's strength profile.

Reflection exercise

➤ Which strengths stood out the most for my child?

➤ Which learning preferences seem strongest?

➤ Did any of the results surprise me?

➤ How do these strengths show up in everyday life (home, school, friendships)?

➤ How can I nurture these strengths through activities, hobbies or learning opportunities?

> How might these strengths help balance or support areas my child finds harder?

> How might I share this profile with my child's teacher so we can work together to support their learning?

Using the Strengths Profile Wheel

The Strengths Profile Wheel (see figure 1.1) is a simple visual tool to help you map your child's scores. 🌐

Shade each bar from 1 to 5 for each category. When you're finished, you'll see a clear depiction of your child's unique strengths at a glance.

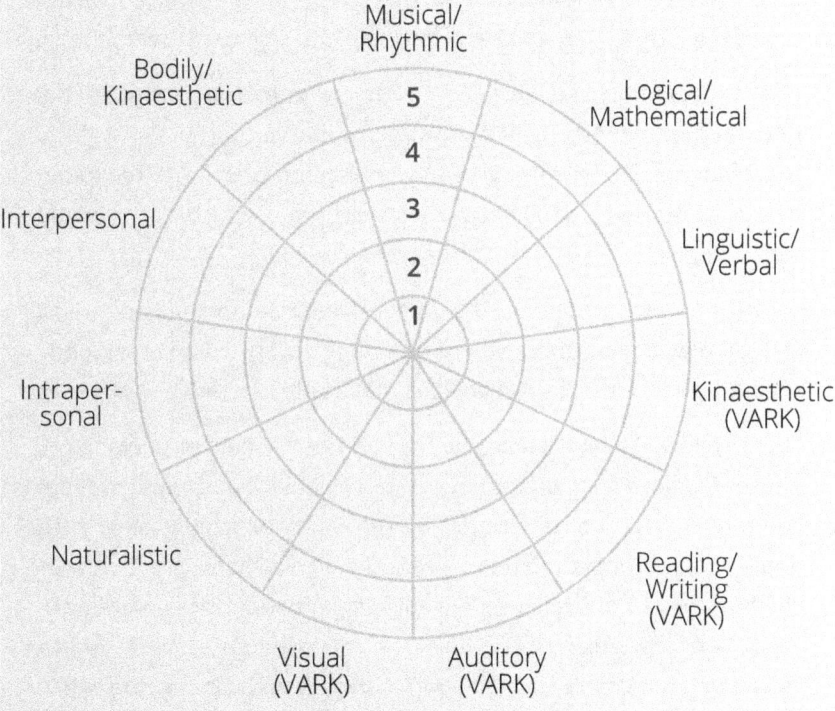

Figure 1.1 *The Strengths Profile Wheel*

(continued)

This isn't about comparing your child, it's about recognising and celebrating what makes them capable, valued and connected.

One parent's reflection

When Sarah filled out the strength profile quiz for her nine-year-old son, she was surprised by what stood out. She had always worried about his struggles with spelling tests, but on the quiz, his highest scores were in logical/mathematical and kinaesthetic strengths. He loved solving puzzles, tinkering with Lego and couldn't sit still unless his hands were busy.

On the strength profile wheel, his bars stretched out strongly in those areas, while his reading/writing scores were lower. For the first time, Sarah realised his difficulties with spelling didn't mean he wasn't 'smart'. He simply learned best by building, moving and experimenting.

Reflecting on this, she began to look for ways to bring his strengths into daily life, like letting him use Lego to model concepts in science, or turning spelling practice into movement games. She also reminded herself to praise his problem-solving skills just as much as she would a good grade.

Seeing her son's profile on the wheel helped Sarah shift her focus: instead of worrying about where he struggled, she could now clearly see and nurture the unique abilities that made him thrive.

Every child will have challenges, that's a normal part of growing up. These struggles don't define your child, but how you respond to them can make a world of difference. By reframing difficulties as growth areas and spotting the hidden strengths within them, you give your children the gift of resilience, encouragement and the belief they are capable of learning and thriving. The following quiz invites you to reflect on your child's struggles with curiosity and compassion, while looking for the hidden strengths within them.

Quiz 2: Reframing challenges as growth areas

Instructions: Take a few quiet minutes to reflect on each question. Write down short notes or examples that come to mind. The goal is not to 'fix' your child, but to see their challenges in a new light and discover gentle ways to support their resilience. Look back at your child's strength profile from quiz 1. Use these short questions to see how their strengths can support them when things feel hard.

Reflection questions

➤ Which strength could help with a current struggle? *Example: My child's energy (strength) can be used in active learning games instead of sitting still.*

➤ Does their learning style suggest a new approach? *Example: My child struggles with spelling, but as a visual learner, they could try colourful word cards.*

➤ How can I bring their interests into tricky tasks? *Example: My child loves animals, so I use animal examples when teaching maths.*

➤ When do I see their strengths shine the most? *Example: They do better with homework in the morning when they're fresh, not at night when tired.*

➤ What makes them feel proud? How can I use that more? *Example: They feel proud when helping younger siblings — I can give them more 'helper' roles at home.*

➤ How can I reframe this challenge as a skill in progress? *Example: 'Bossy' with friends → learning to be a leader with kindness.*

➤ What is one small step I can try this week? *Example: Let them use Lego blocks to practise maths facts instead of worksheets.*

By connecting back to the strengths you've already identified, challenges stop looking like flaws and start looking like opportunities to grow with support.

(continued)

Reflection worksheet: Linking strengths to challenges

This worksheet ⊕ helps you connect your child's strengths (from quiz 1) with their challenges (from quiz 2). By linking the two, you can see how strengths can be used to support growth in harder areas.

INSTRUCTIONS

Look back at your child's strength profile (quiz 1) and write one strength in the first column. Write a related challenge in the second column. In the last column, jot down how you could reframe or support the challenge using your child's strength, so it looks something like the example here.

Strength (quiz 1)	Linked challenge (quiz 2)	Reframe/support
Energetic and loves movement	Finds it hard to sit still during homework	Use movement-based learning games or breaks
Empathetic with others	Gets upset easily when friends are unkind	Role-play calming responses and highlight their kindness as a strength
Curious and asks lots of questions	Becomes frustrated when answers aren't clear	Explore answers together using books, videos or experiments
Creative imagination	Daydreams and loses focus in class	Channel imagination into storytelling or creative projects
Strong sense of fairness	Argues with siblings about 'rules'	Encourage leadership roles (e.g., helping set fair family rules)

You don't need to fill every row. Even one or two linked reflections can give you fresh insight into how to turn challenges into growth opportunities.

Chapter Two

How it works: Understanding your child's brain

Understanding your child's brain is the first step to understanding their brilliance.

What is ADHD?

The DSM-5 (*Diagnostic and Statistical Manual of Mental Disorders*, fifth edition) defines ADHD as:

> *A set of neurodevelopmental differences in brain regions responsible for attention, impulse control and self-regulation. It's characterised by persistent patterns of inattention, hyperactivity, and/or impulsivity that interfere with daily life, impacting how a person manages their thoughts, emotions and actions. It impacts both children and adults, influencing daily life, learning, relationships and overall wellbeing.*[1]

Three key differences exist for people with ADHD in the brain regions responsible for attention, impulse control and self-regulation:

The *prefrontal cortex* is responsible for our executive functioning, the set of mental skills helping us to plan, make decisions and exercise self-control. It's essentially the brain's self-management system. For people with ADHD, the prefrontal cortex may develop more slowly, impairing executive functioning and making it harder to stay organised; manage time; start, finish and transition between tasks; and manage impulses.

Our *basal ganglia* (dopamine-rich areas of the brain) play an important role in movement control, impulse control and executive function due to the way dopamine affects how we process rewards and motivation. People with ADHD often have structural and functional differences in their basal ganglia, which can dysregulate their dopamine levels, making it difficult to sustain attention, complete tasks and assess risks.

The *amygdala* is the area of the brain responsible for processing emotions and managing our stress responses — it's our fight-or-flight part of the brain. Studies show that differences in the functioning and structure of the amygdala in ADHD brains can mean people with ADHD experience more intense emotional reactions to stimuli and find it harder to regulate them.

In combination, these neurological differences are the key drivers of most ADHD symptoms and how they impact the daily lives and overall wellbeing of both children and adults.

How does ADHD present itself?

In practice, the impacts of ADHD on behaviour and emotional regulation might look like a young child who constantly forgets their school bag, a tween who has a meltdown trying to clean their messy room but doesn't know where to start, or a teen who leaves assignments until the last minute despite having good intentions.

Children with ADHD often display behaviours reflecting challenges in impulse control, focus and social interaction, such as:

> *inattention:* easily distracted, forgetful, struggle to follow multi-step instructions
> *hyperactivity:* constant movement, difficulty sitting still, talks excessively

> *impulsivity:* acts without thinking, interrupts, struggles with delayed gratification

> *time blindness:* difficulty understanding time, leading to poor time management

> *social difficulties:* trouble picking up social cues, interrupting conversations, struggling to maintain friendships.

These behaviours are not intentional; they are a result of how the ADHD brain processes information and controls responses.

ADHD also impacts how children navigate emotions, making them more prone to:

> *emotional outbursts:* intense reactions to minor frustrations

> *mood swings:* rapid shifts in emotions from excitement to frustration

> *rejection sensitivity:* deep emotional pain from perceived criticism or exclusion

> *difficulty calming down:* struggle to self-soothe after emotional distress.

Since emotional regulation relies on executive function and impulse control, children with ADHD may need extra support in identifying, expressing and managing emotions in healthy ways.

The various symptoms explained here are commonly organised into three main presentations of ADHD, outlined in Table 2.1.

Table 2.1 *Types of ADHD*

Inattentive type	Hyperactive-impulsive type	Combined type
Difficulty sustaining focus	Excessive movement and restlessness	A mix of both inattentive and hyperactive-impulsive symptoms
Forgetfulness and disorganisation	Interrupting or speaking out of turn	
Easily distracted	Acting without thinking	
Struggles with following instructions	Difficulty waiting for their turn	

Recognising that these everyday difficulties stem from neurological differences rather than disobedience can help you respond with greater empathy. Rather than a cycle of arguments, shame and stress that can impact your child's self-esteem, your goal is to provide scaffolding that helps your child develop crucial skills and management strategies over time.

Gender differences with ADHD

As of 2023, boys were being diagnosed with ADHD at double the rate of girls according to community-based studies, and up to four times in some clinical settings.[2] A large driver of this diagnostic gap is a lack of awareness about how girls can present differently to boys. This can result in long delays in receiving needed support, often until the person is in adolescence or adulthood.

While boys are more likely to show externalised, noticeable behaviours like hyperactivity and impulsivity, girls are more likely to present with the inattentive type. This can look like daydreaming, quietness, forgetfulness or emotional sensitivity — internalised symptoms that are often misunderstood as shyness, anxiety or simply being 'scatterbrained'. Gender norms also mean girls are more likely to mask their neurodivergence than boys, working extra hard to meet expectations and suppressing their symptoms, often with negative impacts on their mental health.[3]

How is ADHD diagnosed in children and teens?

You may recognise many of the behaviours and characteristics discussed here in your child. Perhaps that's why you've picked up this book. If you're yet to receive a formal diagnosis for your child, it's normal to feel unsure about where to start or who to see. The process can feel overwhelming, but knowing what to expect can help you feel more prepared and confident.

Figure 2.1 breaks it down step by step.

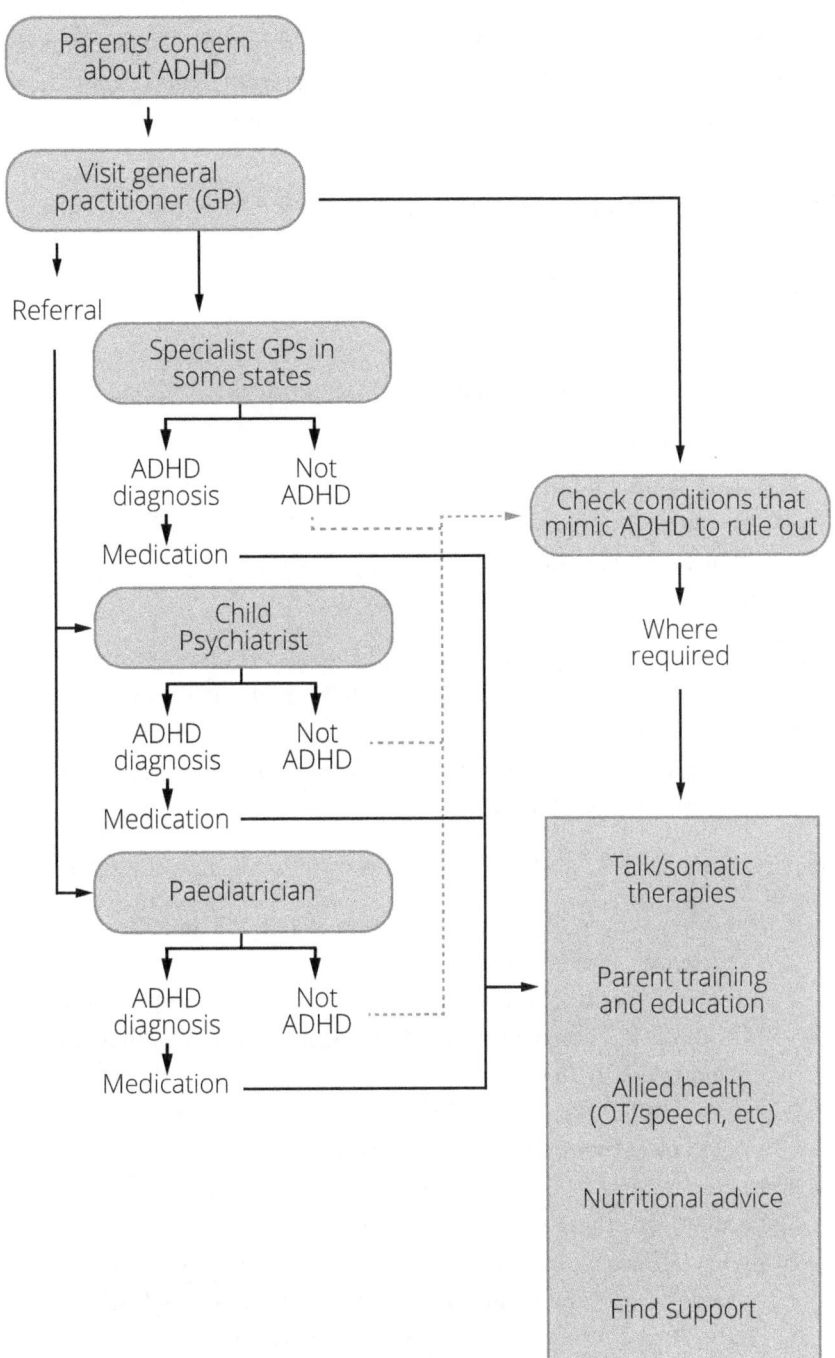

Figure 2.1 *Pathway for ADHD diagnosis and support*

The process differs significantly based on your family's location, needs and preferences. Next we'll cover what to expect from the process to help you navigate and advocate for yourself and your child.

What's involved in an ADHD diagnosis

ADHD is a clinical diagnosis, meaning it cannot be determined by any single blood test, brain scan or checklist. Diagnosis is based on:

> ➤ clinical observation and interviews
> ➤ rating scales and questionnaires
> ➤ reports of your child's behaviour across different settings (home, school, social situations)
> ➤ medical, developmental and family history.

The clinician assesses whether your child meets criteria outlined in the DSM-5 for one of the three types of ADHD: inattentive, hyperactive-impulsive or combined. Symptoms must be present for at least six months, appear before the age of 12, occur in two or more settings (e.g., home and school) and interfere with daily life.

As part of your child's ADHD assessment process, your clinician will likely:

> ➤ interview your child to get a full picture of their thoughts, experiences and behaviours
> ➤ interview you (the parent) to record your first-hand observations of your child's behaviour and challenges at home as well as their development to date
> ➤ review your child's medical and developmental history, taking into account their symptoms over time
> ➤ review reports from allied health professionals, such as occupational therapists, speech pathologists and psychologists
> ➤ review school reports, assessments of academic achievement or under achievement, and reports from teachers or school counsellors concerning behaviour and learning
> ➤ screen for other psychological conditions (anxiety, depression, learning disorders, sensory processing issues, trauma or

attachment-related challenges) and any other medical or psychological concerns contributing to symptoms

➤ consider your child's family and environmental factors, such as parenting styles and strategies; parental stress, mental health or family conflict; the child's ability to form and maintain social relationships.

Your clinician's goal is to gain a full picture of your child's strengths and challenges and the context in which their behaviours occur. This ensures the most accurate diagnosis and helps guide the best support strategies moving forward.

Who can diagnose ADHD?

Several types of professionals can provide an ADHD diagnosis or may be involved (see table 2.2).

Table 2.2 *Health professionals who may offer a diagnosis for ADHD*

Professional	Can they diagnose?	Can they prescribe medication?
Paediatrician	Yes	Yes. This is the most common route. NB: Once a child is 18+ they will need to be referred to a psychiatrist.
Child psychiatrist	Yes	Yes, especially for complex cases or co-occurring mental health conditions.
Clinical psychologist	Yes. Can also assess for neuropsychological and educational issues.	No. They can diagnose and provide psychological therapies and recommendations but not prescribe medications.
General practitioner (GP)	Not usually (specially trained GPs in Qld/WA/NSW can diagnose ADHD), but can initiate a referral.	Sometimes: in some states, under shared care with a specialist. GPs in Qld/NSW/WA (if specifically trained) can prescribe.

Your first step is to see your GP—hopefully one who is knowledgeable and understanding about ADHD. They will ask about your child's symptoms and how they are affecting their daily life. If they don't know your child, they may also ask about their medical history.

If your GP suspects your child may have ADHD, you will be given a referral to a paediatrician, child psychiatrist or psychologist who specialises in diagnosing ADHD, based on your child's needs, local waitlists and available services. They may recommend someone or you can ask them to refer you to someone you have chosen.

At the time of writing, the authority of GPs to diagnose ADHD in children differs between states in Australia as outlined in Table 2.3.

Table 2.3 *Differences in approaches to diagnosing ADHD between Australian states*

New South Wales	In 2025, NSW announced reforms enabling up to 100 specially trained GPs to diagnose/initiate treatment for ADHD in children. Up to 1000 GPs will be authorised to continue prescriptions for stable patients. This GP service starts early 2026 so will take time for GPs to be trained. It's unlikely to be widely available until later in 2026.
Queensland	Certain GPs are permitted to diagnose/prescribe ADHD medications for children aged 4 to 18.
South Australia	Has a GP ADHD Shared Care Program where GPs manage ongoing treatment for patients with established diagnoses. Initial diagnosis and treatment initiation remain under specialist care.
Tasmania, Australian Capital Territory and Northern Territory	GPs are not authorised to diagnose or initiate ADHD treatment. Patients must consult specialists for diagnosis and treatment initiation.
Victoria	GPs are generally not authorised to diagnose ADHD. Diagnosis and initiation of treatment is typically managed by specialists, with GPs involved in ongoing care under shared-care arrangements.
Western Australia	Has a shared-care model where GPs, after completing specific training, can diagnose/prescribe ADHD medications in children aged 10 and older.

How to choose a suitable clinician

Your GP may recommend a suitable paediatrician, psychiatrist or psychologist, but you can research this yourself before making your final choice. Ensure they specialise in diagnosing and treating ADHD, because not all paediatricians, psychiatrists and psychologists do. Ask friends or relatives, join an online community to seek recommendations or search an online directory of ADHD-specific clinicians. ⊕

A psychologist's assessment will give you an understanding of your child's cognitive and psychosocial functioning as well as recommendations for school and home. In a perfect world, an assessment from a psychologist *and* a paediatrician/psychiatrist would be obtained and seen as complementary to each other, but it's often not feasible (financially) to obtain both.

Consider what your most immediate goal is. If it's symptom reduction, you may want to go down the route of accessing medication. If it's improving functioning and wellbeing via psychosocial interventions, then go with a psychologist.

If you have had an assessment/diagnosis carried out by a psychologist, you'll need an additional appointment with a paediatrician or child psychiatrist to access medication as they usually want to perform their own diagnostic assessments.

Check with your chosen paediatrician or child psychiatrist whether they will accept a diagnostic assessment from a psychologist without having to do an additional diagnostic assessment of their own. If a clinician is open to this, it will ultimately be determined by the quality of the assessment. Your paediatrician/psychiatrist may have a working relationship with specific psychologists they recommend — some even share a practice together. If so, ask them to confirm whether they will accept the psychologist's diagnosis.

An increasing number of clinicians offer ADHD diagnosis via telehealth, which is helpful to those in rural or remote areas or who would find it difficult to travel long distances. Advantages include less travel time, less time off work and the ability to bring other caregivers, teachers or professionals onto an online call.

The ADHD Support Australia Directory (adhdsupportaustralia.com.au) and Facebook group (facebook.com/groups/ADHDSupportAustralia) are two online resources to help you find and choose appropriate professionals. ⊕

Other considerations when getting a referral:

> Are they taking new referrals?
> What is the appointment wait time?
> How much will the full assessment cost?
> How much are follow-up appointments?
> How available are they to answer queries outside of appointments (e.g., on medication issues)?

How much will it cost?

The cost of getting an ADHD diagnosis for your child can vary widely depending on who you choose and the complexity of assessment required. It may depend on your location and if you qualify for any rebates through Medicare. Private specialists set their own fees, and these will differ, so it's important to check fees when you enquire.

GP referrals are essential for accessing any Medicare rebates for the assessment, and may cover part of the cost of assessment, but check with the clinician beforehand.

Accessing free or low-cost options

ADHD assessment and treatment through the Australian public health system is available and is more affordable, but there is limited availability, particularly in certain regions. It can also be subject to significant wait times, which can delay the diagnostic process.

If your only option to access a diagnosis is via the public health system in Australia, here's how to get started:

> Visit your GP.
> Share your concerns about your child's behaviour, focus, impulsivity or school issues.
> Ask for a referral to a public paediatrician/child psychiatrist.

- ➤ Be clear you're looking for a referral through the public health system, not private, due to financial reasons.
- ➤ Ask the GP to note any urgency (e.g., school can't, emotional distress).
- ➤ Request a mental healthcare plan. This allows some access to subsidised sessions with a psychologist through Medicare while you're waiting.
- ➤ Speak with your child's school counsellor or wellbeing officer—they may help advocate or offer school-based support.

Get a public health referral

Depending on the state, your GP will typically refer your child to a public paediatric clinic (often based in public hospitals) and/or Child and Youth Mental Health Services (CYMHS) or Child and Adolescent Mental Health Services (CAMHS) for developmental or behavioural assessments.

Call your local health district intake line—they can confirm the referral process or options. Table 2.4 provides some suggested search terms to identify the likely body in your area, if not provided by your GP.

Table 2.4 *Names of health services by state*

New South Wales	Child and Youth Mental Health Service (CYMHS) via your local NSW Health Local Health District (LHD)
Queensland	Child and Youth Mental Health Service (CYMHS) via your local Queensland Health Hospital and Health Service (HHS)
South Australia	Women's and Children's Hospital Child Development Unit
Tasmania, Australian Capital Territory (ACT), and Northern Territory (NT)	Public paediatric or mental health services through your regional health department
Victoria	Child and Adolescent Mental Health Services (CAMHS) via hospitals such as the Royal Children's Hospital
Western Australia	Child and Adolescent Health Service (CAHS)

Once the referral is accepted, you'll be placed on a waiting list. Wait times can vary from several months to two to three years in some areas.

Some services may send you pre-assessment questionnaires to fill out beforehand.

University psychology clinics

Several Australian universities operate psychology clinics offering low-cost or subsidised ADHD assessments for children and adolescents. These clinics are typically staffed by postgraduate psychology students under the supervision of experienced clinicians, providing services at lower fees than private practices.

Availability and wait times vary, so it's advisable to contact the clinics directly for the most current information (see table 2.5). Remember, these are psychology clinics. An assessment via a psychologist will not give you access to ADHD medications.

Note:

> ➤ While some clinics accept self-referrals, others may require a referral from a GP, school counsellor or other healthcare professional.
> ➤ Due to high demand, wait times can be significant. It's advisable to contact the clinics directly to inquire about current wait times and availability.
> ➤ Fees vary between clinics and may be based on a sliding scale. Some clinics offer concession rates for eligible individuals.
> ➤ Some clinics have age restrictions for assessments. Ensure the clinic you choose offers services for your child's age group.

How long does the assessment process take?

It depends on the professional and their process.

> ➤ Psychologist assessments can take several hours over multiple sessions (usually two to three sessions for interviews, questionnaires and report writing).
> ➤ Paediatrician assessments are often shorter (one to two sessions) but rely on structured questionnaires and teacher input.

➤ If co-occurring learning disorders are suspected, additional cognitive or educational testing may be recommended (which adds time and cost).

Table 2.5 *University clinics offering ADHD assessments*

New South Wales	UTS Psychology Clinic provides low-cost psychological services, including assessments, conducted by provisional psychologists under supervision. Offers a broad range of adult and child services.
	Macquarie University Health Psychology Clinic offers high-quality assessments/treatment for children and groups, including ADHD programs. Check directly with the clinic as to whether it is taking on new patients as it does periodically close its waitlist.
	Western Sydney University Psychology Clinic offers assessments for specific learning disorders and ADHD.
Queensland	Bond University Psychology Clinic (Gold Coast) offers counselling services and may provide assessments.
	University of Queensland Psychology Clinic (Brisbane) offers affordable cognitive and neuropsychological assessments conducted by provisional psychologists. A dedicated Neurodevelopmental Clinic for individuals up to age 25 specialising in assessments for ADHD/autism.
Tasmania, Australian Capital Territory, and Northern Territory	University Psychology Clinic at University of Tasmania (UTAS, Hobart and Launceston) provides psychological services, including assessments, conducted by provisional psychologists under supervision.
Victoria	Melbourne Psychology Clinic (University of Melbourne) provides comprehensive assessments for neurodevelopmental conditions, including ADHD/autism, across the lifespan. Assessments conducted by fully registered psychologists.
	Melbourne Psychology Clinic at Australian Catholic University offers comprehensive assessments for individuals under 25 years seeking ADHD and autism assessment if clinically warranted.

Overall, the process can take several weeks to a few months, depending on waitlists and coordination between professionals. Wait times vary greatly between professionals, so some families see a psychologist first for an assessment, then take that report to a paediatrician for treatment planning. However, as mentioned previously, be careful with this route, as many clinicians insist on doing their own assessments, and won't take an assessment from a psychologist or prescribe medication without doing their own assessment. This would mean you end up paying for more than one assessment.

Waitlists can be long, so my advice is to find a few clinicians you're happy with and get on *all* their waitlists. If you're flexible about attending (i.e., if they have a last-minute cancellation and you can get there), you might get in quicker. People are booking appointments so far in advance, chances are that by the time their appointment arrives, they may have gone elsewhere or are unavailable, meaning there will be cancellations.

What documentation will I need to provide?

Being well-prepared will result in the best and most efficient outcome for your child. Set aside time in the months prior to your appointment to gather the appropriate documentation and hunt down anything missing from your records.

Expect to be asked for:

> Your GP referral
> detailed developmental and behavioural history
> parent and teacher questionnaires (e.g., Conners, Vanderbilt or SDQ scales)
> school reports or learning assessments
> notes on your child's behaviour at home, school, socially
> previous reports from speech therapists, occupational therapists etc.
> family mental health history (ADHD is highly genetic).

If your child is older, their own reflections may also be included in the assessment.

Explaining the diagnostic process and what ADHD is to your child

Knowing how to explain ADHD to a child can be daunting. Some parents prefer not to tell their child of any diagnosis they receive because they don't want other people to know due to perceived stigma and/or because they think it will make their child feel bad or they will use it as an excuse not to do well. I believe you should be honest with your child, though the choice is, of course, yours. But how can we ever hope to overcome stigma if people choose to hide their diagnosis?

ADHD is a lifelong diagnosis and your child deserves the opportunity to come to terms with their diagnosis and work with you to explore strategies that work for them to help them overcome any challenges they face.

Once your appointment for a diagnosis is booked, you'll need to plan how best to explain to your child what the appointment is for, why they're going and what the result of the appointment may be in an easily understood way. You don't want your child to worry or think there's something 'wrong' with them. Put their mind at ease with an explanation that helps them understand what ADHD is, and why you think they may have it. Keep it positive so if the diagnosis is confirmed, they can move forward with hope. Now they understand more clearly why they're having difficulties in certain areas, reassure them you'll be working together to overcome those challenges while embracing their strengths.

Use age-appropriate language, reassuring them this isn't a test they can pass or fail, there are no right or wrong answers, and it's definitely not about there being anything wrong with them. It's simply about understanding how they think, feel and focus, and a way of helping them feel more supported and understood.

You might say:

> You know how you sometimes find it hard to concentrate at school or get started on your homework? I'd like to see if we can do anything to help you with that to make your life a bit easier.

I've made an appointment with a doctor who's going to do some tests with you and see if he can find out if there's a reason you find those things hard. It doesn't mean I think you have anything wrong with you—I think you're amazing—and I love you no matter what. This appointment is a way for us to understand how to help you feel more confident and supported in life.

Have you ever heard of ADHD? It's not a bad thing, it just means some brains work differently to others, which can make it harder for people to concentrate, particularly on things they're not that interested in. If you have ADHD, that could be the reason why you find it so hard to concentrate. If we find out you have ADHD, we'll learn more about it and work together to figure out what's going to help you with things you find difficult.

Some people with ADHD are really good at things like sport, art or making things—like you are! You know Simone Biles has ADHD? [insert a successful person with ADHD that will resonate with them]

Books are a great way to discuss what ADHD is with your child. You'll find a selection on the ADHD Support Australia website. ⊕

Chapter Three

Additional conditions: Understanding comorbidities

ADHD is often just one thread in a much more complex tapestry.

Children diagnosed with ADHD commonly have additional emotional, behavioural, learning or development challenges alongside the more familiar symptoms of inattention, impulsivity or hyperactivity because ADHD often coexists with other conditions, known as comorbidities.[1]

A comorbidity means your child is experiencing two or more conditions at the same time. These additional diagnoses sometimes overlap, mask or amplify ADHD symptoms and may influence how your child thinks, learns, behaves and feels.

Understanding and identifying these co-occurring conditions, which are part of your child's unique neurological profile, is crucial for understanding your individual child, developing a whole-child approach and tailoring the best treatment and support.

Common comorbidities

Conditions sharing overlapping symptoms with ADHD can make diagnosis and treatment more complex. I've emphasised the critical importance of understanding your unique child, so being aware of any comorbidities allows you to support your child more holistically, compassionately and effectively. Figure 3.1 shows some common comorbidities.

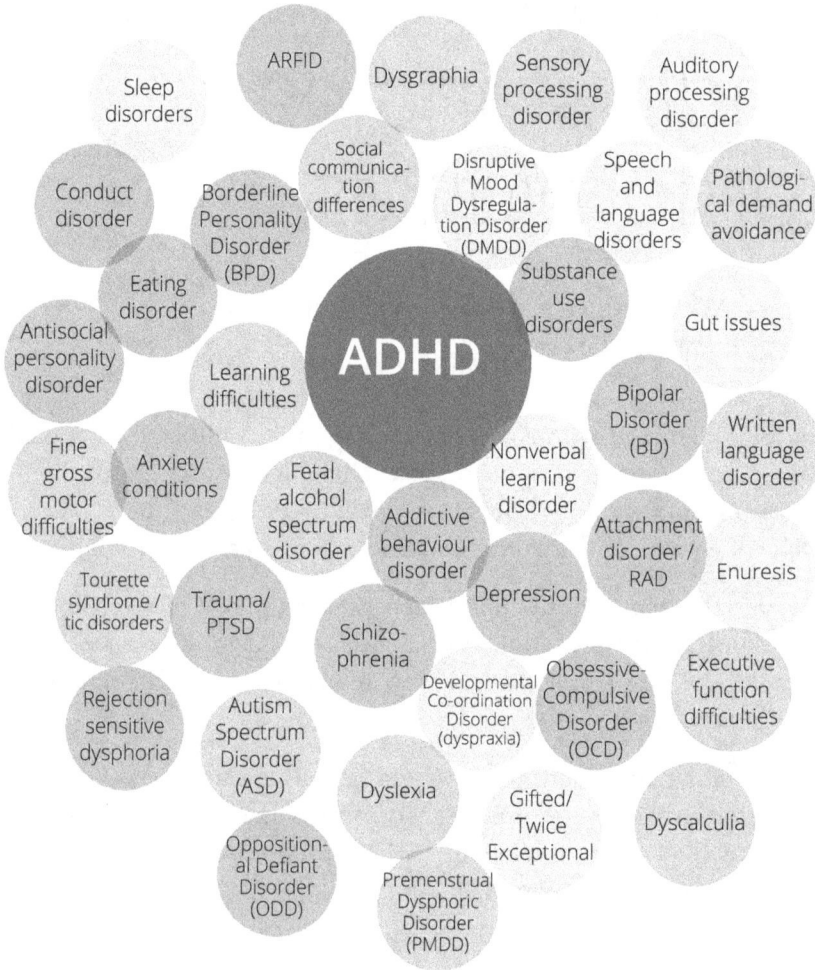

Figure 3.1 *ADHD comorbidities[2]*

Note: Clinical terms are used here for clarity, though many people prefer neuroaffirming language such as 'differences' or 'challenges' rather than 'disorders'.

When you identify comorbidities:

> you can advocate more effectively for your child's needs
> professionals can tailor a more comprehensive treatment plan
> you won't assume everything is 'just their ADHD'
> you'll be better equipped to support them
> your child is more likely to receive comprehensive support, beyond focus and behaviour.

Let's go into more detail on some of the more common comorbidities. For simplicity, I've grouped these into four categories:

> Mental health and wellbeing-related
> Other forms of neurodivergence
> Physical conditions
> Conditions mimicking ADHD

These categories are not mutually exclusive, nor are they necessarily the best fit for some of the comorbidities ascribed to them. Many of these conditions are characterised by symptom clusters overlapping with one another or are connected to each other by the same mechanisms. However, I've grouped them to make the list a little less overwhelming!

For each of these categories, we'll take a deeper dive on a few of the most common conditions, how to spot them and some initial steps to take in response.

In your parenting journal make a note of any comorbidities your child has been diagnosed with, or ones you think they may have, and would like to look into further.

Mental health

Mental illness is increasingly common in all children. However, the brain differences of children with ADHD can make them more susceptible to experience mental ill-health, as can the negative experiences that may occur in relation to their neurodivergence (see Chapter 12 on self-esteem). Table 3.1 lists common comorbidities related to emotional wellbeing and mental health.

Table 3.1 *Common comorbidities related to emotional wellbeing and mental health*

Disorder	Definition
Addictive behaviour disorder	Tendency to become easily addicted to substances or behaviours (e.g., gaming, food, screens), often due to low impulse control and a strong need for stimulation or reward.
Antisocial personality disorder (ASPD)	Long-term pattern of disregard for rules, others' rights or social norms, often with manipulative or aggressive behaviour. Rare in children but may emerge from unresolved conduct issues.
Anxiety disorders	Persistent worry, fear or nervousness interfering with everyday life. May show up as separation anxiety, social anxiety, panic attacks or generalised worry.
Attachment disorders/reactive attachment disorder (RAD)	Emotional or behavioural difficulties arising from early disruptions in bonding or caregiving. Children may struggle with trust, connection or emotional closeness.
Avoidant/ restrictive food intake disorder (ARFID)	Eating disorder where a child avoids or restricts food intake due to sensory sensitivities, fear of choking or vomiting, or low interest in eating. Unlike other eating disorders, ARFID is not related to body image. Commonly seen in children with ADHD, autism or anxiety, it can lead to nutritional deficiencies, growth concerns or social challenges around food.
Bipolar Disorder (BD)	Mood disorder marked by intense mood swings between emotional highs (mania or hypomania) and lows (depression). May be confused with ADHD due to impulsivity and mood shifts.
Borderline personality disorder (BPD)	Characterised by extreme emotional sensitivity, unstable relationships and impulsive behaviour. Emerging symptoms may appear in emotionally intense teens.

Disorder	Definition
Conduct Disorder (CD)	More serious behavioural disorder involving consistent aggression, rule-breaking, lying, stealing or cruelty. Often seen as an escalation from untreated oppositional defiant disorder ODD.
Depression/mood disorders	Persistent sadness, irritability, hopelessness or loss of interest in activities. Common in children with ADHD, especially teens.
Disruptive Mood Dysregulation Disorder (DMDD)	Childhood condition marked by severe irritability and frequent temper outbursts out of proportion to the situation.
Eating disorders (ED)	Serious issues with eating behaviours, body image or food restriction, and includes anorexia, bulimia and ARFID.
Obsessive-Compulsive Disorder (OCD)	Repetitive, intrusive thoughts (obsessions) and compulsive behaviours performed to reduce anxiety. Children may feel trapped in rituals or routines.
Oppositional Defiant Disorder (ODD)	Pattern of angry, argumentative and defiant behaviour, especially toward authority figures. Common in children with ADHD.
Pathological demand avoidance (PDA)	Behavioural profile increasingly recognised within the autism spectrum. Children with PDA experience extreme anxiety when faced with everyday demands or expectations, and often avoid these demands through meltdowns, distraction, negotiation or withdrawal. Unlike oppositional behaviour, PDA is based in anxiety and a need for control, not defiance. Children can appear highly social but struggle with emotional regulation and rigid thinking. Understanding PDA requires low-demand, collaborative approaches rather than traditional reward/consequence behaviour systems, which often escalate distress.
Post-traumatic stress disorder (PTSD)	Emotional and behavioural symptoms following trauma. Includes hypervigilance, nightmares, emotional numbness or behaviour regression.

(continued)

Table 3.1 *Common comorbidities related to emotional wellbeing and mental health. (cont'd)*

Disorder	Definition
Premenstrual dysphoric disorder (PMDD)	A severe form of premenstrual syndrome (PMS) where hormonal changes trigger intense mood shifts, such as depression, irritability or anxiety, that can significantly affect daily life for girls with ADHD who may already struggle with emotional regulation.
Rejection sensitive dysphoria (RSD)	Intense emotional response to perceived criticism or rejection, common in people with ADHD. Reactions may seem dramatic or out of proportion.
Schizophrenia	Serious mental health condition involving hallucinations, delusions and disordered thinking. Rare in children but important to differentiate in complex cases.
Substance use disorder (SUD)	Problematic relationship with drugs, alcohol or other substances. Teens with ADHD are at higher risk due to impulsivity and dopamine-seeking behaviour.

Many factors influence our mental wellbeing, including a combination of psychological, biological and social factors. In children with ADHD some of the contributing factors may include those listed in Table 3.2.

Table 3.2 *Psychosocial and biological factors associated with mental ill-health in people with ADHD*

Category	Symptoms
Psychosocial factors	➤ Feeling misunderstood ➤ Social rejection or exclusion ➤ Struggling to keep up at school ➤ Frequent criticism or punishment ➤ Feeling 'different' or inadequate ➤ Rejection sensitive dysphoria (RSD) ➤ Difficulty regulating emotions ➤ Negative feedback cycles ➤ Family trauma, conflict or stress

Category	Symptoms
Biological factors	➤ Nutrient deficiencies ➤ Gut health and inflammation (gut-brain axis) ➤ Food sensitivities (e.g., gluten, dairy, histamines) ➤ Executive function challenges (forgetfulness, disorganisation, time management) ➤ Sleep deprivation ➤ Blood sugar crashes ➤ High histamine levels
Environmental/ contextual factors	➤ School pressure (fear of failure, sensory overload, undiagnosed learning difficulties) ➤ Difficulty reading social cues ➤ Bullying or peer conflict ➤ High screen time ➤ Family changes (e.g., moving house, caregiver stress)

Depression and anxiety

Children with ADHD are significantly more likely to experience both depression[3] and anxiety[4] over their lifespan. Research indicates that approximately 15 to 30 per cent of children, 20 to 40 per cent of adolescents and up to 50 per cent of adults with ADHD will develop depression, while 25 to 50 per cent of individuals with ADHD also meet criteria for an anxiety disorder. These increased risks are linked to emotional dysregulation, chronic stress, academic struggles and social rejection. Early recognition and integrated support can significantly improve long-term mental health outcomes.

Spotting anxiety/depression in children with ADHD

Recognising signs of anxiety or depression in children with ADHD is essential for providing the right support, as shown in Table 3.3 (overleaf).

If you notice multiple symptoms from these tables lasting more than a couple of weeks, it's important to seek professional help. Your child's life will be impacted in every area if they're suffering from depression, which may increase their risk for self-harm, school can't (formerly called school refusal) and substance use in teens.

Table 3.3 *Signs of anxiety and depression in children with ADHD*

	Anxiety	Depression
Emotional and behavioural signs	➤ Irritability or frequent meltdowns ➤ Avoidance of school, activities or social situations ➤ Excessive worrying or catastrophising ➤ Perfectionism or fear of failure ➤ Reassurance-seeking ('What if I get it wrong?') ➤ Withdrawing from family, friends, or activities they previously enjoyed, increased clinginess, or avoiding new experiences. ➤ Low self-confidence, self-criticism or fear of judgement	➤ Tearfulness or persistent sadness ➤ Increased emotional outbursts or irritability ➤ Withdrawing from family, friends or activities they previously enjoyed ➤ Hopelessness or negative self-talk ('I'm useless', 'I mess everything up') or hopelessness ('I'll never be good enough') ➤ Low self-confidence or guilt
Physical signs	➤ Stomachaches or headaches (with no medical cause) ➤ Muscle tension or fidgeting ➤ Restlessness or difficulty sitting still ➤ Trouble falling or staying asleep ➤ Fast breathing, heart racing or sweating ➤ Nausea ➤ Digestive problems	➤ Excessive sleeping, constant fatigue or low energy ➤ Difficulties sleeping ➤ Appetite changes or loss or gain of weight ➤ Slow thinking or difficulty concentrating ➤ Unexplained aches or pains ➤ School performance declining ➤ Expressing ideas about self-harm, death or suicide (even in a jokey way: always take it seriously)

It's also important to remember, even if your child doesn't meet the criteria for a formal diagnosis, they're still experiencing emotional overwhelm, stress and worry, which affects their daily life. In children, anxiety can manifest in many different ways and is often mistaken for behaviour problems such as aggression or hyperactivity. In Chapter 4, we look at what might be happening beneath the surface when your child is feeling anxious or dysregulated, and how to handle it.

Is it anxiety or OCD?

People who are particularly tidy or orderly often describe themselves as having OCD, but people who have obsessive-compulsive disorder (OCD) have a mental health condition that can be debilitating. Its hallmark feature is recurrent, intrusive thoughts (obsessions) and compulsive behaviours the person feels compelled to perform to reduce their anxiety or prevent a feared event from occurring. The cycle of overwhelming thoughts and rituals can feel uncontrollable and overwhelming for a child with OCD.

Signs and symptoms of OCD in children

While OCD presents differently in each child, some common signs and symptoms cover the following obsessions (recurrent thoughts) and compulsions (repetitive behaviours):

➤ contamination fears (e.g., dirt, germs)
➤ repeated washing/cleaning or handwashing
➤ fear of making mistakes
➤ excessive worry (e.g., did they lock the door, leave something behind?)
➤ excessive checking (e.g. checking the same thing multiple times, such as whether the door is locked)
➤ ordering or arranging things in specific ways believing it will prevent something bad from happening
➤ repeating behaviours or actions a specific number of times or performing rituals until it 'feels right'
➤ mental rituals: repeating phrases or mental checks to avoid intrusive thoughts
➤ unwanted thoughts about violence, harm or taboo topics
➤ intrusive images/worries causing anxiety or discomfort

Supporting your child's mental health

You play a vital role in promoting emotional wellbeing and helping your child feel safe, seen and supported during any episodes of mental ill-health. The most effective support will depend on their specific diagnosis, symptoms, environment and context. However, common strategies to support mental wellbeing in your child include:

> - validating their feelings without minimising or trying to fix them too quickly
> - being present and connected, even in silence or sadness
> - offering structure and routine to create a sense of predictability
> - encouraging small wins (e.g., movement, creative expression, getting outside)
> - supporting restful sleep, balanced meals and hydration
> - limiting screen time, which can worsen low mood and disconnection
> - creating low-pressure opportunities for connection (walks, shared hobbies, board games)
> - modelling your own self-care and emotional expression.

Many of these strategies are explored further in subsequent chapters.

Your child is likely to experience more stress and overwhelm than their peers. It's important you understand that your child's behaviour can be a sign their nervous system is dysregulated and they need support. Working collaboratively with your child on both emotional and physical reasons for their anxiety can support them to manage their anxiety and feel safe in their world.

When to seek professional support

While you can do much to help your child develop positive mental and emotional wellbeing, if symptoms persist, are distressing or interfere with your child's ability to learn, sleep or participate in life, you need to seek professional help. See Chapter 20 for more information.

If your child shows signs of distress, worsening behaviour or sudden changes, don't wait—reach out to a qualified professional. Depending on your child's needs, consider some of these resources:

School staff:

> Wellbeing coordinators, school counsellors or teachers, especially if academic stress, bullying or school can't is a factor.

Medical professionals:

> GP or paediatrician for initial screening, referrals and ruling out physical health issues.
> Paediatrician specialising in ADHD for assessment, diagnosis and care coordination.
> Child psychiatrist for complex presentations or if medication may be considered.

Mental health professionals:

> Psychologist or counsellor specialising in ADHD, anxiety and child/adolescent mental health

Therapists and allied health:

> Occupational therapist (OT) for sensory-related anxiety, emotional regulation and executive function support.

Integrative and nutritional support:

> Naturopath or integrative practitioner specialising in ADHD and mental health for assessing food sensitivities, gut health, diet and nutritional deficiencies.

Can complementary therapies help?

Many parents find holistic approaches to be effective alongside professional care, especially for mild or early-stage depression. Some of the options that could provide some benefit include:

> omega-3 fatty acids (EPA/DHA): some research suggests that omega-3 fatty acids (especially EPA) may help reduce symptoms of anxiety and depression in young people when used alongside other supports, though the evidence remains inconclusive
> vitamin D, zinc, magnesium, B vitamins: deficiencies in these vitamins and minerals are often linked with low mood (see Chapter 8)
> probiotics/prebiotics: improving gut health may influence mood via the gut-brain axis (more on this in Chapter 8)
> mindfulness, yoga, breathwork and body-based therapies: these can support nervous system regulation
> body-based therapies combine movement, breath and physical awareness to help calm the nervous system and build emotional regulation (e.g., yoga, dance, tai chi or simple somatic exercises like mindful breathing and stretching; see Chapter 11 for more)
> general movement: everyday physical activity that boosts mood, reduces stress and helps release excess energy (e.g., walking, playing outside, sports; see Chapter 10)
> creative arts therapy, music therapy and nature exposure: proven mood boosters
> whole-food diet with stable blood sugar: helps regulate energy and mood.

Research indicates that broad-spectrum micronutrient supplementation can significantly improve mood and anxiety symptoms in children with ADHD. See Chapter 8 for a deeper dive.

What to do if your child talks about self-harm or suicide

If your child ever expresses thoughts of self-harm or suicide or is actively self-harming, it's essential you take it seriously and respond with non-judgemental, calm support.

You may think they're saying these things to 'get attention', but, even if they are, the fact they're saying them means they're in emotional pain and need help.

Always give your child your time and presence. Listen with empathy to what they tell you. Reassure them you're there for them, they can tell you anything and you love them unconditionally. Acknowledge (don't dismiss their distress or feelings) and try to learn more. Hard as it is, try not to react with panic!

In Chapter 6 we discuss qualities that contribute to your optimal parenting style and the importance of building a strong relationship with your child, where you keep the communication open between you.

When your child feels emotionally safe to talk to you about anything, without fearing judgement or criticism, they're more likely to share their darkest feelings with you before they reach crisis point. The most dangerous situation is when they stop talking to you and hide their emotional pain, leaving you in the dark. Your relationship is one of the most protective factors against self-harm and suicide.

Be sure to remove access to any means of harm and seek immediate professional support from your GP, psychologist or local mental health crisis services. If you're ever concerned your child may be at risk of immediate harm, don't hesitate to take them to the emergency department or contact a crisis line. You're not alone, and neither is your child. Help is always available and should be sought quickly.

(continued)

Don't make the mistake of thinking signs of depression are just a phase and wait. This is a cry for help from your child requiring calm, non-judgemental support alongside a deeper look at what's happening beneath the surface. With the right care team and support (holistic, physical, emotional and professional) your child can recover and begin to thrive again.

Take your child's words seriously. Listen with care, stay calm and seek professional support immediately.

Other forms of neurodivergence

Many children with ADHD meet criteria for other forms of neurodivergence such as autism, dyslexia, dyspraxia, tic disorders etc. Recognising these co-occurring profiles helps you tailor your whole child support.

Table 3.4 *Common conditions often appear together for neurodivergent children*

Auditory processing disorder	Difficulty processing sounds or spoken language despite normal hearing. Children may struggle to follow verbal instructions or filter background noise.
Autism Spectrum Disorder (ASD)	Neurodevelopmental condition involving differences in social communication, sensory processing, behaviour and flexibility. Many ADHD traits overlap with autism.
Developmental coordination disorder (DCD)/ dyspraxia	Difficulties with motor skills such as writing, catching a ball or coordination. Children often appear clumsy or struggle in physical activities.
Dysgraphia	Learning disorder affecting handwriting, spelling and organising written expression. Children may have difficulty putting thoughts onto paper.

Dyslexia	Specific learning difficulty affecting reading accuracy, fluency and comprehension. Children may reverse letters, read slowly or struggle with spelling.
Executive function difficulties	Challenges with planning, organising, remembering instructions, starting or finishing tasks, and managing time.
Fine and gross motor difficulties	Trouble with small muscle movements (like writing or using utensils) or large movements (like running or jumping), often linked to coordination disorders.
Fetal alcohol spectrum disorder (FASD)	Condition caused by alcohol exposure in the womb, leading to brain, behavioural and learning challenges often resembling or overlapping with ADHD.
Learning disorders/ specific learning difficulties (SLD)	Difficulties in one or more academic areas, including reading, writing or maths, despite average intelligence.
Nonverbal learning disability (NVLD)	Condition where children have strong verbal skills but struggle with visual-spatial tasks, social cues and motor coordination.
Sensory processing disorder (SPD)	Difficulty regulating responses to sensory input. Children may be over- or under-sensitive to sounds, textures, lights, movement or touch.
Slow processing speed	Common cognitive trait where children take longer to absorb, respond to or complete tasks, even if they understand the content.
Socialisation difficulties	Trouble forming and maintaining friendships, interpreting social cues or navigating peer interactions, often overlapping with autism or ADHD. This is more of a symptom than a diagnosis of neurodivergence in itself.
Speech and language disabilities (SLD)	Delays or difficulties with speech clarity, vocabulary, language comprehension or expression. May impact learning and social confidence.
Tic disorders/ Tourette syndrome	Involuntary motor or vocal tics (e.g., blinking, throat clearing). Tics often coexist with ADHD and may worsen with stress or fatigue.

(continued)

Table 3.4 *Common conditions often appear together for neurodivergent children. (cont'd)*

Written language disorder	Difficulty expressing ideas clearly and effectively in written form, often overlapping with dysgraphia or SLDs.
Twice exceptional (2e)	Children described as 'twice exceptional' (2e) have ADHD (or another neurodivergent condition) and are intellectually gifted or talented in one or more areas.

ADHD and autism

ADHD and autism have several shared symptoms including difficulty with attention, impulsivity, emotional regulation, executive function challenges and social communication.

Your child will need an evaluation by a professional specialising in both ADHD and autism to accurately diagnose and differentiate between the two, as well as to develop appropriate interventions tailored to your child's needs.

The main differences between ADHD and autism are shown Table 3.5. It's worth remembering that these are not hard and fast rules. ADHD and autism often overlap and many people experience a mix of traits from both conditions.

Although many children with ADHD struggle with social skills as well, the difference is that children with autism are mainly struggling with interpreting social cues, forming peer relationships and communicating in a socially typical manner, whereas those with ADHD tend to act impulsively or inattentively in social interactions. For more on social skills, see Chapter 15.

Twice exceptional (2e)

Neurodivergent children who are also intellectually gifted or talented in one or more areas are described as twice exceptional (2e). Parents often wrongly assume children who are intellectually gifted do not also have ADHD. Their academic skills can mask ADHD challenges for many years, as they appear to be performing well at school. However, they may not be working to their potential due to their executive functioning or focus issues and may also suffer with emotional dysregulation.

Table 3.5 *Comparison of traits found in ADHD and autism*

	ADHD	Autism
Attention and focus difficulties	✓	✓
Difficulty forming peer relationships		✓
Difficulty understanding social cues		✓
Difficulty with social reciprocity		✓
Emotional regulation	✓	✓
Executive function challenges	✓	✓
Hyperactivity	✓	
Impulsivity	✓	✓
Inflexible in transitions/change		✓
Repetitive behaviours		✓
Rigid thinking		✓
Sensory sensitivities		✓
Social communication challenges		✓

Support your 2e child by helping them develop strategies and coping skills in their challenge areas to nurture their strengths and talents.

Providing gifted children with enrichment activities to spark their interests and allowing them to explore at an appropriately challenging intellectual level nurtures their strengths and talents and is important for their self-esteem.

Carol Dweck, researcher and author of the book *Mindset*, warns against labelling children as 'gifted' or 'smart', as this can lead them to develop a fixed mindset, where they think they achieve success because they're 'smart' not because of the effort they put in. Dweck argues instead that we should praise achievements based on their efforts not on how 'smart' they are. This encourages them to focus on hard work, perseverance and a love of learning, and develops that all-important growth mindset.

For example:

> *I'm impressed with how you chose the harder book and kept going even when it wasn't easy. Effort and curiosity like that will help you keep growing and learning new things.*

When your child is 2e, you'll need to advocate for them at school. Ensure their teachers are aware of their unique learning profile so they understand your child and make the appropriate accommodations to support their organisation, planning and self-regulation.

Acknowledging your child's struggles while embracing a strengths-based approach and providing tailored support will allow your extraordinary child to both thrive and reach their full potential.

Physical conditions

We're becoming more aware of the strong co-occurrence of physical conditions alongside neurodevelopmental conditions showing us the brain and body are always deeply interconnected. Children with ADHD often experience physical health conditions that either mimic ADHD or worsen their symptoms. Addressing these underlying physical health concerns is an important part of supporting a child's overall wellbeing and managing ADHD effectively. Some examples are shown in Table 3.6.

Hypermobility, Ehlers-Danlos syndrome and neurodivergence

Connective tissue disorders like Ehlers-Danlos syndrome (EDS) or hypermobility spectrum disorder (HSD) are examples of physical co-occurring conditions. A study found people with hypermobility disorders are three to four times more likely to have ADHD/autism, and vice versa.[5]

Joint hypermobility means joints move more easily or further than what is considered normal. It's not just natural flexibility, the connective tissues supporting joints are more 'stretchy' than normal, which can lead to instability and an increase in pain or injury.

Table 3.6 *Physical health conditions that can affect children with ADHD*

Enuresis (bedwetting)	Ongoing bedwetting beyond the typical age range, often associated with emotional stress or neurodevelopmental delays.
Gut issues/ gastrointestinal disorders	Chronic digestive problems such as constipation, diarrhoea or bloating. Gut health is increasingly linked to mood and behaviour through the gut-brain axis (see Chapter 8).
Hypermobility, Ehlers-Danlos syndrome	Connective tissue condition characterised by joint hypermobility, frequent dislocations or sprains, chronic pain, fatigue and sometimes digestive or autonomic (nervous system) issues. Can impact energy, focus and emotional regulation due to ongoing physical discomfort and nervous system dysregulation.
Seizure disorders/ epilepsy	Neurological conditions involving recurrent seizures. Some children with ADHD also have seizure activity or overlapping neurological issues.
Sleep problems/ disorders	Difficulty falling asleep, staying asleep or waking rested. Sleep issues can worsen ADHD symptoms and affect emotional regulation (see Chapter 9).

It's not fully understood why neurodivergent people have higher rates of EDS or hypermobility, but research shows several factors may play a role:

> ➤ genetic pathways affecting connective tissues also affect the nervous system
> ➤ nervous system regulation and proprioception (body awareness) differences
> ➤ sensory processing issues or increased sensory sensitivity
> ➤ dysautonomia (a nervous system imbalance) is more common in both neurodivergent people and EDS.

HSD/EDS could fall into the 'comorbid' category or the 'when it's not ADHD' category. Sometimes it's both, and sometimes it's complicated (as always).

Children might meet all the criteria for ADHD/autism and have hypermobility, with overlapping or amplifying symptoms, or children might present with ADHD-like traits entirely due to hypermobility-related factors (e.g., brain fog from postural orthostatic tachycardia syndrome (POTS), sensory overwhelm). Misdiagnosis can happen in both directions so it's vital to assess the whole child, not just their behaviour.

Spotting HSD/EDS in children

Children with hypermobility spectrum disorders (HSD) or Ehlers-Danlos syndromes (EDS) often show a range of physical signs that may be easy to overlook. The following symptoms can help you spot whether your child might need further assessment and support.

Symptoms:

> ➤ highly flexible, 'double-jointed' joints
> ➤ frequent joint sprains or dislocations
> ➤ chronic muscle or joint pain following even mild activity
> ➤ chronic fatigue
> ➤ poor posture, flat feet, other body alignment issues
> ➤ poor proprioception (difficulty knowing where their body is in space)
> ➤ digestive issues (e.g., reflux or constipation)
> ➤ delicate skin, bruises easily
> ➤ velvety skin texture or 'stretchy' skin
> ➤ slow wound healing and/or easy scarring
> ➤ autonomic symptoms: dizziness, rapid heartbeat, temperature regulation issues
> ➤ difficulties with fine motor coordination.

Possible repercussions if HSD/EDS goes undiagnosed

The varied and seemingly unrelated symptoms of HSD/EDS make it easy to see why these conditions get missed and people spend years struggling with symptoms that have been largely dismissed by practitioners. I have family members who fall into this category, who've struggled with symptoms, feeling like hypochondriacs for years, so I understand the importance of getting an early diagnosis!

When HSD/EDS is not identified and supported early, children and, later, adults may experience:

> chronic fatigue and pain
> increased risk of injury or joint damage
> inability to participate in sports and physical activity
> frustration with their body or low self-esteem
> pain or body discomfort resulting in emotional or behavioural challenges
> sensory or autonomic dysfunction causing anxiety and overwhelm.

These symptoms may not be immediately evident. My daughter was talented at sports and dance, and spent most of her time between the ages of ten and 15 playing and competing. She suffered some injuries, but chronic fatigue eventually left her unable to carry on. We never understood why she went from such an energetic child to a teen with chronic fatigue. This may be a small piece of the puzzle we're only learning about years later!

If you suspect your child has HSD/EDS

If you suspect your child may have one of these conditions, it's important to try and get it diagnosed early. Watch them carefully and note down any joint hypermobility symptoms or signs of physical discomfort. Ask your GP for an assessment or a referral to a physiotherapist or occupational therapist specialising in hypermobility and/or a paediatric rheumatologist or geneticist for EDS diagnosis

Our brains and bodies are deeply connected; we need to support our children's physical needs alongside their neurological ones to help them thrive. Identifying hypermobility or EDS early is not about labelling, it's about empowering you with tools to support your child's whole self.

If your child has hypermobility or EDS and also struggles with attention, sensory processing, anxiety or regulation:

> - be cautious before jumping straight to a psychiatric label, such as ADHD or anxiety
> - investigate underlying physical and nervous system issues.

Treatments such as OT for sensory integration, POTS management, pain support and psychoeducation about interoception (the body's ability to sense and understand internal signals, such as hunger, thirst, pain or the need to use the bathroom) may be more appropriate than stimulants or behavioural interventions alone.

Conditions mimicking ADHD symptoms

When children show signs of poor focus, impulsivity, emotional outbursts, fidgeting or forgetfulness, ADHD is the first thing that comes to mind. But not all behaviour that looks like ADHD is ADHD. Many conditions can produce similar symptoms, mimicking, overlapping or even being mistaken for ADHD. Getting an accurate diagnosis is essential for your child to receive effective support.

Conditions commonly mistaken for ADHD:

> - biochemical imbalances: imbalances in neurotransmitters, nutrients or hormones (e.g., iron, zinc, magnesium) can affect energy, mood, sleep and attention
> - fetal alcohol spectrum disorder (FASD): a brain-based condition caused by prenatal alcohol exposure; presents differently in everyone with behavioural, attention and learning challenges
> - food intolerances and sensitivities: reactions to additives, dyes, gluten, dairy, etc. can lead to hyperactivity, mood swings or poor concentration
> - Fragile X syndrome: a genetic condition causing developmental delays and learning difficulties

> giftedness: a high intellectual potential with asynchronous development may lead to boredom, frustration or emotional intensity

> hearing problems: hearing loss can lead to poor attention and behavioural concerns

> medical conditions (e.g., thyroid dysfunction): health issues such as hypothyroidism can impact mood, energy and concentration

> mini seizures (absence seizures): brief lapses in awareness or 'staring spells' that look like daydreaming or inattentiveness but are neurological events

> paediatric autoimmune neuropsychiatric disorders associated with streptococcal infections (PANDAS)/paediatric acute-onset neuropsychiatric syndrome (PANS): sudden onset of OCD-like behaviours, anxiety or tics after infection (e.g., strep throat) caused by immune dysfunction

> post-traumatic stress disorder (PTSD): trauma-related symptoms such as hypervigilance, sleep disturbances or emotional reactivity

> seizure disorders/epilepsy: seizures can impact focus, memory and behaviour

> sleep disorders/sleep disordered breathing: sleep deprivation or poor sleep quality (e.g., insomnia, restless legs) can cause hyperactivity, irritability or reduced attention

> trauma: even without a PTSD diagnosis, chronic stress or traumatic life events (e.g., bullying, neglect) can disrupt emotional regulation, attention and behaviour

> traumatic brain injury (TBI): brain injuries may result in poor memory, impulse control, attention issues or emotional regulation difficulties

> vision problems: uncorrected vision issues may result in task avoidance, headaches or behavioural challenges.

Understanding these conditions helps you and your clinician get a more accurate view of your child's challenges.

While there are many conditions that can sometimes be mistaken for ADHD, I've chosen to focus more deeply on just two: PANS/PANDAS and trauma/ACEs. PANS/PANDAS is still not widely recognised, even among professionals, yet early awareness can make all the difference if sudden symptoms such as OCD appear out of nowhere. Trauma and ACEs also deserve special attention, as their impact is often hidden but profound. By highlighting these, my aim is to give parents the awareness to spot possible signs sooner, seek the right help and address root causes that might otherwise go untreated.

PANS and PANDAS: When sudden behaviour changes might be more than ADHD

If your child experiences sudden, unexplained behavioural or emotional shifts, it's worth asking: Could there be something deeper going on beneath the surface?

Paediatric acute-onset neuropsychiatric syndrome (PANS) and paediatric autoimmune neuropsychiatric disorders associated with streptococcal infections (PANDAS)[6] are not widely known conditions (most people will say 'what the heck is that?'), but they are real and early intervention can make a life-changing difference. Unfortunately, many families face delays in diagnosis due to a lack of clinician awareness or receive a misdiagnosis of 'it's just ADHD' or an 'anxiety disorder'. This is why I've included this section — to flag what to look out for and what to do if you suspect your child has PANS/PANDAS.

These conditions manifest as a sudden onset of neuropsychiatric symptoms triggered by an infection, inflammation or an autoimmune response.

In PANDAS, the trigger is typically Group A Streptococcus (strep throat), whereas PANS may be caused by other infections such as Lyme disease, mycoplasma, Epstein-Barr virus, or even environmental or metabolic stressors.

Instead of targeting the infection, the immune system accidentally attacks the brain, particularly areas like the basal ganglia, which are involved in movement, emotion, behaviour and regulation.

Sometimes behaviour or emotional regulation changes suddenly and drastically — almost overnight. A once calm, happy child might become anxious, aggressive, clingy, moody or obsessive. In some cases, these rapid changes are not part of ADHD or emotional development, and may instead be signs of PANS or PANDAS.

Spotting PANS/PANDAS

PANS/PANDAS symptoms appear suddenly, sometimes within 24 to 48 hours, and often resemble or overlap with ADHD, OCD, anxiety and even autism traits.

Key signs include:

> sudden onset of OCD behaviours
> new or intense tics or involuntary movements
> extreme anxiety or separation anxiety
> irritability, aggression or mood swings
> sensory sensitivities or regression in development
> frequent urination or bedwetting
> decline in handwriting or performance at school
> food restrictions, new eating disorders or fears of choking/germs
> sleep disturbances or night terrors
> ADHD-like symptoms such as inattention, impulsivity, hyperactivity.

Episodes may wax and wane depending on the presence of infections or immune activation. Diagnosis is mostly clinical, based on history and symptom presentation. There is no single test to confirm it but investigations may include:

> throat swab for strep
> blood tests for strep antibodies (ASO, Anti-DNase B)
> testing for other infections (Lyme, Mycoplasma, Epstein-Barr)
> inflammatory markers
> functional brain imaging (in rare cases).

Supporting your child

Treatment for PANS/PANDAS usually involves a multidisciplinary approach aimed at both eliminating the trigger and calming the immune and neurological response. Some common treatments include:

> antibiotics: to treat or prevent infections (especially strep in PANDAS cases)

> anti-inflammatory medication (e.g., ibuprofen or steroids)
> immune-modulating therapies, such as IVIG, plasmapheresis, or low-dose naltrexone in complex cases
> psychological support—cognitive behavioural therapy (CBT), family therapy, OCD treatment
> nutritional and lifestyle support: anti-inflammatory diet, gut healing, stress reduction
> treatment of coexisting conditions (e.g., ADHD, anxiety, OCD)
> environmental detoxification: supporting immune and nervous system regulation holistically.

It's important to work with a team, including a GP, paediatrician, immunologist, neurologist and/or integrative medicine practitioner familiar with PANS/PANDAS.

Trauma and adverse childhood experiences (ACEs)

As you'll discover in Chapter 4, trauma can sometimes mimic or overlap with ADHD symptoms.

Dr Bessel van der Kolk, an expert in the trauma field and author of *The Body Keeps the Score*, explains how traumatic experiences in childhood, such as neglect, abuse or highly stressful events, can have a neurobiological impact on the developing brain. These changes can affect areas such as the prefrontal cortex and basal ganglia, which are also involved in attention, impulsivity and emotional regulation. This is why trauma can produce behaviours that look very similar to ADHD.

There is, however, an ongoing debate. Some experts, including Dr Russell Barkley, a leading clinical psychologist and one of the world's foremost experts on ADHD, emphasise that ADHD is a distinct neurodevelopmental disorder with well-documented genetic and biological markers, and is not caused by trauma.

The clearest way to think about it is this: trauma does not cause ADHD, but it can create ADHD-like symptoms or intensify existing ADHD symptoms. This overlap makes it especially important that children are assessed by an experienced clinician who can carefully differentiate between ADHD and trauma-related conditions or recognise when both are present.

Chapter Four

Influencing factors: Understanding factors that influence ADHD and its symptoms

Supporting your child with ADHD means looking beyond the diagnosis—because both biology and environment shape behaviour.

While there's no one 'cause' of ADHD, a number of factors influence or exacerbate the presence and/or severity of ADHD symptoms. The sheer volume of intersecting and overlapping pieces of the puzzle make it difficult to know where to start, as you read in Chapter 3.

ADHD is a complex neurodevelopmental condition and no child with ADHD is the same as another. It's easy to see your child's surface behaviours (impulsivity, emotional regulation or distractibility) without exploring the deeper layers. When you dive beneath the surface, you'll get a much richer understanding of your child and be able to support them accordingly.

In this chapter, you'll explore the key factors shaping how ADHD presents in your child: genetic predispositions, environmental factors, trauma and the effects of adverse childhood experiences (ACEs). You'll gain valuable insight into elements contributing to your child's symptoms and possibly your own.

Parenting Hierarchy of Needs

Figure 4.1 presents my Parenting Hierarchy of Needs, an adaptation of Maslow's renowned Hierarchy of Needs from developmental psychology. My Parenting Hierarchy framework illustrates which of your child's needs take priority over others, and why starting at the bottom is essential before moving on to higher levels.

The Parenting Hierarchy of Needs can be applied to any child, but it is especially valuable for children with ADHD. Their unique challenges, such as emotional regulation, executive functioning and heightened sensitivity, make a structured, layered approach to support even more important.

Each of the needs in the hierarchy must be addressed in order. There's no point focusing on strategies to change behaviour until more foundational needs have been met. Higher-order needs, such as meaningful relationships, developing self-esteem and, eventually, reaching self-actualisation cannot be achieved if basic physiological and security needs like sleep, food and safety are not in place.

For example, if your child is exhausted, anxious, dysregulated or hungry, you can't expect them to concentrate on schoolwork or cooperate calmly at home.

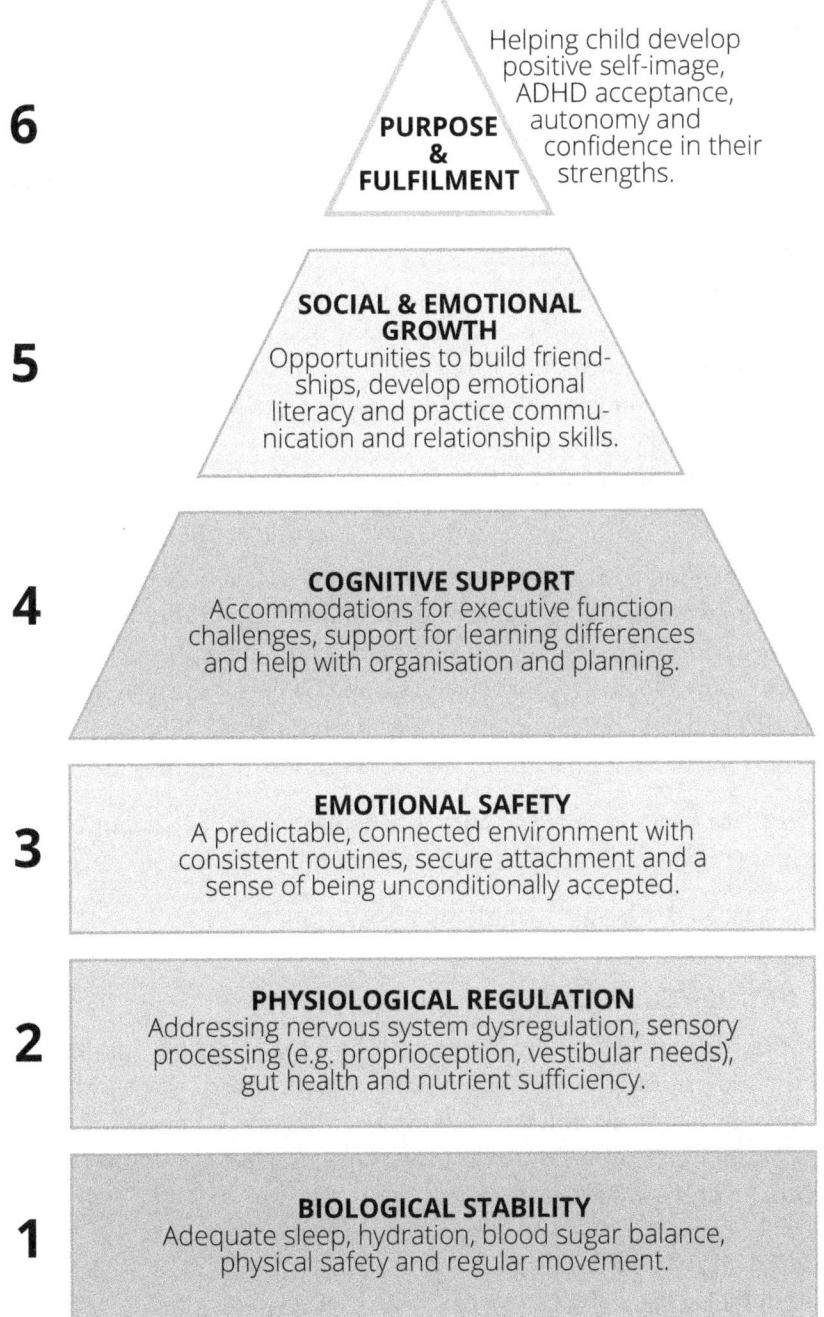

6

PURPOSE & FULFILMENT Helping child develop positive self-image, ADHD acceptance, autonomy and confidence in their strengths.

5

SOCIAL & EMOTIONAL GROWTH Opportunities to build friendships, develop emotional literacy and practice communication and relationship skills.

4

COGNITIVE SUPPORT Accommodations for executive function challenges, support for learning differences and help with organisation and planning.

3

EMOTIONAL SAFETY A predictable, connected environment with consistent routines, secure attachment and a sense of being unconditionally accepted.

2

PHYSIOLOGICAL REGULATION Addressing nervous system dysregulation, sensory processing (e.g. proprioception, vestibular needs), gut health and nutrient sufficiency.

1

BIOLOGICAL STABILITY Adequate sleep, hydration, blood sugar balance, physical safety and regular movement.

Figure 4.1 *Parenting Hierarchy of Needs*

Overview of the tiers

> Biological stability: Your child's most basic physical needs: sleep, nutrition, movement and rest.

> Physiological (nervous system) regulation: Helping your child feel calm, grounded and safe in their body.

> Emotional safety: Secure, supportive relationships that make children feel understood and safe.

> Cognitive support: Building learning and problem-solving once the body and emotions are steady.

> Social and emotional growth: Developing friendships, resilience and collaboration skills.

> Purpose and fulfilment: Confidence, identity and reaching one's full potential.

If you're dealing with homework battles or school behaviour concerns, it's natural to want to start at the level of cognitive support. But learning sits higher up in the hierarchy. The first three foundational tiers (biological stability, physiological regulation and emotional safety) must be supported first. If your child is tired, anxious or dysregulated, they simply can't engage effectively with learning, no matter how capable they are.

Once these lower tiers are stabilised, schoolwork and behaviour become far more manageable and less stressful for both you and your child.

Now, let's walk through each tier in more detail.

1. Biological stability

The first tier of the Parenting Hierarchy is biological stability. This includes your child's most basic physical needs: sleep, nutrition, rest and healthy movement. These are the foundations of wellbeing. If your child's body and brain aren't supported at this level, everything else higher up the hierarchy will feel harder to achieve.

Biological factors

Within biological stability, we start with biological factors that influence ADHD. These include inherited traits (genetics), environmental influences and everyday lifestyle elements, such as sleep, screen use and nutrition.

Together, these factors shape how symptoms present and how your child feels day to day.

Genetics

The most well-established factor is genetics, so let's start there.

Research shows ADHD tends to run in families. Most parents discover they have ADHD after discovering their child has ADHD. This was the case for me and has been the case for many parents I work with. If your child has ADHD, there's a strong chance at least one parent or close relative does too (whether they have been diagnosed or not).

If you have ADHD, it doesn't automatically mean your child will too; however, neuroimaging studies have shown that differences in brain structure and function (particularly in the prefrontal cortex and basal ganglia, which are involved in executive functioning) can be inherited.[1]

The heritability of ADHD has been found to be around 74 to 80 per cent in twin studies, making it one of the most genetically influenced mental health conditions,[2] but there is often more than genes at play with ADHD, which we will explore next.

Genes aren't the whole story though. How those genes are switched 'on' or 'off' by lifestyle and environment (epigenetics; see page 167) also matters. I'll dive deeper into this in Chapter 8.

Environmental influences

While ADHD is primarily genetic, researchers also recognise that certain environmental influences can play a part in how it develops and how severe symptoms may become. These influences are not causes of ADHD on their own, but rather factors that can shape a child's overall development. Some of the areas scientists have studied include:

> *In utero:* Maternal stress, alcohol use, smoking or exposure to toxins such as lead or pesticides may slightly increase risk.
> *Birth and early years:* Complications at birth, premature birth or low birth weight have also been linked to a higher likelihood of ADHD. Because the brain develops so rapidly in the early years, disruptions during this period may have lasting effects.

It's important for parents to know that these factors are not something to blame themselves for. But recognising that things like low birth weight or early complications can increase the likelihood of ADHD means you can be more vigilant, seek early support if challenges arise, and give your child the best chance to thrive.

Biological processes

Beyond genetics and early environmental influences, everyday biological processes also play a major role in how ADHD symptoms show up. Factors such as nutrition, gut health, sleep and screen time can either make symptoms harder to manage or, when well supported, ease them.

While these environmental factors are not the *cause* of ADHD, they can contribute to symptoms or, if addressed, improve symptoms.

Nutrition and gut health

Research is starting to link nutrient status with ADHD symptoms, and deficiencies in omega-3 fatty acids, iron, zinc and magnesium have been observed in some children with ADHD.[3] The gut-brain axis is also an increasingly recognised factor where poor microbial diversity in the gut may impact mood and attention[4] (see Chapter 8 for more).

Sleep

Children with ADHD are more vulnerable to sleep disturbances. Unfortunately, poor sleep quality can also exacerbate symptoms of ADHD[5,6] (see Chapter 9).

Screen time

Excessive, or even minimal screen use in some sensitive children, can dysregulate and worsen their ADHD symptoms. When used before bedtime, it can impact sleep quality, worsening ADHD symptoms (see Chapter 16)

2. Physiological (nervous system) regulation

The second tier is physiological (nervous system) regulation. This is about helping your child feel calm, grounded and safe in their own body. For children with ADHD, their nervous systems are more easily thrown off balance, which means they may become overstimulated quickly, struggle to calm down or find it hard to cope with everyday stress. This means co-regulation strategies, calming routines and predictable rhythms are essential. When children feel regulated, they are better able to navigate emotions, behaviour and learning.

Before working on learning or behaviour, supporting your child's nervous system is key. Simple practises like routines, predictability, physical activity or calm connection with a caregiver can make a big difference in how safe and regulated your child feels.

We'll explore this in much greater detail in Chapter 11, where you'll find practical strategies to help your child, and yourself, stay regulated. For now, it's important to remember that regulation is the foundation for focus, cooperation and emotional wellbeing.

3. Emotional safety

The third tier is emotional safety. Children thrive when they feel seen, heard and understood. For children with ADHD, who may encounter more criticism, rejection or misunderstanding, emotional safety is especially important. It provides the buffer they need to take risks, learn resilience and bounce back from challenges.

The impact of trauma and chronic stress

Trauma is a key influence in ADHD-like symptoms. Symptoms such as inattention, hypervigilance and impulsivity can occur in children who have experienced trauma. However, ADHD and trauma can coexist, with ADHD even contributing to the severity of trauma.

The brain's natural response to a stressful situation (the fight-flight-freeze response) is meant to protect us from danger. However, when children are exposed to stress or trauma, their brains can become chronically activated, which can impair their executive functioning and emotional regulation. These areas are already vulnerable in children with ADHD, hence why ADHD could contribute to more severe trauma experiences.

Additionally, children with ADHD are more prone to trauma due to impulsivity, emotional regulation challenges and social difficulties, which increase their risk of bullying, academic failure and punishment.

Recognising these aspects helps you move away from blaming your child for their behaviours and towards a trauma-informed parenting approach.

Adverse childhood experiences (ACEs)

A study into ACEs highlighted how early childhood stress and trauma, such as exposure to violence, neglect, abuse or even caregiver mental illness, can have profound effects on a child's mental and physical health.

Screening for ACEs involves a questionnaire asking children and their caregivers about their exposures to emotional stresses. This yes/no screening generates an ACE score by giving one point for each 'yes' answer. A high ACE score is linked to an increased risk for ADHD, anxiety, depression and substance use.

Chronic exposure to stress and trauma changes how the brain and body respond to stress, which can lead to emotional dysregulation and difficulty with focus and attention.

If your child has experienced trauma, it's not too late to reshape their path by providing a strong caregiver bond, practising responsive parenting and creating a safe environment. These protective factors mitigate the effects of these ACEs and promote healing for your child.

Curiosity is your friend! Every behaviour you see from your child is communication. Your job is to understand the 'why' behind the 'what' so you can respond more effectively and compassionately.

Minimising the impacts of trauma:

> ➤ Understand your family history of ADHD or trauma.
> ➤ Build healthy routines for sleep, screen time, nutrition, movement and support self- and co-regulation.
> ➤ Find trauma-informed therapists trained in developmental trauma and ADHD who employ strategies to help your child feel safe enough to thrive.

> ➤ When you're calm, present and attuned to your child (remembering you don't have to be perfect) this can be a wonderful antidote to your child's stress.

Understanding this complex puzzle of factors contributing to your child's symptoms allows you to show more empathy towards them. With that empathy comes that crucial feeling of safety for them, and a new mindset for you, enabling you to adapt and nurture your unique child and advocate for them in the wider world.

As we've seen, ADHD doesn't arise from a single cause, it's shaped by biological and environmental factors.

4. Cognitive support

The fourth tier is cognitive support. Once the body and emotions feel steady, children are ready to engage in learning, problem-solving and academic growth. Parents often want to start here because school struggles feel urgent, but lasting progress only happens when the first three tiers are in place.

Children with ADHD often face unique learning challenges, such as difficulties with attention, organisation, working memory and following through on tasks. Cognitive support means giving them the right scaffolding, whether that's using visual schedules, breaking tasks into smaller steps, offering extra movement breaks or providing supportive teaching strategies. It also includes knowing when to advocate for school accommodations or tutoring tailored to their needs. We'll look at these supports in more detail in Chapter 14.

5. Social and emotional growth

The fifth tier is social and emotional growth. At this level, children develop friendships, collaboration skills and resilience. Children with ADHD may face extra social challenges, such as difficulty reading social cues, managing big emotions in friendships or coping with rejection.

Supporting their social and emotional growth means helping them build empathy, resilience and skills for navigating relationships. This might involve role-playing social scenarios, encouraging strengths-based activities where they can connect with peers or accessing structured social skills programs. We'll explore these areas further in Chapter 15.

6. Purpose and fulfilment

The final tier is purpose and fulfilment. At this level, children develop confidence, a strong sense of self and the ability to reach their full potential. These stages cannot be rushed. They naturally unfold once the lower tiers are met and the focus shifts toward building confidence, a strong sense of identity and eventually reaching their full potential.

For children with ADHD, who may hear more negative feedback than their peers, fostering self-esteem is especially vital. This means celebrating their strengths, recognising effort as much as achievement and helping them see themselves as capable and valuable. Self-actualisation grows from this foundation, as your child begins to pursue their passions, develop resilience and build a vision for their future. We'll explore these themes further in Chapter 12.

Your unique child

No two children with ADHD are the same because, despite all these interacting factors — genetics, environment, social and experiential factors — ADHD looks different in every child depending on the factors at play. Children's symptoms may intensify in stressful periods or settle down when they feel safe, supported and understood.

While understanding the ADHD brain and any co-occurring conditions is essential, it's only part of the picture. Your child is so much more than a diagnosis. To truly support and connect with your child, it helps to step back and look at the whole child: Who they are beyond their challenges? What are their strengths? What lights them up? What are their unique interests, quirks and talents? Recognising their gifts not only builds their confidence, but also helps you advocate for them more effectively, shape learning and parenting strategies and celebrate them as a developing person.

Considering your child's temperament, personality traits and even their love language is important. Some children thrive on physical affection, while others light up when they receive words of affirmation or quality time. Noticing how your child gives and receives love, how they handle transitions or express emotions and what truly motivates them helps you tailor your parenting in a way that resonates for them. This holistic understanding fosters deeper emotional safety and connection—something every child, and especially a neurodivergent one, needs. When you see your child as a whole person, rather than a collection of symptoms, you build the foundation for a relationship that nurtures both their growth and your confidence as a parent.

Part II

Being a calm, connected, compassionate parent

Effective parenting isn't about being perfect—it's about creating connection and showing up with calm, compassion and consistency.

Now that you understand your child's brain, strengths and challenges, it's time to turn the focus to you. Part II is where knowledge becomes action, introducing my 6Cs of ADHD parenting: calm, compassion, consistency, collaboration, curiosity and connection. These flexible, human-centred values will help guide you through the everyday chaos and beauty of parenting.

You'll learn how to bring these principles to life at home with practical, ADHD-friendly tools and strategies. Most importantly, you'll discover why supporting yourself is key—whether you're parenting solo, with a partner or managing ADHD yourself—so you can build a family culture rooted in emotional safety and mutual respect.

Chapter Five

Changing perspectives: My parenting philosophy

You can't act on what you don't yet know —but understanding changes everything, bringing wisdom and compassion for your past self.

Your child doesn't come with an instruction manual. Your parenting approach comes, for the most part, from how you were parented yourself and perhaps a few books you've read or courses you've taken over the years. But parenting a child with ADHD is not usually what you expected, and much of the traditional advice is outdated or doesn't apply to your unique situation.

Like many parents I've worked with, I've felt the stark mismatch between traditional parenting approaches and what neurodivergent children truly need. This often leads to parents feeling overwhelmed, burnt out and lost. I've lain awake doubting myself, cried after school drop-off and questioned where I was going wrong —just as you probably have.

When my daughter was diagnosed with ADHD at 14, things started to make sense, but I still didn't realise that I needed to parent differently. I panicked, thinking what you might be thinking now: 'I've messed it up', 'It's too late' or 'I don't know how to do this'.

If you're having these same thoughts, take a deep breath—it's never too late to start fresh. Traditional parenting may not work for your child with ADHD, but with the right strategies, life can improve for you and your family. I've seen things shift beautifully, even with small changes.

There's no such thing as a perfect parent—I've made plenty of mistakes and I'm still learning. Parenting advice changes over time, but what matters most is showing up with empathy, understanding and a willingness to learn from our mistakes.

In Part I, we explored your child's ADHD and its impacts. Now, we shift the spotlight to you. Parenting a child with ADHD isn't just about learning new strategies, it's about becoming the steady anchor your child needs. This isn't about blame, but about discovering how to respond in ways that support both you and your child.

This part of the book is your invitation to pause, reflect and reset—not with pressure, but with hope.

In this chapter, I'll share my Calm, Connected, Compassionate Parenting Philosophy—a mindset shift, not a one-size-fits-all approach—that underpins the strategies in this book and the foundation of your relationship with your child.

This philosophy consists of six core principles (the 6Cs):

> ➤ Connection 🫁
> ➤ Compassion ♥
> ➤ Curiosity 🔍
> ➤ Calm 🪷
> ➤ Collaboration 👥
> ➤ Consistency 🔋

These principles draw on neuroscience, lived experience, research and wisdom I've gleaned from many experts over the years. The goal is to empower your child, not control or change them. The 6Cs offer a consistent approach to support the practical strategies shared throughout this book. Let's look at each one in depth.

1. Connection 🙌

Your relationship with your child is the most powerful tool you have as a parent. When that connection feels strong and supportive, your child feels safe and understood. Children who feel safe and calm are better able to think clearly, manage their emotions and cooperate. In this settled state, they are more open to learning, listening and sharing with you.

Your relationship with your child should be at the heart of your parenting. You want a loving, respectful bond with your child that weathers life's inevitable ups and downs, but parenting a child with ADHD can place extra strain on your connection. Misunderstandings and overwhelm can create distance, but it's never too late to repair the relationship. You are your child's strongest advocate, greatest coach and the person who matters most.

Many children with ADHD grow up feeling misunderstood, but practising unconditional love can change that. While almost all parents would argue that, of course, they love their child unconditionally, sometimes—especially in harder moments—we can forget to actively demonstrate this to them. Unconditional love means not only that you love them, but you *let them know you love them,* no matter what. Show love, not only when your child behaves the way you want them to or when they succeed, but in all their most challenging moments. They must never feel unloved or unlovable.

Create quality time
In the busyness of daily life, even a few minutes of genuine, unrushed time with your child can make a big difference—especially for kids with ADHD, who often receive more correction than connection. Spending quality time with your child, even if it's just for a short period each day, where it's

just the two of you, is beneficial. It shows you enjoy their company, value their world and love them as they are. Make sure you allow your child to choose an activity they enjoy and keep the time positive, without criticism. Allowing them to show you something they're good at, or teach *you* how to do something, is also a boost for their self-esteem. When your child feels truly seen and valued, they're more likely to open up, cooperate and feel safe in your presence. This is how you build a relationship where your child feels safe telling you the *small* things now and the *big* things later.

Quality time for younger children

When you have younger children, quality time should be simple and playful. Let your child pick the game/activity, even if it means building lopsided Lego or role-playing a superhero scene for the tenth time. This is about connection, not perfection.

You might read a story together at bedtime, sing silly songs during bath time or have a dance party in the kitchen. Even five minutes of fully engaged play (without multitasking or distraction) can go a long way. If you have more than one child, aim to spend a little one-on-one time with each of them regularly, even if it's just a short cuddle and chat before bed. These moments communicate, 'You matter to me. *I see you.*'

Connecting with your teen

Quality time with teens looks a little different, but it's just as important. They may not ask for it, but they still deeply crave your interest and presence. Connection often happens *side by side* rather than face to face, so think about chatting while driving, walking the dog or doing chores together. Let your teen take the lead. Ask them about their music, hobbies and opinions. Be curious without being critical. If they invite you into their world, say, to watch their favourite show or try a game they love, say 'yes'. Go out for hot chocolate, visit a local market or cook a meal together. Let them see you enjoying their company. That shared time builds a bridge of trust that will carry you through the harder moments.

Whether your child is five or 15, the key is to slow down and make time. Don't wait for the perfect opportunity—create it, even in the small pockets of your day. Put down your phone. Leave the dishes for later. Let them feel your presence. These moments are how you build a relationship where your child knows they can come to you with anything because they've learned you care about *everything*, even the little things.

Strengths-based parenting

As we explored in Part I, a strengths-based parenting approach focuses on what your child does well rather than what they struggle with. Children with ADHD often receive constant correction and criticism in their daily lives, which can erode self-esteem and motivation. A strengths-based approach helps restore balance by noticing and nurturing their gifts, whether that's creativity, problem-solving, empathy, humour, determination or enthusiasm.

By shining a light on their strengths and celebrating effort and progress (not just outcomes), you help your child build a positive self-image and strengthen the connection between you. In Chapter 12, we'll look at how to build self-esteem and resilience.

Repair and reconnect

We all lose our cool sometimes—we're human after all. Even with the best intentions, you might yell, say something you regret or walk away in frustration. What matters most is what you do next. Show your child relationships can be mended, mistakes are part of being human and your love for them doesn't disappear in moments of anger.

Mending the relationship helps your child feel emotionally safe again. It teaches them conflict doesn't mean disconnection, and models accountability and empathy. A simple, heartfelt 'I'm sorry I shouted. I was feeling overwhelmed. I love you and I always will' goes a long way in rebuilding your connection.

Don't wait for your child to be 'okay' first. They may not have the tools yet, but you do. Reconnection can be a hug, shared laugh, invitation to play or simply sitting together quietly. These small moments lay the foundation for trust, showing your child no matter how big the emotions get, your connection is never lost.

Many parents experience periods of deep disconnection. It's painful, but relationships *can* heal. Start by gently acknowledging the disconnect: 'I know things have felt hard between us. I'd like to understand how we got here and how we can reconnect.' Even if your child doesn't respond right away, simply showing up with openness (and without blame) plants the seed for repair.

One mum I worked with had a teenage son who stopped speaking to her after years of tension. She let go of trying to fix everything and simply invited him for walks—no pressure, just presence. At first, he stayed silent but, over time, he opened up, sharing that what hurt most was feeling like she only saw what was wrong with him. That honest moment sparked change. She began focusing more on his strengths and giving him more space, and their connection began to return. Reconnecting takes time, but small, consistent efforts rebuild trust and show your child how to do the same in their own relationships.

2. Compassion ♥

By now, you've started to develop a deeper understanding of your child: diagnosis, co-occurring conditions, strengths, sensitivities and what makes them beautifully themselves. But even with all this insight, parenting can still feel overwhelming.

You may be doing your absolute best, yet still find yourself caught in daily battles over chores, homework, behaviour or sibling conflict. School might feel like a source of disappointment instead of pride, and your child's social world may be marked by exclusion or loneliness. Perhaps the hardest thing of all is seeing your child begin to internalise these struggles, and feeling different, discouraged or broken.

Compassion is the emotional anchor of parenting a child with ADHD. It's essential, not just for your child, but for you. Compassion helps you shift your mindset from seeing your child *as the problem* to understanding your child is *struggling with* a problem. Instead of thinking, 'He won't concentrate', you begin to see, 'He's having a hard time concentrating'.

This simple but profound shift externalises the problem and allows you to work *with* your child, not against them. You move from frustration to partnership, from blame to understanding.

True compassion doesn't mean lowering expectations or being permissive, it means:

> ➤ meeting your child where they are, with kindness and patience—walking beside them as they build the skills they need
> ➤ holding space for their big emotions, recognising their behaviour is often an expression of dysregulation, not defiance
> ➤ noticing when your child is hurting, even if that hurt comes out as anger, avoidance or meltdowns, and responding with curiosity rather than criticism
> ➤ recognising when systems and environments present structural barriers to your child's wellbeing and ability to thrive, and becoming partners in finding ways to succeed anyway and advocate for change and inclusion.

When you approach parenting with compassion, you create emotional safety, and that's the foundation your child needs to thrive. Compassion allows you to show your child: 'You're not broken. I'm here with you. We're in this together.' Compassion is the balm for your own heart, too. It reminds you that you're not failing, you're facing something hard, and doing it the best you can and with love.

3. Curiosity ⌕

Most, if not all, of the strategies outlined in this book rely on you having a baseline understanding about ADHD and a curiosity about what that means for your child's experience of the world. By stepping into your child's shoes and seeing the world through their eyes, you're able to foster a deeper connection and sense of compassion that will carry you through even the toughest times.

As discussed in Part I, by understanding the physiological and neurological workings of your child's brain, you can better show up with empathy, awareness and the right tools to help your child flourish exactly as they are. As clinical psychologist Dr Ross Greene argues, 'children do well if they can', so your job is to identify and address whatever it is that's getting in the way of them doing well—and to do this effectively, you need to get curious.

A useful way to conceptualise this is through the iceberg metaphor, described by Dr Mona Delahooke in her book *Beyond Behaviours* and illustrated in Figure 5.1. Your child's 'behaviours' are on top of the iceberg—but this is just part of the picture. Beneath the surface of the iceberg lurk unmet needs, sensory sensitivities, trauma or other emotional struggles. If you only focus on correcting the behaviours on the top, you'll miss the opportunity to explore the clues to what's going on for your child underneath, and what will help them feel safe and supported.

Gathering this information puts you in a great place to support your child where needed, while encouraging them in their particular interests, talents and strengths. Understanding what makes your child tick will enable you to see their behaviours as the tip of an iceberg with the reasons that trigger it below. Could it be anxiety? Overwhelm or a still-developing skill? Could they be hungry, tired or overstimulated? The better you know your child, the better you're able to identify what factors affect their life (which we will cover in Part III) and how to support them in everyday situations (discussed in Part IV). In Chapter 11, we'll explore how to identify signs of dysregulation and help your child return to a calmer state.

A curious, compassionate approach is critical when concerning behaviours or setbacks arise. Modern neuroscience tells us much of what we've been labelling as 'bad behaviour' is a stress response, not a deliberate act of defiance and, therefore, requires different tools to ensure your child gets the support they need. Shift your lens to view behaviour as communication and approach it with curiosity and compassion and seek a deeper understanding of what's going on beneath the surface.

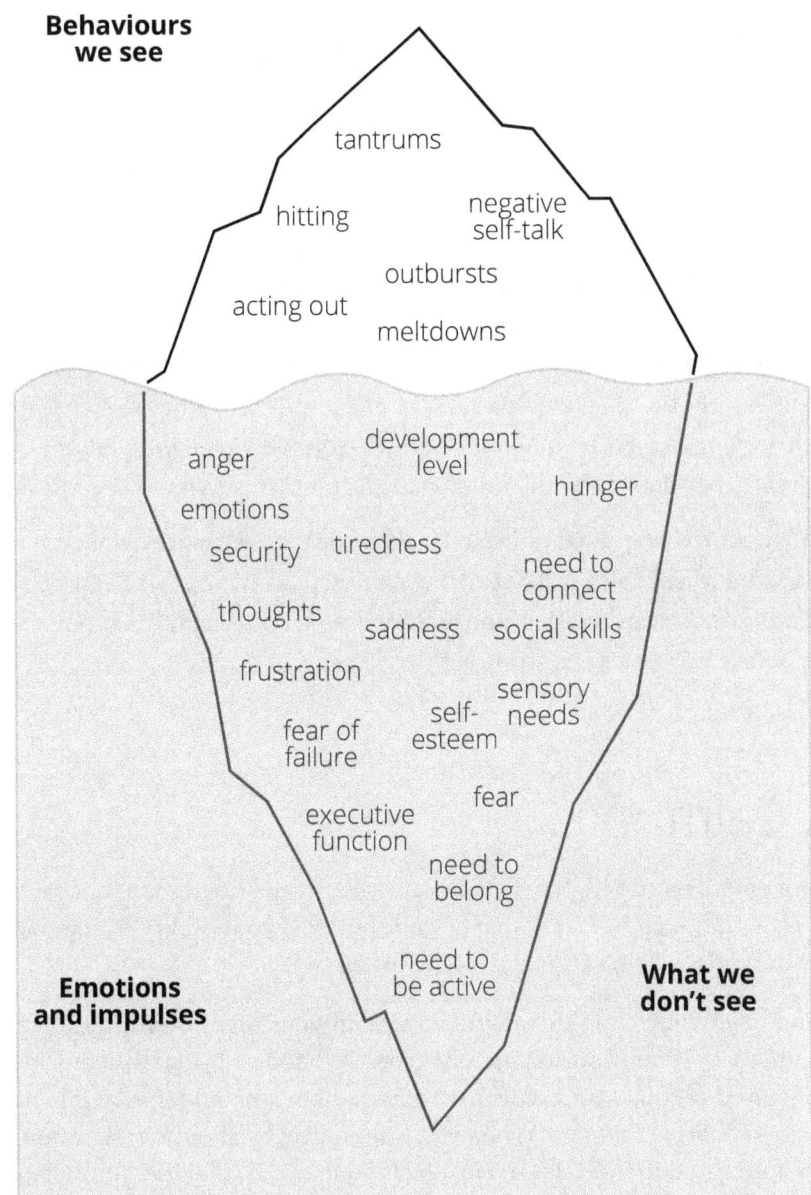

Figure 5.1 *Iceberg metaphor*

Understanding Oppositional Defiant Disorder (ODD)

ODD is often diagnosed alongside ADHD. It's not a neurobiological condition like ADHD, but a label for a set of behaviours that can manifest in children with ADHD. Those behaviours usually include anger, defiance, irritability, arguing, frequent outbursts and resistance to authority. As we've just explored, when a child exhibits behaviours, they're giving us clues. It's important to understand that they're not necessarily being defiant for the sake of being difficult, they're simply struggling to regulate emotions or feeling overwhelmed in situations where they don't have the skills or coping mechanisms to succeed.

Rather than labelling them as 'difficult' or 'defiant', it's more helpful to explore what's going on beneath the behaviour with the goal of finding out what skills are missing, and teach those skills in a supportive, non-punitive way, using the strategies in this book.

4. Calm 🪷

When emotions run high, whether your child is melting down, unable to cooperate or pushing every one of your buttons, your ability to regulate _your_ nervous system can make all the difference.

If you meet your child's dysregulation with your own, it only escalates the situation. When you stay steady, grounded and emotionally available, you help co-regulate your child's nervous system and model what it looks like to handle big feelings. When you lose control by shouting, slamming or snapping, your child doesn't just hear your words, they _feel_ your chaos and it makes them feel unsafe. That sense of emotional unpredictability damages connections and makes it harder for your child to calm down. It's okay to have moments where you lose it—we all do. What matters most is how you repair, reflect and keep practising. I refer to this as regulated parenting, which looks like:

> ➤ *Recognising and regulating your own emotions.* Calm starts with you, which can be difficult when concerning behaviours surface or when you're feeling dysregulated yourself.
> ➤ *Viewing your child's behaviours as clues, not misbehaviour.* Pause to ask yourself what's going on for your child underneath and how you can offer support.
> ➤ *Helping your child calm down* and feel safe and connected enough to move forward.

This approach builds emotional safety over time, strengthens your relationship and teaches your child how to regulate themselves more effectively.

This is easier said than done, especially when you're exhausted or overwhelmed! In Chapter 6, you'll explore strategies for creating a calm home environment and practical examples of co-regulation. These are explored further in Chapter 7, which looks at how understanding yourself and prioritising self-care is essential to remaining calm for your child. In Chapter 11, you'll learn about nervous system regulation.

When it comes to your child's behaviour, become a detective. Look beyond the surface and consider what might be driving those big reactions or tricky moments, especially the things that may be outside their control. Behaviour will often be a symptom of a dysregulated nervous system—an overwhelmed brain or body. Children with ADHD are often more easily overstimulated or experience greater distress as a result of dysregulation, which can, in turn, drive less than ideal behaviours or coping mechanisms. For example, if your child melts down after school, pause to ask yourself: Are they just trying to push my buttons or are they struggling with anxiety or emotional overload? They may have been holding it together all day in a loud, demanding environment, leaving their nervous system overloaded and exhausted by the time they get home. When you identify signs of dysregulation in your child, your job is to create a calm, supportive environment and support your child to regain their calm.

5. Collaboration

Traditional methods of parenting focusing on compliance and consequences are far less effective for children with ADHD and often backfire. Adopting a 'coach approach', focused on collaborative skill-building rather than a command approach, helps to build your child's skills and self-esteem and strengthen your relationship with them, rather than simply managing their behaviour.

Rather than seeing yourself as the boss and your child as someone who should comply with your instructions no matter what, the coach-approach positions you as a guide and mentor who provides support. This doesn't mean giving up on rules, boundaries or expectations, but it does shift how you work with your child to meet those goals.

Many children with ADHD have oppositional tendencies or struggle to regulate their emotions, meaning they often won't do as you say, just because you said so. This is usually not because they're intentionally disrespectful or defiant, but because there is some reason why they're unable to meet the expectation placed on them. Getting into a debate or 'putting your foot down' simply won't work, it will only escalate tension and disconnect between you. Rewards and consequences have their place (see Chapter 7), but when overused or used at the wrong times they will be ineffective, feel like punishment and impact your child's self-esteem.

In contrast, as a coach, you meet your child where they're at and help them to do their best. From a place of connection and compassion, you can see your child is often not *choosing* to behave in a certain way or not to complete a certain task. Instead, you need to discover what is going on for your child and help them solve their challenge accordingly. They may need more support to build certain skills or get their executive functioning and impulse control working to do as you ask. Once you understand where the unsolved problem or the developing skill is, scaffold your child and teach those developing skills or help them to solve the problem.

A coach doesn't expect perfection, they identify what needs work and break it down into manageable steps, offering support and encouragement along the way.

As a coach, you might:

> ➤ scaffold tasks so your child doesn't feel overwhelmed
> ➤ guide, model and support your child, rather than command
> ➤ acknowledge your child's effort above their outcomes
> ➤ validate your child's feelings while still holding appropriate limits.

Being a parent-coach means a shift in your parenting mindset from giving orders to guiding skill-building. Your role as a coach is to help your child develop the skills they need to become independent in life, rather than focusing on gaining their compliance. It's a long-term strategy prioritising connection, collaboration and capability over control. As a coach, you don't jump in to do the work for your child, nor do you shame them when they make a mistake. You observe, support and guide improvement with patience and encouragement.

When you employ coach-approach parenting, you're offering guidance and structure while still honouring your child's autonomy. You validate their feelings and involve your child in the problem-solving process. As a coach, you're working alongside your child towards shared goals in day-to-day life.

In the next chapter, we'll explore how this approach aligns with Dr Ross Greene's Collaborative and Proactive Solutions Model, which provides practical tools to work with your child on unmet needs and developing skills before the escalation happens.

6. Consistency 👣

Consistency in your parenting approach is critical to build trust between you and your child. Consistency doesn't mean rigidity; flexibility remains important. Consistency demonstrates you'll remain calm, compassionate and connected no matter what and that's the key to a strong relationship. When your child knows how you respond to different behaviours and scenarios, it helps them feel less anxious, supports them to make informed choices and encourages them to overcome setbacks and mistakes without shame.

Consistent parenting also helps provide your child with the predictability and structure their brains sometimes struggle to create for themselves. Consistent expectations, routines and boundaries help your child feel safe and secure, even when things get messy around them. Without these, children with ADHD can become overwhelmed or dysregulated. Repetition and routine also strengthen neural pathways supporting executive functioning tasks such as planning and self-regulation.

It's important this consistency is mirrored by everyone involved in parenting your child, whether that's a partner, co-parent or other family members and carers. While it's natural for parents or caregivers to have differing approaches, it's important that everyone is aware of some of the slightly different strategies you may be using with your neurodivergent child. Presenting a united front with other caregivers creates a sense of safety and predictability for your child, while conflicting approaches can increase anxiety, confusion or oppositional behaviour. Take the time to get on the same parenting page (see Chapter 6). Part V provides further detail on taking a whole-of-family approach and building and communicating with your support network.

In Chapter 6, we'll discuss how to effectively set, communicate and maintain boundaries as a family in a way that allows your child to know what is expected from them, but also what they can expect from you in different situations. I'll also provide some tips for getting on the same page with other caregivers.

A parenting philosophy grounded in hope

My parenting philosophy has calm, connection and compassion at its centre. It doesn't focus on behaviour, which is where a lot of advice for parenting with ADHD focuses. Using my philosophy, you'll change your narrative from 'What's wrong with my child?' and 'How can I get them to behave?' to 'How can I support my child's growth and development in the best way possible?'

At the end of the day, your child doesn't need you to be the perfect parent—there's no such thing! They need you to believe in them, especially when they don't believe in themselves. You're going to have tough days and you'll lose your calm sometimes—as will they.

This philosophy teaches that our relationship with our child is the most powerful tool we have and the one that brings most satisfaction to all involved. Every situation has multiple moments where we have the chance to improve our connection with our child.

Your child needs you to be calm, compassionate and connected. Using my philosophy, you're not just 'managing' ADHD, you're supporting your child to build important life skills, nurture their self-esteem and help them reach their potential. In this way, you raise your child not just to survive but to fully thrive!

My philosophy is more than a strategy, it's a new mindset, a new lens with which to view your child and your parenting journey with a perspective that your child is not broken—they are perfect—just wired differently.

Chapter Six

The 6 Cs: Putting calm, connected, compassionate parenting into practice

The 6Cs are your daily anchors—every time you choose calm, connection and compassion, you're gently transforming your family from within.

Now you've had a chance to explore my Calm, Connected, Compassionate Parenting Philosophy informed by the 6Cs, this next chapter is where we bring it to life.

You may be wondering, 'What does this look like in everyday life?' That's exactly what we're going to dive into here. While the previous chapter laid the foundation of mindset and relational intention, this chapter is all about the *how*—the practical tips, real-life strategies and adjustments that will help you embody this philosophy in your home. It's one thing to understand your child differently, and another to know what to *do* in the heat of the moment, or how to set up your environment and routines in a way that supports everyone's wellbeing.

I'm not giving you a rulebook, I'm equipping you with tools and flexible approaches that meet you and your child where you are. You'll find encouragement, examples and small changes that can make a big difference so you feel more confident, capable and connected in your parenting every day.

Some core strategies can be applied across almost every parenting situation. These form your core parenting toolkit. Pick a different drill bit or screwdriver head depending on your child's individual context or the situation at hand, but these form the basic ingredients of your parenting know-how.

> Curious, collaborative problem-solving
> Effective communication
> Setting and maintaining boundaries and routines
> Using rewards and consequences
> Creating calm and supportive environments
> Working together as parents

Resisting the urge to rush

A quick note before we begin: take things *one step at a time.*

In this book you'll come across many ideas, strategies and perspective shifts. It's tempting to want to try to fix *everything* all at once. I encourage you not to try to tackle every problem at once. Doing so will likely leave you feeling discouraged and burnt out. Spreading your energy too thin will backfire and prevent you from making meaningful progress.

Just choose one thing that feels doable and start there. *A journey of a thousand miles begins with a single step,* as they say. Begin by brainstorming specific challenges you're currently facing: morning routines, sibling conflict, homework battles or emotional outbursts.

Ask yourself: Which of these, if improved even slightly, would make the biggest positive difference to my day-to-day life?

Lasting change doesn't come from doing everything perfectly; it comes from small, consistent efforts over time. Give yourself permission to go slow and trust every step forward is progress.

Curious, collaborative problem-solving

In the previous chapter, we talked about the importance of curiosity and collaboration as core principles embodied in the idea of coach-approach parenting. Rather than stepping in as an enforcer, the coach-approach positions you as a guide who stays regulated and helps your child return to calm while building their skills over time. It's about becoming a detective not a disciplinarian, leading with empathy, structure and insight.

We'll dive deeper into what that looks like in practice through a framework for collaborative problem-solving developed by clinical psychologist Dr Ross Greene and apply the CPS Model across a range of scenarios (not just conflict scenarios) when you're dealing with challenging behaviour.

Greene identifies three main ways adults usually respond to concerning behaviour:

> ➤ *Impose their will*: traditional top-down, punitive approach, often leading to power struggles
> ➤ *Let it go temporarily*: setting an issue aside, if your child isn't ready to manage it
> ➤ *Problem-solve collaboratively*: working together to find a mutually satisfying solution.

Dr Greene's model is called Collaborative and Proactive Solutions because it aims to solve problems *collaboratively* with your child and *proactively* find solutions for their unsolved problems.

It requires you to view your child's behaviour as an unsolved mystery, a need to be met or a skill to be developed rather than a behavioural problem. Your goal is to find out which skills your child needs help with, help your child develop those skills and scaffold them as they learn, instead of focusing on modifying behaviour and trying to coerce them with rewards and consequences.

Dr Green's mantra is 'children do well if they can', which makes so much sense! Why wouldn't your child want to do well? The opposite way of thinking is 'your child does well if they *want* to', which assumes that difficult behaviour is a matter of choice or willpower rather than a developing skill or underlying challenge. If you believe your child's behaviour is intentional, then you'll focus on attempting to modify their behaviour using rewards and consequences — rewarding the behaviours you like and punishing or using consequences for the behaviours you don't.

Imagine if I said I'll give you $100 to walk a tightrope (which you lack the skill to do), and if you don't manage it, I'll impose a consequence for not doing so. That would be extremely frustrating, wouldn't it? You would probably want to earn the $100, show me you *can* walk the tightrope, while avoiding a consequence. If you don't have the ability to do the task, it's a lose-lose situation. Being asked to do this task will leave you facing a consequence simply because you don't have the skill to perform it — even if you try as hard as possible. Being asked to do so might elicit a range of emotions such as anger, frustration, embarrassment, resentment, a sense of injustice and so on.

So, if your child wants to do well, but can't because they are yet to develop that ability, then getting punished or missing out on a reward for doing something they do want to do but can't is just going to make them feel angry or frustrated.

Dr Greene argues that when a child displays concerning behaviour, it's often because they're unable to meet an expectation being placed on them and that their skills are still developing in some way. These emerging skills he calls 'unsolved problems'. With this perspective, you can now view your child's concerning behaviour as difficulty meeting an expectation rather than an intentional action.

How does it work?

Greene proposes a three-step process to implement Collaborative and Proactive Solutions.

Step 1: The empathy step

Your objective in step 1 is to gather information from your child's perspective and find out what their concerns are. It's vital you ask your child for this crucial information because without their input you won't know exactly what is going on for them and, thus, how to solve the problem.

You won't always be able to identify the cause of a behaviour on your own, and nor should you make assumptions on behalf of your child—you could be wrong.

Listen to, and understand, your child's perspective. Ask open-ended questions and stay curious about what's going on for them beneath their behaviour. For example: 'It seems like getting started on homework has been tough lately. What's been going on?'

You may need to dig down to find the heart of the problem, because if you don't identify the core issue, you'll end up with a less effective solution—or no solution at all. You'll know you've reached the heart of the problem when your child's answer feels specific, makes sense and truly matters to them; for example, moving from '*I hate homework*' to '*I don't understand the instructions and I feel stupid asking for help*'. A good sign you've reached the core is when your child seems calmer or relieved after sharing—that's often a sign they feel understood.

To help get there, use gentle digging questions such as:

> ➤ 'Can you tell me more about that?'
> ➤ 'What's the hardest part?'
> ➤ 'When does it usually feel toughest?'
> ➤ 'What would make it a bit easier for you?'

The extra time it takes to do this is worthwhile, as it will save you time in arguments, improve your relationship with your child and strengthen your child's self-esteem and problem-solving skills.

Get curious

When your child is melting down over what seems like nothing, or unable to do something you've asked them to do a hundred times, your approach should be to ask: _What's really going on here?_ Your child's behaviour is giving you clues. They're not just displaying unwanted behaviours to annoy you or push your buttons. These behaviours often happen for a reason. Your job is to become a detective and find out what could be triggering those behaviours so you can respond effectively. Get curious — not reactive!

Think about the last time your child behaved in a concerning way. Why do you think they behaved that way? Think about what came _before_ the behaviour. Common reasons for concerning behaviour include your child feeling:

➤ hungry

➤ tired

➤ thirsty

➤ anxious

➤ frustrated

➤ angry

➤ overwhelmed

➤ unnoticed.

Think about the circumstances preceding the behaviour. Ask yourself:

➤ Where were they?

➤ When did it happen?

➤ Who were they with?

➤ What were they doing or being asked to do?

➤ What else was going on at the time?

> Had they been using screens?

> What had they eaten or drunk?

> Is there anything else that may have contributed?

This is not an exhaustive list, but these are common behavioural triggers, especially for children with ADHD, and a great starting point. In Part III, we'll explore in detail the factors that can affect your child's ADHD symptoms and behaviours, from nutrition to screen time, to support you on your detective journey.

Start asking yourself these questions and see if you find any patterns. Does it always happen after screen time, a particular lesson at school, before homework time, with certain people, in certain places, after eating certain foods and so on? When you start identifying patterns, you start getting a better idea of what might have been behind their angry outburst, rude behaviour or meltdown, and this will help you know how to react more compassionately or to solve any problems you identify in a more sustainable way. Your child's behavioural triggers are likely caused by still-developing skills such as:

> executive function

> social skills

> academic ability

> problem-solving strategies

> self-reflection

> study habits

> time management

> organisational skills

> planning

> flexibility to change task

> emotional regulation.

Step 2: Define adult perspective

This step focuses on expressing your *adult* perspective. This is where you calmly and clearly share what's important to you, whether it's safety, learning, routines or values, so your perspective is *part* of the solution. It's not about laying down the law, it's about making sure your perspective is heard and considered alongside your child's. For example: 'I understand it's hard, but I also want to make sure your schoolwork gets done so you can keep up.'

Now, instead of reacting to their behaviour, you're going to pre-empt it happening by proactively collaborating with your child to identify the 'unsolved problem' driving their behaviour. This shift in focus helps reduce blame and gets to the heart of what's going on.

For instance, if your child resists bedtime because they feel it's 'boring' or 'too early', you might say:

> *'I hear that bedtime feels boring to you, but my concern is that you need enough sleep to have energy for school and to feel good the next day.'*

Or, if homework leads to tears, you might explain:

> *'I understand that homework feels frustrating because the instructions are confusing. My concern is that you still need to hand it in, and I want to help you feel confident doing it.'*

These conversations should only ever happen when everyone is calm and regulated. Trying to solve problems in the middle of a meltdown or conflict will not only fail, as your child's logical brain is not in control at those times, but you may end up escalating the situation and making your child and yourself feel worse. This should be a proactive, not reactive, approach.

Step 3: Invitation to collaborate 👥

Work together with your child to brainstorm realistic solutions that address both of your perspectives.

Once you discover your child's emerging skill or the reason for their behaviour, you'll be able to support them. Concerning behaviour becomes predictable once you identify your child's unsolved problem, and realise their behaviour is due to placing expectations on them that exceed their skills. For example: 'Can we think of a way to make homework a bit easier for you while still making sure it gets done?'

Adults tend to solve problems unilaterally, that is you decide what your child's problem is and come up with a solution, without even talking to your child about it. When you try to solve their problems this way, you're unlikely to be successful. Your problem-solving must be done *with* your child—collaboratively—to successfully solve their problems. Do it *with* your child, not *to* your child.

Your first solution may not work perfectly (or at all), and that's okay. Problem-solving is a process not a one-time fix. You simply return to the table together, reflect on what didn't work and try again—collaboratively.

Don't attempt to address too many issues at once, you'll only become overwhelmed. Start small by choosing one or two high-priority issues and focus your energy on those to increase your chance of success and help build your child's trust in the process.

We've looked at how to become a parenting detective, seeing behaviour as a clue to what's happening beneath the surface and explored the CPS approach. Together, these ideas shift the focus from controlling behaviour to understanding needs and building skills. This approach takes effort but so does living in constant conflict. By embracing collaboration, you reduce overwhelm, strengthen connection, and help your child build the lifelong skills they need to thrive. CPS encourages you to move from reacting with consequences to proactively solving problems *with* your child—a win-win for both regulation and relationship.

Effective communication

One of the biggest shifts you can make is learning how to communicate in ways that reach your child. Children with ADHD often struggle with auditory processing, working memory, emotional regulation and impulse control, so when we talk *at* them (especially when they're already dysregulated), it can feel like throwing words into the wind. They either tune out, get overwhelmed or react defensively, and this can escalate situations and lose trust.

When our words become too frequent, too long or too negative, children with ADHD tend to either shut down or push back. Effective communication isn't about saying more, it's about saying less but with more clarity and intention. How you speak *to* your child shapes how they see themselves and how safe they feel with you.

Let's explore a few practical ways to build trust through your words and actions.

Say less, act more

Many of us fall into the habit of over-explaining, lecturing or repeating ourselves when our child doesn't do what we've asked. ADHD brains often struggle to hold on to too much verbal information at once. Long-winded explanations, especially when layered with emotion, are usually ineffective.

Instead, keep it short, simple and calm. Say what you need to say once and then follow through with action if needed. Fewer words often have more impact.

Instead of saying: 'How many times do I have to tell you to put your shoes on? We're going to be late again and I'm tired of reminding you every single day. This is ridiculous!'

Try: 'Please put your shoes on now.' (Then walk over and gently guide them if needed.)

When you speak less and act more, you eliminate the power struggle and reduce the emotional intensity.

Tell them what to do versus what not to do

The ADHD brain responds better to *positive directives* than negative commands.

Take the focus off the don'ts and focus on the do's. If you're constantly telling your child what not to do, you're not telling them what they *should be doing*. Telling them what you want them to do and why can be effective:

Instead of saying: 'Don't yell like that; it's embarrassing me.'

Try: 'Please lower your voice. We're in a library, so we need to be quiet.'

Instead of saying: 'Don't run inside!'

Try:' Walk inside, please.'

Instead of saying: 'Stop yelling!'

Try: 'Use a calm voice.'

These small tweaks in language can significantly reduce confusion, especially when your child is already emotionally charged. ADHD brains benefit from clear, actionable guidance.

Telling them what to *do* helps anchor their behaviour in the moment and makes it more likely they'll succeed, which, in turn, boosts their confidence and sense of safety with you.

Give clear, specific instructions

Children with ADHD often struggle to follow multiple instructions and often miss or misunderstand vague or long instructions. Instructions such as 'Get ready for school', 'Clean your room' or 'Be good' are too abstract. What does 'Get ready' mean? What's the first step? What counts as 'good'?

Instead, be specific and break it down into manageable chunks; for example, 'Put on your school uniform, then come to the kitchen for breakfast' or 'Put the dirty clothes in the basket and the books on the shelf'.

If possible, get your child's attention first before giving instructions. Say their name, get on their level, make eye contact, touch their shoulder gently before speaking and then give your short, clear instruction.

Where possible, reduce competing distractions such as screens, TV or radio noise. Asking your child to repeat your request ensures you know they've understood what you've asked, while reinforcing it in their mind.

Following these tips will help you cut through distractions and improve the chance your child will process and act on your requests.

When your communication is predictable, respectful and clear, your child starts to feel safer with you. They know what to expect. They're less likely to feel overwhelmed, confused or ashamed. This reduces friction and emotional situations, making it easier for your child to comply because they know exactly what's being asked.

Over time, when your child experiences you as someone who is fair, consistent and easy to follow (not someone who floods them with frustration or corrections), they'll trust you more, and trust is the foundation that allows all the other parenting strategies to work.

Catch them doing well

Children with ADHD often hear far more corrections than compliments throughout their day: 'Stop that', 'Pay attention', 'Why can't you just…?' Over time, this chips away at their self-esteem and motivation. Actively noticing and naming the positive behaviours you want to see more of (even the tiny ones) is one of the simplest, most powerful ways to shift this dynamic.

Sometimes, when things are going well, we may feel we don't want to jinx it, so we say nothing. But, if we want them to do more positive things, we need to notice and comment when they do. Acknowledge it right then and there:

> ➤ 'Thanks for starting your homework without me asking—that shows responsibility.'
> ➤ 'I saw you give it another go—that was really brave.'

Your praise should, of course, be genuine and sincere, but make it a habit to notice the positives at the time, particularly in those areas your child has difficulty with, such as following instructions, playing quietly, waiting their turn, helping out and so on. Be specific; for example, 'I appreciate how you tidied up after the game today—that's really helpful', and see how this impacts your relationship with your child moving forward.

Always praise their positive behaviour, even when there's also unwanted behaviour. For example, 'Thank you for saying sorry about the fight. Other than that, you've played really well with your brother this afternoon.' Don't harp on about any lapse in behaviour and keep any discussions about it short.

Offer support when appropriate or needed; for example, try 'You've done a great job with that artwork. Shall I help you put it on the table, out of the way' rather than just asking them to clear it away. In this way, you're supporting them while teaching them the right thing to do.

Positive reinforcement not only builds confidence, it also reinforces the behaviours you're trying to encourage. When your child believes you see the good in them, not just what's going wrong, they feel safer, more connected and more willing to cooperate. This is how trust and motivation grow.

Managing difficult conversations with responsive parenting

You may face a constant stream of situations demanding decisions, some small, some explosive and many somewhere in between. The truth is, you don't have to respond to *everything* and you certainly don't need to respond immediately. One of the most impactful parenting tools you can develop is the ability to pause and *choose* how (or whether) to respond.

Instead of jumping straight to discipline or correction, ask: *What's driving this behaviour?* Many concerning behaviours are simply symptoms of unmet needs, sensory overload, anxiety, tiredness or developing skills.

It helps to:

> ➤ name the behaviour clearly (e.g., 'It's not okay to hit' or 'You're shouting')
> ➤ stay curious: Why might they be acting this way?
> ➤ respond to the need *behind* the behaviour rather than just the behaviour itself.

By taking this pause, you shift from reactive parenting to responsive parenting, something that supports long-term emotional growth and connection. Figure 6.1 (overleaf) gives a clear visual of the responses available in given situations, and which will be explained more fully.

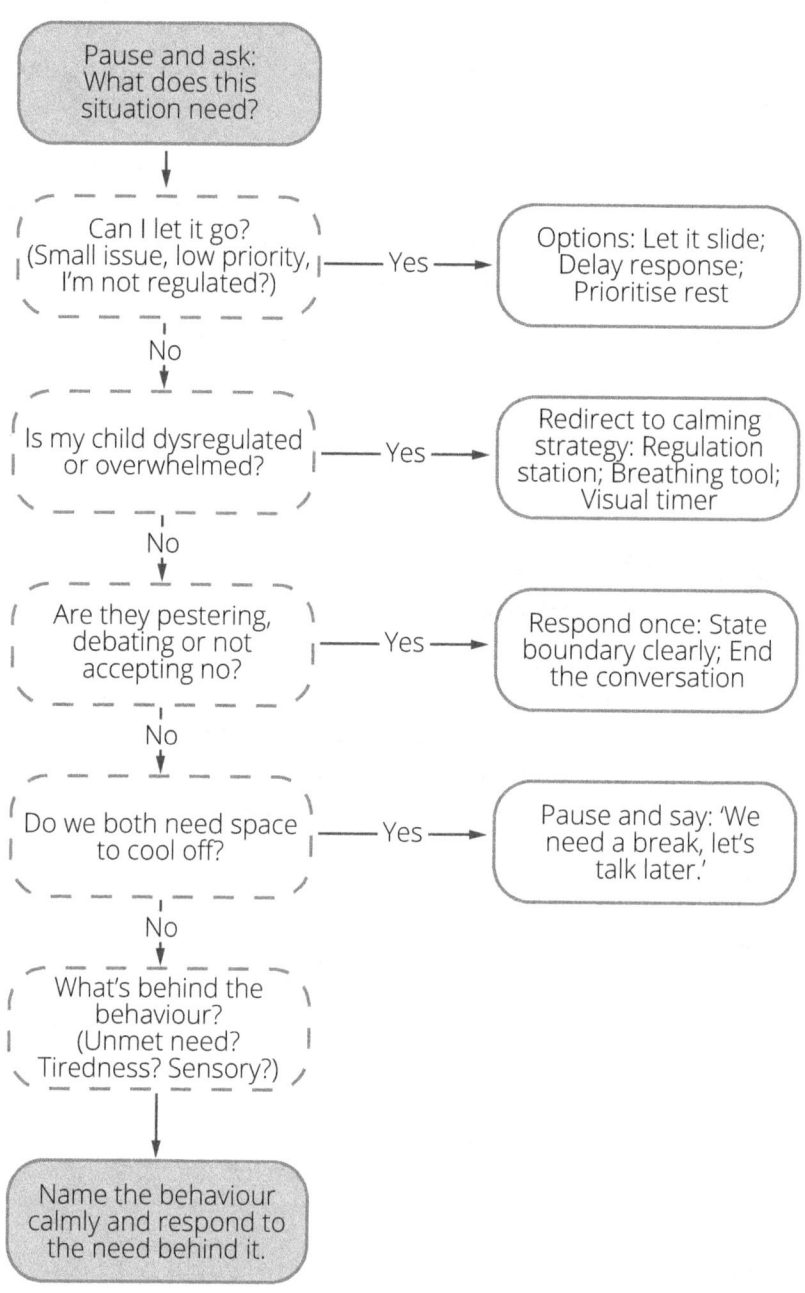

Figure 6.1 *Responsive parenting decision chart*

This sort of intentional decision-making can be the difference between a day that spirals and one that ends in reconnection. It's not about getting it right every time (none of us do), but about gradually learning to parent with both empathy and clarity.

Letting it go

Not everything needs to be a teachable moment. Some things are just not worth the emotional energy. Ask yourself:

> ➤ Is this small in the big picture?
> ➤ Is it more about my own triggers than my child's behaviour?
> ➤ Am I feeling too tired, dysregulated or overwhelmed to deal with this effectively?

If so, it's okay to:

> ➤ let it slide for now (don't sweat the small stuff)
> ➤ say, 'This isn't a priority today'
> ➤ tell yourself, 'This might sort itself out without me intervening.'

Giving yourself permission to *not* react to everything doesn't mean you're being permissive, it means you're being intentional.

Create a calming strategy

Before jumping in with consequences, questions or instructions, ask: *Is my child in a place where they can hear me?*

If they're dysregulated, they likely can't process logic, reason or requests because their logical brain has gone offline and their fight-or-flight response has taken over. Because they're unable to respond logically at this time, what they need is your calm presence to help them coregulate and feel safe again.

Co-create a calming strategy with your child in advance that your child feels comfortable with and you know will be effective. Your child will know what to expect, and you'll feel more confident in helping them regain their calm in the heat of the moment.

The goal is not to control their behaviour but to support them in returning to a state of regulation. Only then can teaching, problem-solving and learning happen.

For more on emotional regulation and managing meltdowns, see Chapter 11.

Debating limits

Sometimes your child won't take no for an answer. If they keep engaging in further debate, whining or pestering on a specific topic after you've made a decision, it can be tempting to keep engaging, explaining or justifying your decision. But often, less is more. Set a calm, firm and respectful limit; for example, 'We've already talked about this, and the answer is "no". I'm not going to keep discussing it.' By doing this, you're simply choosing not to give energy to a conversation that's already been resolved.

If you've given a clear answer, especially a 'no', it's important to:

> ➤ say it once
> ➤ set a boundary
> ➤ avoid entering a debate.

Importantly, you should continue to engage warmly with your child in all other areas of conversation and activity.

This approach helps reinforce boundaries without turning everyday challenges into ongoing power struggles, while also modelling boundaries and emotional regulation to your child.

Reflection/cool down time

Sometimes things are clearly heading towards a blow up, and both you and your child need time to cool off. Say:

> ➤ 'We both need a break. Let's take some time apart and talk when we're calm.'
> ➤ 'Let's press pause and come back to this later.'

Your child, depending on their age, might like to head to their 'regulation station' (see page 118 for more on this) or other safe space. If your child is older, or it's safe to do so, you might remove yourself from the situation and regulate yourself.

This approach isn't a 'time out' or a 'punishment' for your child, it's the opportunity for all involved to regulate themselves before a situation escalates and to have a chance to reflect on the interaction. It models emotional intelligence and helps avoid power struggles or unproductive yelling matches.

Establishing effective boundaries and routines

Parenting a child with ADHD can feel a bit like trying to steer a boat in choppy, unpredictable waters. Some days flow smoothly: your child's focused, things get done, you almost feel on top of it. Other days? Total chaos. Getting out the door, bedtime, even basic routines can feel like uphill battles.

Children with ADHD thrive on structure, clarity and consistency while struggling with impulse control, time management and focus. This can make following rules or routines challenging and, as a result, they may push back against boundaries or forget routines entirely. However, these very boundaries and routines are essential in helping them develop the skills to navigate their behaviour and emotions.

Boundaries can be considered 'the rules of the game'. They provide a set of expectations and limits for your child to ensure they know how to navigate the world safely and with respect. They clearly tell your child what is and isn't acceptable, and what the consequences are if those limits are crossed. This helps reduce confusion and anxiety, supports them to learn decision-making skills and enables you to hold them accountable for their choices.

Routines are more like the flow of the day—repeated sets of tasks or steps that help your child move through daily life. Routines tell your child what to expect and what comes next. They can turn daily tasks into habits, making life more manageable and less chaotic and encouraging focus even when distractions arise. Routines support independence by allowing children to practice tasks on their own, for example, getting dressed or packing their backpack, which builds confidence.

Both boundaries and routines help create structure and predictability for your child, who may struggle with executive function, impulse control and feelings of overwhelm. Clear, kind and consistently reinforced boundaries, combined with predictable routines, create a sense of safety and reduced anxiety for children with ADHD.

Setting effective boundaries as a family

Though definitions vary, the core principles of setting, communicating and maintaining boundaries share common themes.

> ➤ *Agree together and plan ahead.* If you have set your boundaries collaboratively, as a family, and everyone has a clear idea of what any rewards or consequences might be in a given situation, this will save energy and emotional upset in the moment. You simply need to say: 'We decided the rules. You've decided not to follow the rules knowing what the consequence would be.' This takes the emotion out of the situation, because it's not you being angry or unfair in their eyes, it's just you following through on the agreed upon plan.
> ➤ *Keep it simple.* Too many rules can be overwhelming. Focus on a few key non-negotiables and build from there. List some boundaries you would like to include in your family (e.g., around behaviours at bedtime or in the morning) in your parenting journal.
> ➤ *Be clear and specific.* Be extremely clear and specific about what you want your child to do, using language your child can understand to avoid confusion and misunderstandings (e.g., 'We clean up our toys after playtime' rather than 'Be neat'). Review the section on effective communication on page 97 to avoid overcomplicating instructions.

➤ *Be consistent but flexible.* Consistency is key. If a boundary is crossed, respond predictably with a calm, clear reminder or a logical consequence. If no screens before homework is a rule, apply it every day to avoid confusion. It's important to remember that consistency does not mean rigidity. Children with ADHD need structure but they also need compassion and flexibility when things don't go to plan. Life is unpredictable, and it's okay to bend the boundary when necessary, as long as the overall structure remains strong.

➤ *Focus on positive reinforcement.* Notice and acknowledge when your child is *using their skills* or *making an effort*, and make daily routines feel positive with praise for effort and progress. 'Thank you for following our rule about putting toys away. Now we have more space to play tomorrow.' Or you may use rewards for specific tasks you're working on. This keeps rules/routines from feeling like punishments. Still, acknowledge your child's feelings, while holding the boundary: 'I know you're disappointed we have to leave the park, but it's time to go now.'

➤ *Role model.* Children learn boundaries by watching you. If they see you respecting your own limits, such as setting aside time for rest, they're more likely to respect their own boundaries and those of others.

When boundaries are used with empathy and intention, they don't just make life easier, they provide the scaffolding your child needs to feel calm, capable and connected. They create a rhythm that helps your child thrive, even when the world feels overwhelming.

Creating routines in your child's day

Routines provide a predictable rhythm that helps reduce overwhelm and anxiety. They take the guesswork out of daily tasks, support executive functioning and make transitions smoother.

View routines as something you set up to make your life easier. Once you perform the routine often enough, it becomes a habit. Once a task becomes a habit, it starts to become more automatic and, therefore, easier to do on autopilot. It gives your child's brain less to remember. Routines used for everyday situations, like brushing teeth, are so normalised they become habits, which are rarely forgotten and we do with hardly a thought. In others, where there are many steps or tasks in a process, such as getting ready for school, create structured, predictable routines with clear rules that will become habits. With these routines in place, life becomes easier for you and your child.

You might feel creating structured routines seems very regimented and too strict, but clear, loving guidelines are a form of support, helping your child feel secure and understood.

That said, many children with ADHD respond best not just to structure but to structure with *a dash of novelty*. Predictability helps reduce chaos, but too much sameness can become boring and lead to resistance or disengagement. Keep routines fresh by incorporating small, fun twists, such as using a silly voice during morning checklists, letting your child pick a 'transition song' for tasks, changing up the order occasionally or turning routines into games. Think of novelty as the spark that keeps engagement alive, while routine provides the container. Together, they create both consistency and flexibility—an ideal combo for an ADHD brain.

Some handy hints to bear in mind when creating routines:

> ➤ *Work with your child and family* to figure out what will work best for everyone to ensure the routine runs smoothly. Involving them, as much as you can, helps them understand why you make decisions and that you've taken their opinions into account, gives them buy-in to the whole process and means they are more likely to cooperate.
> ➤ *Establish boundaries and expectations as the bones of your routine.* As part of the routine, there will be some rules (boundaries) and expectations involved. For example, your morning routine may have a rule of no screens or TV before school. There will also be expectations, such as being ready to leave the house by 8am.
> ➤ *Break tasks into smaller steps.* Instead of saying 'get ready', which is several steps in one instruction, ask your child to do one task at a time (e.g., 1. Brush teeth; 2. Get dressed; 3. Pack bag).
> ➤ *Include time for movement breaks.* Allow time for sensory release between tasks or movement as part of your routine.

- ➤ *Build in buffer time.* Rushing increases stress and dysregulation. Don't expect everything to run smoothly and on time—expect life to happen sometimes!
- ➤ *Create rituals, not just routines.* Create a ritual by adding the chance for connection with your child (e.g., a goodbye hug or a special bedtime song) to make routines feel warm and secure.
- ➤ *Reflect and adjust.* Routines aren't static. They need to evolve as your child grows. At the end of each week, take a few moments to reflect on what's working and what isn't. Involve your child in this process by asking them for feedback: 'What part of our bedtime routine do you like best?' Small adjustments can make a big difference and get their buy-in.
- ➤ *Review routines.* Regular family meetings provide a space to discuss routines and rules and solve any problems collaboratively. Involving your child in problem-solving when things aren't working improves their problem-solving skills and elicits their cooperation; for example, 'What could we do to make mornings easier?'

Keeping routines consistent takes effort, but these tools can help:

- ➤ *Visual reminders and checklists.* ADHD brains benefit from external structure, so visual tools are powerful supports. Picture schedules, whiteboards, laminated checklists, or simple signs (e.g., by the door reminding your child to pack their hat or drink bottle) can keep routines flowing without constant verbal reminders, especially helpful for children who struggle with working memory.
- ➤ *Timers.* Use a timer for routines, especially during transitions between activities. Visual timers showing the passage of time are effective for children with ADHD.

What does this look like in practice?

Establishing consistent routines for key parts of the day, such as mornings, after school, mealtimes and bedtime, can make a world of difference. When your child knows what comes next, they're less likely to resist, forget or become dysregulated.

Here are a few examples of different routines you could implement.

Morning routine: Setting the day up for success

Your morning routine often sets the tone for the rest of the day. A chaotic start can make it harder for children to stay focused and regulated and leaves everyone feeling frazzled. Morning routines often start the day before.

> ➤ Ensure everyone has had sufficient sleep (see Chapter 9).
> ➤ Prepare what you can the day/evening before.
> ➤ Wake your child up early enough to give them time to fully awaken.

Build in time for some movement and exposure to morning light to wake up their brain and give them a good start to the day and sleep better later (see Chapters 9 and 10).

Use a visual checklist for each step (one they carry around is great as it stays with them). Children can tick off tasks, flip cards on a ring or move Velcro/magnet pieces from a 'to do' side to a 'done' side as they complete each step. These small actions give them a satisfying sense of progress and even a little dopamine boost, which helps keep them motivated. The exact steps will depend on their age and stage of development but could include. . .

> ➤ get dressed (or put on each individual item of clothing)
> ➤ eat breakfast
> ➤ clean teeth
> ➤ wash your face
> ➤ go to the toilet
> ➤ pack your backpack (break it down: what do they need in there?)
> ➤ put your shoes on.

Celebrate small wins. Encourage your child to check off each step they complete. Praise and reward their progress with simple affirmations like 'Great job! You got dressed all by yourself!' or, if they're at the stage of struggling with a particular task, like getting their socks on, praise that part of the process.

Make it fun. Gamify your morning routine by setting a timer for each task (five to ten minutes for each step). For some children, upbeat music can help keep them moving.

Set up a launch pad. An inexpensive modular storage unit creates a handy 'launch pad' by the front door. Have your child place everything they need to remember for school in their cubby the night before (e.g., backpack, shoes, homework, instrument) to avoid searching for things at the last minute.

Tips

> The less *you* have to do, the more you can supervise your child.
> If possible, organise yourself the night before (lunches, your clothing/items).
> If possible, get up earlier to get organised. It will help if you're not rushing yourself.
> Be in the same area as your child to convey short, clear instructions.
> Separate siblings, if possible, so they're not fighting over the basin etc.

Homework routine

Homework can be tough for children with ADHD, especially after a long day at school. Here's how to make it more manageable:

> *Create a dedicated workspace:* Choose a distraction-free space with all the materials they need (pencils, erasers, etc.).
> *Be or find a body double:* Body doubling is a simple yet effective strategy where someone else is physically present while your child works. The body double doesn't need to do the task for them — or even with them — but their presence acts like an anchor, helping your child stay focused, regulated and on track. It could be you, another caregiver or an older student you employ.
> *Set a timer:* Encourage your child to start at a consistent time and use a timer to keep track of focus time (e.g., 15 to 20 minutes of work followed by a five-minute break).

(continued)

➤ *Use a to-do and done list:* Break down homework into smaller tasks; for example, 'math worksheet' and 'spelling practice' each get their own line. As your child completes a task, they physically move it from the 'to-do' side to the 'done' side — this could be as simple as shifting a sticky note across, crossing it off and rewriting it in the done column, or dragging it on a digital app. This small but visible action gives them a sense of accomplishment and helps their brain register progress, which is especially motivating for children with ADHD.

➤ *End with a positive note:* After homework, take a moment to acknowledge their effort, not just the outcome. 'You worked so hard on that math sheet! I'm proud of you.'

➤ *Utilise supports where needed:* Some kids focus better with headphones and white noise or classical music playing. Experiment to see what works best.

Bedtime routine

Predictable bedtime routines help children transition from their day's activities to a restful night. Here are some tips that can help:

➤ *Go screen-free:* Turn off screens at least 90 minutes before bed as they make it harder for children to wind down. Blue light from screens disrupts circadian rhythms and impacts sleep, and online content is often dysregulating and/or overstimulating.

➤ *Keep the light environment dim:* Use warm red-orange lighting only, if possible, to help melatonin release.

➤ *Create soothing rituals:* Try a calming sensory activity like a warm Epsom Salts bath with essential oils (lavender or vetiver), a gentle massage or some deep-breathing exercises.

➤ *Look for connection:* Read a bedtime story together or play soothing music, which can signal it's time for sleep.

- > *Offer an outlet:* Make sure they've downloaded any worries and thoughts before they try to sleep by chatting with them or encouraging them to journal or write them down.
- > *Routines are your ally:* Consistent bedtimes help your child's internal body clock adjust, making it easier for them to fall asleep.
- > *Think about sleep distractions:* Ensure their room is completely dark, install block-out blinds if necessary and remove light-emitting devices.
- > *Keep tech out of the bedroom:* Do not allow mobile devices in your child's room overnight.

While it may take time and patience to set up effective routines and boundaries, doing so provides your child the structure they need to feel safe in navigating their world with self-confidence and a growing sense of independence.

Using rewards and consequences

Rewards and consequences are not your first parenting tool, especially when parenting your child with ADHD. As we've explored earlier, behaviour is about communication. Your child's behaviour is a clue signalling their unmet needs, sensory overload, developing executive function or emotional dysregulation. Your first response should be to ask: 'What is my child's behaviour telling me?'

If you miss this step and head straight to consequences or rewards, you risk missing the root cause, and perhaps damaging your relationship with your child in the process.

Bearing that in mind, when used with intention and thought, rewards and consequences can still have a supportive role. Just consider them a tool to give encouragement for effort or provide structure to the foundations you've already laid, rather than tools to control.

Understanding intrinsic and extrinsic motivation

It's useful to understand the difference between intrinsic and extrinsic motivation when considering offering rewards. Intrinsic motivation is when your child does something because they want to, because it feels good to them, like finishing a book they're enjoying. This is the motivation we want to foster. You want your child to do things because they simply *want* to.

On the other hand, extrinsic motivation is the motivation you get when a reward is offered—a task you might not do because you want to but you do because of some incentive. For your child that could be stickers, pocket money or praise. Some people don't believe rewarding children in this way is helpful because it can mean they come to expect a reward to do things, and it will diminish their natural internal motivation.

However, the reality is, especially for children with ADHD, some tasks are boring, difficult or overwhelming, and in these cases, incentives are helpful. Let's be honest, adults rely on external motivation to go to work and do other things they wouldn't otherwise just do for the love of it!

Rewards can definitely help motivate your child in a way that builds momentum over time; for example, if you reward them for getting their shoes on, it incentivises getting their shoes on. Later on, as they grow and develop, getting their shoes on is much easier and they can do it without thinking about it so much, and then they no longer need the incentive to get that specific task done.

Using rewards effectively

If you're going to use rewards, make sure you create a reward system that works *with* your child's brain not against it. Some ideas that might work for you include the following:

> *Keep it simple:* If your reward system is too complicated, you won't keep it up, and your child will quickly lose trust in it. Start small and build on it as needed.
> *Be specific:* Clearly define what your child is working towards; for example, 'Start your homework within ten minutes of being asked', and what the reward will be for achieving it.

> *Make it visual:* Being able to see their progress helps ADHD brains stay engaged. Use tokens, stickers, jars with marbles or a visual chart to show how close they are to earning their reward.

> *Co-create the reward system with your child:* Agree on the expectations, rewards or consequences together to ensure they have a sense of ownership and buy-in. This reduces conflict when consequences occur: 'You knew the rule, and you chose the action, so now the consequence follows.'

> *Gamify it:* Make it fun by engaging your child's imagination to keep their motivation high—use levels, badges, themed charts etc.

> *Choose rewards that matter:* Any reward offered must be important to your child, not just what's convenient for you. Don't be afraid to ask what they'd like to work towards.

> *Let them feel success:* Start with easy tasks so rewards feel *attainable* and the system gains traction. As tasks become a habit/easier for your child, gently raise the bar.

> *Update rewards/goals frequently:* As your child masters a skill (like getting ready on time), change the focus to a new area they're working on. Change the rewards to keep your child motivated. This keeps the system relevant and rewarding.

> *Don't make them wait:* Give rewards immediately or as soon as possible.

Not every reward has to be extra screen time (see Chapter 16 for avoiding over-reliance on screens), though, as most parents know, this shows the power of a reward they want. Make your child's rewards something you feel good about such as an outing to the park, choosing what they eat for dinner, a Lego piece towards a full set or a special game with you.

Handle consequences with care

Consequences can be useful but, again, they must be handled with care. ADHD brains struggle with impulsivity and cause-and-effect reasoning, so delayed or unclear consequences often fall flat. Avoid vague threats like 'You've lost your iPad for the rest of the week!' or dramatic declarations like 'Christmas is cancelled!' These are hard to follow through on and your child will quickly learn not to take you seriously.

Using consequences effectively can include strategies such as:

> *Link the consequence to the behaviour.* When the consequence directly relates to what your child did, it feels fair and makes the connection clearer in their mind. For example: *'You threw the toy, so it's going away for the afternoon.'*

> *Keep it immediate or as close as possible.* Children with ADHD find it hard to connect a consequence at bedtime to something they did in the morning.

> *Decide consequences in advance and explain them calmly.* When your child knows the expectations *ahead of time*, they can make more informed choices, and you're less likely to react emotionally or make unrealistic threats.

> *Make it meaningful.* If the consequence doesn't matter to your child, it won't change anything.

> *Let the punishment fit the 'crime'.* Keep it proportionate and always delivered with empathy, not shame.

Frequent feedback is key

One final (and crucial) piece of the puzzle: children with ADHD need frequent feedback to know how they're going. They often don't realise whether they're off track or doing well without external cues. Waiting until the end of the day, or even the end of a lesson, is too long.

Instead, check in often with small prompts and praise:

> 'You've already packed your bag. Great job, just shoes to go.'

> 'You're staying focused. That's not easy, but you're doing it.'

These moments help your child stay on course, feel seen and build internal awareness over time. It's like bumpers on a bowling lane, not to control the outcome, but to guide them towards success.

Rewards and consequences are not the *foundation* of ADHD parenting, but when used wisely, they can be incredibly helpful tools. The goal is to support behaviour without shame, build motivation without manipulation, and create a family culture where expectations are clear, effort is recognised and consequences are predictable. Start small, stay consistent and always lead with connection.

Here's an example: If your child struggles to get ready in the morning, you might offer a small reward, like choosing the playlist in the car, *if* they're dressed and ready by a certain time. Over time, you phase out the reward and replace it with intrinsic motivators: the satisfaction of being on time, a calmer start to the day or more time for breakfast.

Creating calm, supportive environments

Once routines are in place, the next step is to consider the environment around your child. Because while structure matters, so does the space they live, learn and grow in. Children with ADHD thrive in calm, organised environments.

It's impossible for most families to keep their home in complete order all the time, but it can be helpful to create a designated calm space in your home where your child can go to self-regulate when they need to. Fill it with comforting, sensory items to help your child manage overwhelming emotions.

While we can't always control the outside world, we *can* shape our home to better meet our child's needs. When that space feels predictable, calming and supportive, it becomes a powerful ally in reducing stress and building success.

Children with ADHD often thrive in structured but not rigid, calming but not sterile environments. ADHD brains are more easily distracted by visual and auditory input, so creating a home that reduces overwhelm and supports regulation makes a real difference.

Here are some key principles for a supportive home environment.

Declutter and simplify

Visual clutter increases stress and distractibility for children with ADHD. Limit the number of items in open view, especially in work and rest areas. You don't need a minimalist home, but simplicity helps ADHD brains focus better.

Tip: Use labelled storage bins, colour-coded drawers or cubbies, and keep commonly used items in consistent places. As the saying goes: 'A place for everything, and everything in its place.'

Create a distraction-reduced work space

Designate a low-stimulation zone for homework or focused tasks. Ideally, this area should be away from noisy siblings, TVs or other competing distractions. Noise-cancelling headphones, visual timers and fidget tools help too.

Research shows children with ADHD perform better on cognitive tasks in distraction-free environments and that environmental modifications can reduce off-task behaviour.[1]

Create a regulation station

Every child needs breaks, especially those with ADHD. Creating a sensory-friendly 'regulation station' offers your child a safe retreat when they feel overwhelmed, angry or dysregulated.

This isn't a 'time out' or punishment space, it's a regulation station designed to help your child reset. Allow your child to create their regulation station in a quiet corner of a room or in whatever comfortable space is available. Let them choose what goes inside, giving them ownership and safety. Help them make it feel inviting and calming, free from screens or loud noises.

This space may include:

> sand timer (helps with timing quiet moments or breaks)
> weighted blanket/cushion/lap toy for deep pressure and calming
> textured fabrics or sensory toys
> soft rug/blanket
> fidget toys (e.g., stress balls, putty, tangle toys)
> calming colouring books/plain paper and drawing/colouring materials
> comforting books/picture books about feelings
> noise-cancelling headphones
> soothing music/white noise

> feelings chart/emotion cards (help your child identify how they feel)
> a calm-down bottle (glitter jar/water bottle filled with liquid and floating items)
> scented playdough or calming essential oils (using child-safe, pre-diluted roller blends)
> breathing prompts/visual aids for mindful breathing
> soft cushions or a beanbag
> dim lighting or a small lamp.

This space helps your child develop emotional awareness and regulation skills over time. It gives them a non-judgemental place to pause, regroup and return to their day feeling more centred—and it gives you a proactive alternative to reactive discipline.

Use visual schedules and predictable routines

Children with ADHD do better when they *know what to expect*. Visual schedules for daily routines (e.g., morning, after school, bedtime) give structure and reduce arguments. Use checklists, picture cards or a whiteboard—whatever works for your child's age and learning style. According to research, predictable routines and external structure can significantly improve behaviour and reduce emotional dysregulation in children with ADHD.[2]

Support movement and play

Movement helps regulate attention and mood in children with ADHD (see Chapter 10). Make it easy for your child to move their body at home, whether that's on a small trampoline, balance board, yoga mat or just encouraging regular outside time. You might also consider a 'wiggle seat' or resistance bands on chair legs in their study area to provide sensory input while they work.

Balance calm

Your home is not going to be a silent Zen retreat with children around, but you could designate certain times as 'quiet times', for example, before bedtime. During these times, encourage family members to pursue calm, non-screen activities, helping them wind down and avoid overstimulation. Similarly, you could implement this for family connection times, during meals or an evening chat to help your child feel emotionally safe and grounded.

A well-organised, low-stimulation, sensory-friendly home environment isn't about perfection, it's about intention. When your child knows where things belong, what's expected and that they have a safe space to retreat to, they can begin to regulate better, focus longer and feel more in control of their world.

Planning ahead

A game-changer for your child with ADHD is learning to plan ahead, not in a rigid, over-controlling way, but in a thoughtful, supportive, 'let's set you up for success' way. Whether it's a birthday party, family gathering, trip to the shops or even a new after-school activity, anticipating what might be tricky for your child *before* it happens makes all the difference.

Children with ADHD often struggle with transitions, sensory overload, unpredictability and social expectations. These aren't 'bad' behaviours, they're nervous system challenges. When you plan ahead, you're helping your child navigate the world more safely and successfully.

Involve your child in the plan

The goal isn't to micromanage your child, it's to partner with them. Let them know you're not trying to control the situation, you're trying to help it go well. You might say something like, 'Hey, I know birthday parties can sometimes feel loud and crazy for you. Let's make a plan so it feels easier.' This teaches your child their experience matters and gives them a sense of agency. Some ways to do this might include:

> *Talk through what to expect:* Tell them what's going to happen, how long it'll last and who will be there. Visual schedules or simple step-by-step verbal run throughs work wonders.
> *Create an exit strategy:* Maybe they only stay for the first hour of the party or you pick them up early. That's okay! Leaving on a high note is better than pushing through until they melt down.
> *Adjust the environment:* Avoid overstimulating places (noisy shopping centres or crowded events) if they're already tired or dysregulated. Can it wait for another day, be done online or without them?

> *Bring what they need:* Bring your own snacks if your child has food sensitivities, noise-cancelling headphones if they're sound-sensitive or even a small comfort item. Always check in with the host where necessary.
> *Create a secret signal:* A prearranged hand squeeze, a tug on the shirt or a discreet visual cue lets them say, 'I need help' or 'I want to leave' without embarrassment.
> *Praise their effort:* Notice when they follow the plan or work through big feelings. Say, 'I noticed you were overwhelmed, and you used our signal. Great job using your tools.'

Planning ahead might seem like a boring extra chore, but it's preferable to your child (or you) having a negative experience. It also helps your child develop the skills they need to handle specific situations. Each time they try a new or previously challenging situation and succeed, their confidence grows. You don't want your child to end up avoiding situations due to past negative experiences. Each time they try challenging situations, they learn and grow from the opportunity, so supporting them in these ways is important to help them build the foundations of emotional regulation, social awareness and self-advocacy—skills they'll use for the rest of their life.

Let's be honest, your sanity matters too. When you plan, you're less likely to be caught off guard and are more able to respond effectively instead of reacting poorly, which creates a calmer experience for everyone. So, take a little extra time to plan out your next outing together proactively. It shows your child you've got their back, no matter what.

Parents working together

When two or more caregivers are involved, it's crucial to get everyone on the same page. Consistency is key and when caregivers present a united front, it creates a sense of safety and predictability for your child. On the other hand, conflicting approaches to parenting can increase your child's anxiety, confusion or emotional resistance.

It's pretty normal for parents to have differing approaches to parenting, especially when raising a neurodivergent child, which demands slightly different parenting strategies. The key is to put supporting your child's development and emotional wellbeing at the centre of your approach. It's not about being right, it's about what works best for your child. Work on your shared goal of supporting your child above all.

Share this book

After you've read this book, ensure you do your utmost to have your partner or other relevant caregivers read it too. Discuss how you plan to move forward with your parenting, and create a protocol or a plan that works for everyone. Explore areas where you agree or disagree and try to resolve your differences. Do this without your child being present.

Support each other

The first step to creating a unified parenting protocol is to ensure you're communicating openly with your partner. Acknowledge each other's feelings, frustrations and perspectives without criticism. Set aside regular times for calm discussions about parenting, focusing on solutions rather than problems. This allows each of you to understand what the other is experiencing and how to support each other.

Using active listening skills:

> ➤ Allow your partner to share their perspective—don't interrupt.
> ➤ Understand their perspective better by asking them open-ended questions.
> ➤ Use 'I' statements rather than 'you' statements to avoid pointing the finger of blame and encouraging greater cooperation; for example, 'I feel overwhelmed when we have no routine', rather than 'You never stick to the routine'.

Learn about ADHD together

Sometimes, the biggest challenge in parenting your child with ADHD is not understanding enough about the condition itself. If one, or both of you, are unfamiliar with ADHD and how that affects your child, it can lead to frustrations or unrealistic expectations. It's important to learn about ADHD parenting together—you've made a massive start by reading this book. You can also attend workshops, webinars, ADHD-specific parenting courses or ADHD parent coaching for extra support.

To achieve the best outcomes, sit down together and set clear, consistent goals for your child and your parenting approach. Discuss topics such as:

> - What are our non-negotiables? These could be your family values around safety, respectful behaviour or household responsibilities.
> - Which areas are you happy to be flexible over (e.g., what time they go to bed)?
> - What strategies will you decide to implement in your home?

When you're both firmly on the same page in your parenting, your child receives consistent messages about your expectations, helping them feel safe.

Caregivers may possess different parenting strengths: one may be better at emotional regulation, while the other might shine in creating structure and routines. Make sure you leverage each other's strengths to create the most balanced approach.

Create a parenting plan together

Any parenting plan you and your partner create should be flexible — a document that changes over time, not set in stone. It should outline the general strategies you both agree on, which may include:

> - Which boundaries and routines will you agree on?
> - How will you handle concerning behaviours?
> - What are your family values?
> - What will your child be rewarded for and what will the reward be?
> - What will they receive a consequence for and what will it be?
> - How will you communicate and keep each other informed about your child?

Adapt and compromise

Parenting is a dynamic process and the routines and structures you agree on will require constant adjustment over time, both as your child grows and matures and because, sometimes, what works today might not work tomorrow. Be willing to adjust your strategies as you learn more about your child and their changing needs. Keep having ongoing open discussions and revisit your parenting plan to tweak it as needed.

If you find creating and implementing a plan that works too daunting, consider attending an ADHD parenting course or one-on-one ADHD parent coaching session to help get you started. Getting everyone who has responsibility for caring for your child on the same page will create a more aligned, supportive parenting team. Gaining greater insight into how ADHD affects your family allows you to all work together to develop an effective parenting strategy that aligns with your child's needs.

Seek help from others

If either parent feels like they're becoming overwhelmed, it's important to acknowledge this. It's okay to say you need help or that you aren't coping—we all feel that way sometimes. Supporting each other is crucial, but you can also seek professional help. If you feel you need to, reach out to a therapist, couples counsellor, ADHD parent-coach or support group for families of children with ADHD. Sometimes external perspectives provide valuable insights into how to balance the needs of you, your partner and your child. See Chapter 20 to explore how to build your support village.

Model teamwork

When your child sees you and your partner working together as a team and modelling collaboration and cooperation, this helps them feel more secure. In addition, it teaches them important lessons about working together to solve problems. When they see both parents respectfully handling disagreements and coming to mutual agreements, it shows them how to use similar strategies when navigating their own challenges.

Parenting your child with ADHD is a constant juggling act—it's demanding without doubt. However, when you work together, communicate openly and create a unified parenting protocol, you can build a supportive family environment where everyone feels valued and heard. Be patient with one another, acknowledge the strengths each of you bring to the table, and always be willing to adapt and grow as a unified team.

Chapter Seven

The regulated parent: Self-care as the foundation of calm, connected, compassionate parenting

When you care for yourself, you parent from strength—not survival—and that's a gift to both you and your child.

Before you dive further into ways to understand, connect with and support your child, you need to pause and look at yourself. We've talked about the importance of your knowledge and mindset in underpinning an empathetic, strengths-based parenting approach, but this isn't enough on its own.

While it may feel counterintuitive, finding ways to appropriately prioritise your own wellbeing is foundational to your child's success and the wellbeing of your whole family. Without enough support or self-awareness, you can easily become overwhelmed, reactive or burnt out. Your own past experiences, triggers and emotions can significantly influence your parenting and your responses to your child's behaviour and emotions.

Your journey must start with understanding and strengthening your own mental health, mindset and capacity. You'll be familiar with the 'put your own oxygen mask on first' analogy—make sure you're okay before you start assisting others. The same applies to parenting—you need the strength, resilience and self-regulation to cope with the demands of parenting. You require more patience when parenting a child with ADHD, which means you're going to need to address your own regulation and wellbeing first so you can show up consistently and compassionately to support your child.

When you make your self-care a priority, you'll find you're more emotionally regulated and better able to respond to your child with calm, connection and compassion (as we've discussed) instead of with frustration, anger, shame or guilt.

Your stable foundation allows you to foster a more positive family dynamic, with reduced conflict and a stronger sense of connection between you and your child. When you model what healthy emotional regulation, self-advocacy and self-care looks like for your child, you're providing them with powerful real-life examples of the skills they need to learn. When your focus shifts from 'fixing' your child to supporting their whole environment, the result not only benefits your child's outcomes and a more resilient, compassionate family unit, but it benefits your own emotional wellbeing—and that's a huge win.

The importance of self-care for parents

You experience constant high-level parenting requirements that parents of neurotypical children don't usually experience. You face a variability and unpredictability of behaviour and problems where you often don't know what to expect at the start of each new day, and that's a cause of daily stress.

When you're constantly having to plan, prepare, be more structured and organised, help them navigate overwhelming moments and advocate at school, all while remaining cool, calm and collected, you're having to work way harder than other parents, particularly if you also have ADHD. It's easy to put your own wellbeing last on the list, but you can't pour from an empty cup. When you're running on empty, everything around you begins to unravel: your emotional regulation, your health, relationships and your ability to parent with calm, compassion and connection.

When your stress levels rise and your nervous system is dysregulated, it becomes incredibly difficult to remain calm, empathetic and responsive. You may find yourself snapping more easily, feeling constantly overwhelmed, or struggling to show up as the parent you want to be. Stress reduces your emotional bandwidth, and instead of responding to your child's behaviour with curiosity and compassion, you're more likely to react with frustration and irritability. Over time, this emotional load leads to exhaustion, resentment, disconnection or even burnout.

You're so busy trying to meet the needs and demands of your child and life in general, you find little time for yourself. You feel the pain and difficulties of your child acutely and chronically, perhaps even more deeply than they do themselves, because they're your child and you worry about them. Are they going to be okay? Do they have friends? Are they getting bullied? All of this worry can lead to parental burnout.

Parental burnout

Parental burnout, or any burnout, looks like:

> exhaustion: fatigued, even after rest
> feeling numb, irritable, hopeless or detached
> overwhelm
> losing interest in things you used to enjoy
> feeling emotionally shut down
> emotionally reactive or dysregulated
> greater difficulty planning, organising and making decisions
> having a more negative mindset
> physical symptoms such as headaches, digestive issues or sleep disruption.

If you're experiencing any of these symptoms, it's time to radically address your self-care. But even if you're not experiencing these symptoms at the moment, don't wait until you get there! Act now and avoid starting down that path.

When you are under chronic constant stress, it doesn't just affect your mood. Adrenaline and cortisol (our stress hormone) will increase in your body, which, over time, creates downstream effects: gut issues, allergies, food intolerances, weight gain, hormonal dysregulation and maybe anxiety and depression (see Table 7.1). You may experience more headaches or have trouble falling or staying asleep and your immune system may be affected, making you more prone to illness.

Table 7.1 *Impact of chronic stress*

Symptom	Effect on the body
Increased cortisol	Disrupts sleep, impairs memory, worsens anxiety
Lower serotonin and dopamine	Affects ability to feel motivation and joy and regulate emotions
Disrupted blood sugar levels	Contributes to mood swings, cravings and energy crashes
Impaired immune function	More prone to illness and burnout
Increased inflammation	Linked to fatigue, chronic pain and poor mental health
Hormonal imbalance	Affects everything from mood to metabolism, menstrual cycles and libido
Poor sleep	Worsens emotional dysregulation, reduces resilience and contributes to weight gain and irritability
Elevated blood pressure and heart rate	Increases long-term risk of cardiovascular disease
Muscle tension and physical exhaustion	Headaches, general aches and pains, physically drained and more reactive

This is not what you want for your mental or physical health, and it also means you will be less effective in your parenting. When you're mentally worn down and overwhelmed, you're less able to respond to your child in a calm, connected and compassionate way. If you struggle to put yourself first for the sake of yourself (as many parents do), make *your child* the reason. If you don't, you'll experience a vicious cycle where your ability to parent effectively suffers, your child's behaviours and challenges increase, and you become even more exhausted and begin to wonder how you can possibly turn things around. Your self-care should be front and centre in your parenting protocol.

What is effective self-care?

Effective self-care isn't just about the odd bath or treating yourself to a manicure every now and then, even though that's part of it—it's a whole lifestyle approach. True self-care is about building small, consistent habits that support your emotional, physical and mental wellbeing.

When you feel you're in the midst of chaos, looking after your own needs can seem like the last thing on your to-do list, but it should be at the top, because it's going to enable you to cope better.

By looking after yourself, you're also acting as a role model for your child while giving yourself the opportunity to feel your best, and build the resilience you need to cope with the extra challenges you face in parenting your child with ADHD.

You can quickly become emotionally dysregulated when you're exhausted, overwhelmed or burnt out. Let's look at some effective self-care strategies.

Prioritise sleep

At the very top of your self-care list should be sleep. Sleep is one of the most overlooked aspects of wellbeing. When your sleep quality is not optimal, it doesn't just result in you feeling tired, its effects are far more wide reaching. Lack of quality sleep disrupts your hormones, affects your weight, increases your cortisol levels and reduces your capacity for empathy and emotional regulation. When you're tired, you're less patient and more reactive in your responses with your child. You're also more vulnerable to feeling overwhelmed and developing anxiety or depression. Some tips for improved sleep (see Chapter 9 for more):

> *Set a consistent bedtime:* Going to bed at the same time each night trains your body and brain to recognise when it's time to sleep.
> *Create a wind-down ritual:* Reduce artificial light, switch off screens, listen to calming music, read a book.
> *Drop non-essential evening tasks:* Rest is productive.

Find support and connection

Parenting is a hard road to travel on your own. It takes a village as they say — although these days it's harder to find a village to support you! (I talk more about this in Chapter 20.)

It's much easier when both parents/carers agree on the strategies they'll implement. Make sure you discuss and agree on your parenting protocol with your partner and/or other caregivers. Effective parents have each other's back and they present a united front to their child, so get on the same page (see Chapter 6 for tips on how to do this), avoid arguing over parenting and, whatever you do, don't argue over parenting in front of your child!

Gather a supportive network of close relatives, extended family, friends and neighbours and ask for help. Finding people who are in the same boat, and who get it to talk to about what's going on for you, helps you feel less lonely and isolated. Find this support in other mums you know, at local ADHD support networks or online ADHD parenting support forums (such as ADHD Support Australia ⊕).

Another important part of your support team might be psychological support or counselling or an ADHD coach who understands what it's like parenting with ADHD. See Chapter 20 for more on building a support team.

Create healthy boundaries: Learn to say 'no'

If you've got enough on your plate already and you're not coping, it's okay to say 'no'. Self-care involves being assertive, including learning to say 'no' to others when they ask you for help, even if they're family. Always say 'no' to things that drain your energy.

Look at your current commitments. Is there anything you can let go of right now? Is there anything you can delegate to someone else? Get as much off your plate as possible to leave space for yourself and your family. Only say 'yes' to tasks or activities that restore you.

Embrace progress over perfection. Lower your bar and learn to accept when something is 'good enough'.

Take a break

Everyone needs time away from their children. It's normal and healthy. If your child is well cared for and you spend plenty of quality time with them, it's not going to harm your child to take the occasional break — it's the quality and quantity of time you spend together that counts. Get out, socialise, make time for fun in your life. Think about things that make you happy and do them. Remember: you're a role model for your child.

Practical self-care ideas

I know you're busy and exhausted and protesting that you don't have time for you, but I hope what I've said here will motivate and inspire you to start small and build your self-care habits consistently over time. It's not just about 'feeling better', it's about functioning better. When you nourish your body, rest your mind and protect your energy, you'll be better able to show up as that calm, connected, compassionate parent. You functioning better will create a ripple effect on your child's behaviour and the whole mood of your household.

Just as setting solid foundations for your child to thrive is vital, this principle also applies to you. Look at your lifestyle to see where you could make small changes.

Here are some practical, doable self-care ideas that don't require large chunks of time, but can make a big difference in how you feel and show up.

Improving your nutrition and gut health

Take small steps towards a healthier, more nutritious diet by:

> focusing on a whole food, nutrient-dense diet
> introducing pre- and probiotic foods into your diet
> preparing healthy snacks ahead of time to fuel you on the run
> meal prepping in advance and cooking large batches to save time
> staying hydrated with plenty of filtered water
> reducing high carbohydrate, sugary snacks, junk foods and alcohol.

Nutrition and gut health are covered in Chapter 8.

Increasing movement and exercise

You don't need a hard workout, just keep your body moving in gentle ways (see Chapter 10 for more tips):

> dance in the kitchen, stretch while your child plays or go for a short walk
> do five minutes of yoga or squats between tasks
> if you feel stuck emotionally, try moving your body — it helps shift mood and tension.

Micro-moments of self-care

Tiny moments of regulation sprinkled throughout your day can reset your nervous system and reduce stress. Try:

> taking a few deep breaths in the car before school pick-up
> stepping outside for two minutes of fresh air and sunlight
> keeping a water bottle nearby throughout the day
> putting your hand on your heart and saying, 'I'm doing the best I can.'

Mindfulness

Mindfulness helps shift your nervous system from survival mode to calm presence. Increase your relaxation by:

> practising a three-minute mindfulness meditation (many free apps can guide you)

➤ writing down your thoughts, frustrations or wins in a journal—getting it out helps clear mental clutter
➤ trying a gratitude list: three small things that went well in your day.

Make time for you

Caring for a child with ADHD can be all-consuming, but looking after yourself is just as important. Building in moments of joy and rest helps you recharge, making it easier to show up for your family with patience, energy and compassion. You could:

➤ listen to your favourite podcast, music or audiobook while doing chores
➤ make time for small things that bring joy: gardening, reading, crafting or simply doing nothing for ten minutes
➤ give yourself permission to rest; not everything must be productive, but adequate rest can ultimately improve your productivity anyway.

Joy is a legitimate form of nourishment.

Name and acknowledge your emotions

You don't have to be calm and composed all the time. Feeling moments of frustration, guilt, anger or sadness are normal. Notice your emotions without judgement. When you name your emotions, you release pressure and begin the process of regulation. Say:

➤ 'I'm feeling overwhelmed right now.'
➤ 'I'm sad that parenting feels so hard today.'
➤ 'I love my child, and I also feel exhausted.'

Don't feel guilty

Don't feel guilty if you're struggling emotionally. Just because other people may have it worse, your experience is still valid. It's okay to get frustrated, feel sad or want a break. Having these emotions is not a reflection of how much you love your child, but a sign you're human.

Build in daily stress-release rituals

Little releases throughout the day prevent stress from building to unmanageable levels. Include one daily stress-reducing activity, such as:

> ➤ deep-breathing or grounding exercises
> ➤ a short walk outside or stretching
> ➤ music, journaling or quiet tea time
> ➤ venting safely to a trusted friend or support group.

Check in with yourself

Regularly tune into your own needs before getting overwhelmed. Ask yourself:

> ➤ 'What do I need right now?'
> ➤ 'How is my body feeling?'
> ➤ 'Where am I holding tension?'
> ➤ 'What emotion is showing up for me today?'

Reflect and reframe: Don't criticise yourself

Perfection is not the goal: presence, progress and self-kindness are. Have compassion for yourself by reflecting on difficult days:

> ➤ 'That was a tough moment, but I'm learning.'
> ➤ 'I didn't get it perfect, but I showed up.'
> ➤ 'Tomorrow is a new day. I can repair and try again.'

How can parental trauma and triggers affect parenting?

Experiences from your own past and upbringing can significantly influence the way you parent your own child. These, often subconscious, patterns may dictate how you react to your child's challenging behaviours and emotions. Any unresolved trauma or difficult past childhood experiences you have can, unfortunately, influence your emotional regulation and, therefore, your ability to have patience and respond empathetically to your child. Sometimes referred to as 'intergenerational trauma', this can unintentionally see the cycle of emotional dysregulation and behavioural challenges in your family continue.

Dr Gabor Maté, who has researched how parents' unresolved emotional wounds can lead to reactive and overly emotional parenting, explains that when parents' chronic stress or unprocessed childhood trauma can lead to the triggering of disproportionate responses to their child's behaviour. These reactive and emotional responses can result in more conflict, emotional distress and anxiety in families. Dr Shefali Tsabary, in her book *The Awakened Family*, agrees and highlights the importance of parents exploring and healing their own unresolved wounds so they can start to shift away from reactive parenting.

As we saw in Chapter 4, studies on adverse childhood experiences (ACEs) support the idea that when children experience emotional or physical abuse, neglect or unstable home environments, they often struggle as adults with regulating their own emotions.

If you have difficulty regulating your own emotions, one result of this will be that what your child says or does may cause you to overact in the moment. It can cause big feelings to come up for you that perhaps afterwards you're not sure where they came from. In the moment, you may interpret them as a personal affront or challenge to your authority and you may become angrier or more upset than is warranted in the situation.

The second result is you'll not be teaching your child how to effectively regulate their own emotions by modelling for them. Thirdly, your response will likely escalate the situation and cause your child to internalise these emotional responses, leading them to feel unsafe, insecure, anxious or angry.

Your own unresolved emotional issues may be unexplored, and you may be unaware of what's going on for you. You may ask, 'What can I do about my past experiences? I can't change them.' It's true—your past is your past. However, the first step to healing intergenerational trauma starts with acknowledging it's happening. Once you're able to identify your specific triggers, you're on the first step of a road to healing.

Start to notice what it is your child says or does that makes you more angry, upset or frustrated than it should. See if there's a pattern that emerges.

Explore why these situations seem to press a button in you that sends your reactions over the top. Get curious about those feelings.

Once you notice your feelings and reflect on them, the next time you're in a similar situation, pause, reflect, name and acknowledge your emotions before trying to respond in a less emotionally charged way. Understanding what's happening is the first step. Reflecting and attempting to change the old patterns is the next.

Other ways to work towards better regulation of your own emotions is to engage in activities such as mindfulness, meditation, breathwork or journaling. A systematic review found that mindfulness and meditation practises impacted mental health and caused increased cortical thickness in brain regions involved in emotion regulation and sensory processing, leading to reduced anxiety and better emotional regulation.[1]

Regular journaling can also help develop self-awareness, a key component of emotional regulation. By consistently checking in with yourself and recording your emotional experiences through regular journaling, you'll start to notice patterns and triggers. Developing greater self-awareness will go a long way to helping with regulating your emotions.[2,3]

If it's available to you, seeking therapy or counselling will allow you to address unresolved emotional traumas in a professional setting, while gentle breathwork supports calming the nervous system in the moment, making not only your parenting journey easier but also your life generally.

We'll explore more about nervous system regulation, emotional safety and supporting emotional regulation in Chapter 11.

When you have ADHD yourself

Since ADHD is highly heritable, it's common for one or both parents to be navigating their own ADHD symptoms while also trying to support their child. Parenting a child with ADHD comes with challenges, but when you or your co-parent also have ADHD, those challenges can multiply.

You have to be more organised, scaffold your child's executive function, learn new or different parenting techniques, and create routines and structure, all while coping with your own symptoms, which can create a perfect storm of overwhelm, frustration and missed cues on all sides.

It doesn't mean you can't create a parenting journey that supports your family to thrive, it just means you need a parenting approach that accounts for *everyone's* needs, including your own. The key is recognising the dynamics and implementing strategies to create a more organised, calm and supportive environment for both parents and children.

Let's look at some practical ways to parent effectively when ADHD is part of your story too (see Table 7.2).

Table 7.2 *Added challenges for parents who have ADHD themselves*

ADHD challenge	Possible outcome	Strategy
Difficulty with consistency	Parents struggling with forgetfulness; impulsivity; and maintaining consistency in rules, routines and expectations results in difficulty creating clear, predictable routines	Use visual schedules, alarms, checklists Simplify routines to essential steps Consider co-parenting apps or shared calendars Repair with your child when things go off track and model trying again
Emotional dysregulation	Parents prone to emotional reactivity make it harder to maintain calm in stressful situations, resulting in escalation of situations and inability to help their child regulate	Practice daily self-regulation strategies (e.g., breathing exercises, mindfulness or body movement) Pause before responding: use a mantra like 'calm first, solve second' Get support (therapy, coaching) to help process emotions outside of parenting moments

(continued)

Table 7.2 *Added challenges for parents who have ADHD themselves (cont'd)*

ADHD challenge	Possible outcome	Strategy
Disorganisation	May struggle with organisation/planning, lose track of appointments, tasks etc., which can increase family stress and fuel anxious feelings or exacerbate their child's symptoms	Use external supports (e.g., whiteboards, digital reminders, family command centres) Build shared routines (e.g., Sunday set up for the week) Delegate/outsource where possible Keep systems visible and simple
Difficulty with follow-through	Finishing tasks can be challenging, leaving household chores incomplete, for example, causing further stress and frustration	Use timers or body doubling (see page 111) to stay on track Break tasks into small, achievable steps Celebrate partial progress ('I got halfway through; that's better than nothing') Prioritise tasks with greatest impact on family wellbeing

Practice emotional regulation

Since both parents may struggle with emotional regulation, setting aside time to practice self-regulation techniques is vital. Mindfulness, deep-breathing exercises and time for yourself are strategies you can model for your child to help everyone stay calm during stressful moments (see Chapter 11 for more on this). Encourage family members to take breaks when needed and learn how to recognise when they're becoming overwhelmed.

Work on self-care

When you're juggling your ADHD symptoms along with those of your child, it's easy to neglect your own needs. But self-care is essential. Make sure you're carving out time for your physical, emotional and mental wellbeing. Prioritise healthy eating (more in Chapter 8), regular exercise (Chapter 10), and sleep (Chapter 9). Taking care of yourself will allow you to be more present and effective in your parenting.

Get support

Don't hesitate to seek professional support when you need it. ADHD coaching, family therapy, psychology or support groups for parents of children with ADHD can help you navigate your challenges more effectively (I cover this further in Chapter 16).

When you and your child both have ADHD, it definitely makes life more challenging and can seem daunting. However, by embracing the challenge with creativity and using your ADHD strengths to turn what might seem like chaos into a dynamic, engaging home environment for your family, you can support everyone's needs — including yours. Remember, you're not alone and it's okay to ask for help when you need it.

Normalisation and self-compassion

Have compassion for yourself. When you have ADHD, you may find running a household, holding down a job and general adulting a challenge. Add the demands of ADHD parenting (one of the most demanding jobs we have) and it's not going to be a walk in the park.

You're doing one of the hardest jobs in the world, and you don't have to do it perfectly. It will require resilience, but also compassion — for your child and for yourself. By tending to your stress, protecting your energy and regulating your own emotions, you're not only looking after yourself but providing a role model for your child to learn these important life skills.

Embrace the art of self-care — it's a non-negotiable!

Part III

Building strong, positive foundations

A strong foundation supports your child's lifelong wellbeing, nurturing their brain, body and sense of self so they can thrive in every part of life.

People often focus on attention, mood and behaviour when talking about ADHD, and for good reason, as those are hallmark challenges. But ADHD affects the whole child, including their emotional and physical wellbeing.

In the next few chapters, we'll take a holistic, integrative look at ADHD — one that supports your child's body and mind alongside conventional strategies. There's no one-size-fits-all approach; every child is unique, with different genetics, sensitivities and environments. But small, everyday changes in routines, food, sleep, movement and support can make a real difference in reducing symptoms and supporting your child's wellbeing.

I'll walk you through evidence-based options, such as gut health, nutrition, sleep, exercise and nervous system regulation, as well as complementary therapies, such as mindfulness, breathwork and mindset work. We'll explore how your child's overall physical health impacts their brain function, mood regulation and overall ADHD symptoms.

By embracing a more holistic lifestyle, you're not just managing symptoms, you're laying the foundation for your child's lifelong health and happiness.

Let's begin.

Chapter Eight

Nourishing the brain: How nutrition and gut health impact ADHD symptoms

Food fuels more than our body—it shapes the brain, steadies the mood and supports the foundations of focus and regulation.

It's often said that food is medicine. Supporting children with ADHD often revolves solely around strategies, therapies or school accommodations—all of which are important. However, there's a deeper, often overlooked foundation that can influence your child's symptoms: what they eat, how their body digests food and how well their gut and brain communicate.[1] Nutrition and gut health form the biological foundation in the Hierarchy of Parenting Needs, sitting at the level of physiological regulation.

Imagine you want to grow healthy plants for abundant flowers or produce. You would ensure each plant has the right soil pH, fertiliser, temperature, sunlight and water. Your child similarly has unique requirements for optimal functioning of their brain and body.

Food, nutrition, gut function and even genetics impact your child's ADHD symptoms and overall wellbeing.[2] Let's start with the easy changes: balancing blood sugar, identifying common food sensitivities, reducing artificial additives, and then move onto a more in-depth look at nutrition and gut health.

Blood sugar balance

Rapid spikes and crashes in blood sugar lead to mood swings, irritability, poor focus, hyperactivity and emotional outbursts, making it much harder for your child to regulate behaviour and attention throughout the day.[3] To keep their blood sugar stable, aim for meals and snacks including real, whole foods, such as eggs, meat, nuts, seeds, vegetables and healthy fats like olive oil or avocado. These provide slow-burning energy, keeping the brain steady. Avoid sugary cereals, white bread, sweetened yoghurts, fruit juice and processed snack foods, which cause sharp blood sugar spikes and crashes. A simple rule of thumb is to include protein and fibre with every meal and choose foods as close to their natural form as possible.

Timing and meal structure

When your child eats can be just as important as *what* they eat. Regular meals and snacks spaced every two to four hours helps maintain stable blood sugar levels. A common side effect of ADHD medication is suppressed appetite. If your child skips meals or goes too long without food, it affects their blood sugar balance. Ensure you work around medication: eating prior to taking it and ensuring what they do eat is low sugar and nutrient dense as mentioned previously. A simple structure of balanced meals and nourishing snacks throughout the day provides a predictable rhythm, helping your child's body and brain function more smoothly.

Protein intake

Protein is essential because it provides the building blocks (amino acids) needed to make key neurotransmitters such as dopamine and serotonin.

Starting the day with a protein-rich breakfast helps support focus and reduces impulsivity, while regular protein intake throughout the day prevents energy dips. Children with ADHD often do better with more protein than the standard diet provides, so aim to include good-quality protein (eggs, meat, poultry, fish, legumes, nuts or seeds) at every meal and in their snacks.[4] This steady supply supports not only better brain function, but also more stable moods and improved behaviour.

Healthy fats

Healthy fats, particularly omega-3 fatty acids (EPA/DHA), are essential for building brain cells, supporting communication between neurons and regulating inflammation in the brain.[5] Research shows many children with ADHD have lower levels of omega-3,[6] which can impact attention, impulse control and mood. The best food sources include oily fish (salmon, sardines and mackerel) as well as grass-fed meats and pasture-raised eggs. For picky eaters or those who don't eat fish, high-quality fish oil supplements can be a helpful alternative. It's also important to reduce excessive omega-6 fats, such as processed vegetable oils (like soybean, sunflower and canola oil), as a high ratio of omega-6 to omega-3 drives inflammation and worsens symptoms.[7] Increasing omega-3 intake and cutting back on ultra-processed foods can make a meaningful difference to your child's mental and emotional wellbeing.

Avoid processed foods

Processed and ultra-processed foods are often high in added sugars, artificial additives, unhealthy fats and refined carbohydrates, which can contribute to blood sugar spikes, inflammation and gut dysbiosis (an imbalance of micro-organisms) and have a significant negative impact on ADHD symptoms, as well as overall mental and physical health.[8] These typically nutrient-poor, chemical-laden foods can worsen hyperactivity, inattention, mood swings and sleep disturbances. Replacing them with whole, minimally processed foods gives the brain the fuel it needs to thrive, and supports better regulation, learning and emotional balance.

Choose organic where possible

Choosing organic, pasture-raised, wild-caught and grass-fed foods is important because it helps minimise exposure to harmful chemicals like pesticides, antibiotics, hormones and synthetic additives. Pesticides, such as organophosphates and glyphosate, have been linked to attention problems, hyperactivity and disruption of the gut microbiome and nervous system. These chemicals can interfere with neurotransmitter balance and detoxification, making ADHD symptoms harder to manage.[9]

Hydration

Proper hydration is essential for children with ADHD, as even mild dehydration affects attention, mood, energy levels and the brain's ability to regulate impulses. However, the quality of water matters too—filtering water helps remove chlorine, heavy metals, pesticides and other contaminants that can burden the nervous system and gut, especially in sensitive children. Always encourage water over sugary drinks or juices.

Dietary triggers and food sensitivities

Some parents notice certain foods or ingredients trigger physical discomfort, behavioural challenges or dysregulation in their child.

Food sensitivity or allergy?

Food sensitivities and intolerances are different from food allergies. Allergies (often called *IgE reactions*) involve a rapid immune system response and can cause immediate and serious symptoms (like hives or even anaphylaxis). Sensitivities and intolerances (sometimes referred to as *IgG reactions*) usually affect the body more slowly—they can build up in the digestive system or even affect mood and focus over time. Because they don't always cause obvious or immediate reactions, they can be much harder to spot and connect to certain foods.

Symptoms of a food sensitivity or intolerance may include:

> anxiety or social withdrawal
> irritability, aggression or frequent emotional overwhelm (breakdowns)
> hyperactivity or restlessness
> low mood or emotional volatility
> brain fog or concentration issues
> sleep difficulties or night waking
> physical reactions, such as rashes.

Symptoms can be mistaken as part of ADHD, when in fact they're exacerbated by certain foods or food chemicals.

Common sensitivities and intolerances

Don't assume only junk foods are to blame—even foods considered 'healthy' can cause issues in sensitive children. Some children might be sensitive to natural food chemicals, such as oxalates or salicylates found in common foods like tomatoes or berries and otherwise nutritious foods. The foods children are most commonly sensitive or intolerant to include gluten, dairy/lactose, soy, eggs, corn and sulphites—all of which can cause a range of symptoms.

According to Australian resource Fed Up, artificial flavours, colours and preservatives, as well as naturally occurring food chemicals, like salicylates, amines and glutamates, have been linked to a range of reactions, especially in sensitive children.[10] Table 8.1 (overleaf) outlines some naturally occurring food chemicals that may impact ADHD and/or mental health symptoms.

Some children are more sensitive than others for many possible reasons.

> *Gut dysbiosis,* which can reduce the body's tolerance for food chemicals.
> *Nutrient deficiencies* make it harder for the body to break down/ process food chemicals and certain compounds.
> *Genetic variances* can limit the body's ability to detoxify or metabolise food chemicals.

Table 8.1 *Common natural food triggers that can cause food sensitivity or intolerance*

Compound	Foods	Symptoms
Oxalates[11]	Spinach, beetroot, almonds, raspberries, sweet potato, dark chocolate	Gut irritation Inflammation Neurological symptoms like sensory overload or anxiety happen when oxalates build up in the body, leading to disrupted mineral absorption (calcium and magnesium), and added stress on the nervous system.
Histamines	Fermented foods, aged cheese, canned fish, vinegar, bone broth, leftovers	Headaches Irritability Anxiety Sleep disturbances
Salicylates	Apples, grapes, berries, citrus, tomato, herbs and spices	Restlessness Aggression Hyperactivity Mood instability
Amines	Bananas, chocolate, aged cheeses, soy sauce, avocados	Migraines Behavioural issues Sleep disturbance Low mood
Phytic Acid	Nuts, seeds, beans, legumes	Nuts contain phytic acid, which can block nutrient absorption and irritate the gut. Soaking or 'activating' them neutralises this, making them easier to digest.

To identify these sensitivities, some families explore elimination diets such as the RPAH Elimination Diet or the FAILSAFE diet, which carefully remove high-salicylate, high-amine and additive-rich foods before systematically reintroducing them. While these diets can be complex and should be undertaken with professional guidance, they can be incredibly revealing and life-changing for children whose symptoms are driven by food chemical sensitivity.

Coeliac disease vs gluten sensitivity

Emerging data[12] indicates a higher-than-normal rate of coeliac disease in children with ADHD, making it prudent to consider screening, especially in the presence of digestive symptoms or nutrient deficiencies.

Undiagnosed coeliac disease can lead to a wide range of issues, including nutrient deficiencies, poor growth, fatigue, mood and behavioural problems, digestive issues, skin conditions and even autoimmune disorders.

Early diagnosis and a strict gluten-free diet is essential to prevent long-term complications. If coeliac disease is not diagnosed, but symptoms persist after eating gluten, your child may have non-coeliac gluten sensitivity and a gluten-free diet will improve symptoms.

Artificial additives

Artificial additives and preservatives are commonly found in many processed foods, which, for some children, can be highly problematic. A Southampton study[13] found certain combinations of food dyes and preservatives significantly increased hyperactive behaviours in all children, not just those with ADHD.

Artificial colours such as tartrazine, sodium benzoate (preservative), and monosodium glutamate (MSG) have been linked in several studies to increased hyperactivity, impulsivity and behavioural challenges in sensitive individuals. These additives don't *cause* ADHD, but they can exacerbate symptoms or trigger behaviours closely resembling ADHD. For sensitive children, removing these additives can lead to noticeable improvements in mood, focus and self-regulation.

Reading food labels is vital—artificial additives often lurk in foods marketed as 'health foods', such as flavoured yoghurt, muesli bars, fruit juices and veggie chips. Choosing additive-free products (using apps like

Chemical Maze) and focusing on whole, unprocessed foods is a simple, effective way to support your child's wellbeing.

Some diets aim to reduce ADHD symptoms by targeting underlying biological triggers.[14] The Feingold Diet[15] eliminates artificial colours, flavours, preservatives[16] and certain salicylates. The Few Foods Diet, also known as an oligoantigenic or elimination diet,[17] takes things further by removing almost all potential trigger foods and then slowly reintroducing them one at a time to identify sensitivities. This approach has shown promising results in reducing symptoms for a significant subset of children.

Your child may not be sensitive to anything, or you may find small changes in diet result in a massive positive change for them, so it's worth looking into. Working with a practitioner can help determine if food sensitivities are playing a role in your child's symptoms.

Tracking food sensitivities

Explore how food affects your child by following these vital steps to identify any diet-related symptoms.

Step 1: Keep a diary

Write down everything your child eats and drinks. Look for behaviours such as:

> ➤ mood changes
> ➤ focus and attention issues
> ➤ energy highs or lows
> ➤ digestion issues
> ➤ sleep changes
> ➤ meltdowns
> ➤ other behaviour challenges.

Watch for symptoms, especially with commonly reactive foods. Symptoms might not be immediately obvious and could, instead, build up over days. Be observant about every ingredient consumed—even 'healthy' foods.

Step 2: Look for patterns

> ➤ *Reflect on diary entries:* Check for consistent reactions linked to specific foods or ingredients.
> ➤ *Notice the timing:* Some reactions happen quickly (within minutes to a few hours), while others may take up to 24 to 48 hours to show up. Quick reactions can sometimes suggest an allergy, but although intolerances and sensitivities can also happen fast, delayed reactions are more often linked to sensitivities.
> ➤ *Identify the type of reaction:* Is it always the same (e.g., stomach upset, rash, mood changes) or did it vary? Consistent patterns make it easier to identify triggers.

Step 3: Eliminate suspected problem foods

> ➤ Remove the foods you suspect for at least two to four weeks.
> ➤ Keep the rest of your child's diet and daily routine as normal as possible. If you make lots of changes at once, like cutting out safe foods, adding supplements or shifting sleep and activity patterns, you won't know what's really driving any improvements or setbacks. Keeping everything else steady helps you clearly see whether the eliminated foods are the true triggers.

Step 4: Record changes

Keep using the food and behaviour diary to track improvements or continuing symptoms. Note any new behaviours, sleep or mood changes etc. during elimination period of the trigger foods.

Step 5: Reintroduce (if safe) for testing

If symptoms improve during the elimination period, carefully reintroduce the trigger food in a small amount to confirm it is the cause (unless reaction was severe/dangerous). Watch for a return of symptoms within one to three days.

Step 6: Decide long-term avoidance, if necessary

If a food was a clear trigger for negative outcomes, you may choose to avoid it long-term. If necessary, find nutritional replacements to replace it to ensure your child maintains a balanced nutritional diet.

Step 7: Seek professional support

If you're unsure whether certain foods are affecting your child's behaviours, you may want to consult a professional, such as a:

> ➤ naturopath experienced with ADHD or sensitivities
> ➤ functional medicine practitioner
> ➤ paediatrician or integrative doctor.

Professionals will assess any nutrient gaps, gut health, intolerances or whether further food allergy testing or elimination diets are needed, and help you work through the next steps to find out what may be influencing symptoms. If a suspected ingredient has no nutritional value, it's a no-brainer to remove it long-term.

From theory to table: Real-life ADHD eating made simple

As you can see, food is one of the best tools in your arsenal to support your child. Nutrient-dense, whole foods help build neurotransmitters, stabilise energy, reduce inflammation and fuel learning and regulation. Try exploring various dietary patterns shown to support ADHD, such as the Mediterranean diet.[18]

Simple changes add up to a big difference over time. This isn't about perfection, it's about small, sustainable shifts. All children benefit from better nutrition—so whether or not it shifts ADHD symptoms for your child, it will still support your whole family's wellbeing.

Let's see what this looks like in real life.

Breakfast

> ➤ Egg muffins or scrambled eggs with cheese/veggies
> ➤ Half a banana or a few berries
> ➤ Slice of seeded toast with avocado or nut butter
> ➤ Smoothie: berries, coconut milk/yoghurt/protein powder
> ➤ Leftovers from last night's dinner are okay!
> ➤ Water or a warm drink like lemon and honey or caffeine-free tea

Morning snack

> ➤ Handful of activated nuts or trail mix (nuts, seeds, coconut flakes)
> ➤ Boiled egg or a slice of cheese
> ➤ Berries or veggie sticks
> ➤ Seed crackers and liver pate, hummus, guacamole

Lunch

> ➤ Wholegrain sandwich/gluten-free wrap with chicken, cheese or egg
> ➤ Nori rolls with cooked rice, veggies and fish/meat
> ➤ Frittata with cheese/veggies
> ➤ Soups/stews
> ➤ Cucumber sticks, cherry tomatoes, carrot sticks, olives
> ➤ Hummus/guacamole
> ➤ Berries or small fruit salad
> ➤ Water bottle with lemon slices

Afternoon snack

> ➤ Homemade bliss balls, paleo muffin or unsweetened yoghurt with chia and berries
> ➤ Seed crackers or veggie sticks with guacamole or hummus
> ➤ Meat stock as a soup/drink

Dinner

> ➤ Salmon/oily fish/chicken/slow-cooked beef/lamb/nutrient dense organ meats
> ➤ Sweet potato wedges
> ➤ Cauliflower rice
> ➤ Streamed or roasted vegetables
> ➤ Sauerkraut/kimchi (if tolerated)

Optional bedtime snack

> ➤ Warm milk of choice with cinnamon/sugar-free cacao
> ➤ Slice of banana with nut butter
> ➤ Small homemade treat (e.g., sugar-free muffin or cookie)

Also important is to ensure your child has plenty of filtered water throughout the day.

Keep it simple. Start with one meal at a time. Focus on whole, colourful, nutrient-dense foods, balance protein with slow-release carbs, and add good fats and fermented foods when possible.

Remember: Any food can cause sensitivities: use your diet/symptom tracker from page 150.

Meal-planning tips

> ➤ *Plan in advance:* Use a weekly meal planner to prepare balanced meals and snacks ahead of time.
> ➤ *Batch cook where possible:* Make extra portions, like veggie-packed pasta sauces, soups or curries, and freeze them.
> ➤ *Include protein and fat* in every meal/snack to stabilise blood sugar.
> ➤ *Have go-to healthy snacks ready* and easily accessible.
> ➤ *Involve your child in planning,* shopping and preparing food to increase their interest and willingness to try healthy options.
> ➤ *Avoid food battles.* It's okay to allow occasional treats; it's the overall pattern of eating that matters most.

∞ ∞ ∞

Figure 8.1 summarises what to increase and what to avoid in an ADHD diet.

✔ Increase	✖ Avoid
☐ Nutrient-dense whole foods	☐ High-sugar and refined carbs (bread, pasta, potatoes, cereals)
☐ Low-GI carbs (sweet potato, carrots, cabbage, cauliflower)	☐ Ultra-processed foods and snacks (preservatives, additives, flavours and colourings)
☐ Colourful veggies and low-sugar fruits (greens, berries, broccoli)	☐ Industrial seed oils and unhealthy fats
☐ Protein (eggs, meats, fish, legumes, nuts)	☐ Inflammatory ingredients and refined grains
☐ Healthy fats (omega-3s, avocado, olive oil, seeds)	☐ Caffeine/energy drinks (even small amounts can overstimulate)
☐ Fermented foods (live yoghurt, kefir, miso, sauerkraut, kimchi)	

Figure 8.1 *What to increase and what to avoid in an ADHD diet*

Metabolic psychiatry

A newly emerging field of study, metabolic psychiatry is slowly changing our traditional view of mental health from a purely psychological model to a holistic whole-body approach. Metabolic psychiatry looks at how brain energy metabolism and nutrient balance impacts mental health and, therefore, neurodevelopmental conditions like ADHD. Instead of focusing on symptoms and neurotransmitters alone, it explores how our body systems (mitochondria, gut, levels of inflammation and blood sugar regulation) all combine to influence our brain function.

Since the gut plays a central role in regulating metabolism, inflammation and nutrient absorption, poor gut health may underlie or worsen mental health challenges. This approach encourages looking beyond symptoms and addressing the root biological imbalances that affect the brain.

This means supporting gut health isn't just about digestion but is a strategy to improve behaviour, focus and mood.

Early research and clinical experience from pioneers in this field, including Dr Georgia Ede (Harvard-trained psychiatrist and author of *Change Your Diet, Change Your Mind)* and Dr Chris Palmer (assistant professor of psychiatry at Harvard Medical School, researcher and author of *Brain Energy),* is showing that when root causes such as inflammation, nutrient deficiencies and metabolic stress are addressed, many children show marked improvements in focus, energy, emotional regulation and overall wellbeing.

Metabolic psychiatry is still an evolving field, but for families seeking a more holistic, biology-based approach to improving symptoms, it shows exciting promise.

Micronutrients for brain health

Nutrition plays a central role in supporting children with ADHD. While much attention is given to medication and behavioural strategies, growing research shows that the brain also needs the right building blocks (nutrients) to function well. Many children with ADHD have higher nutritional needs or may be functionally deficient in key vitamins and minerals, so it's important to prioritise a nutrient-dense diet with a variety of whole foods, and, when necessary, consider targeted micronutrient supplementation with professional guidance.

Supplementation

Eating a varied, nutrient-dense, whole-food diet should always come first (see page 152); however, strong arguments exist for additional micronutrient supplementation.

> minerals depleted from soils (due to farming practises that deplete the soil), storage (during which nutrients naturally break down) or cooking (especially by boiling)
> genetic factors may cause higher individual demand for certain nutrients
> children often have specific likes, dislikes or sensitivities when it comes to food

> avoidant/restrictive food intake disorder (ARFID) or other
  eating disorders
> reduced appetite or nutrient depletion as a side effect of medication
> nutrient imbalances/deficiencies
> other medical reasons.

With these factors in mind, it's clear certain supplements may provide much-needed additional nutrients.

Are multivitamins enough?

One of the leading researchers in the area of micronutrients, Professor Julia Rucklidge, has conducted ground-breaking studies on the impact of broad-spectrum micronutrient supplementation for children with ADHD and other mental health conditions.[19]

Professor Rucklidge and her team have published numerous peer-reviewed studies showing a carefully formulated multivitamin and mineral supplement leads to significant improvements in attention, mood regulation, emotional stability, aggression and overall functioning in individuals with ADHD, especially when used over several weeks to months.

Unlike single nutrient supplementation (like just taking zinc or magnesium), Rucklidge's approach uses broad-spectrum micronutrients (a combination of vitamins, minerals, trace elements and amino acids) because the brain needs many nutrients to work together synergistically.

Her research shows that, for some children, these micronutrient formulas are as effective as medication and, in some cases, better tolerated.

What was used in the studies?

Professor Rucklidge's trials used a formula called Daily Essential Nutrients by Hardy Nutritionals, a high-dose, broad-spectrum micronutrient supplement that includes:

> all B vitamins in active forms
> vitamins C, D, E
> essential minerals like zinc, magnesium, iron, selenium, iodine, calcium, copper, manganese, molybdenum and chromium
> amino acids and trace elements to support neurotransmitter and enzyme function.

The dosage used in the studies was higher than standard, over-the-counter multivitamins, often spread over three to four capsules taken three times a day. These levels were chosen based on clinical effectiveness, not just to meet the minimum recommended daily intake.

While this may sound a lot, the research showed this comprehensive, therapeutic approach was well tolerated and had a strong safety profile. As promising as this research sounds, it's important to discuss any medication changes with your child's doctor first.

Is a regular multivitamin enough?

Not all supplements are created equal. Many over-the-counter brands contain low-quality forms of nutrients that are poorly absorbed and contain unnecessary additives, artificial sweeteners or ingredients that can aggravate the digestive systems of sensitive children. They typically provide very low doses of nutrients—just enough to prevent deficiency, but not enough to create therapeutic benefits for brain function or mood regulation. While these are fine for general health, they're unlikely to deliver the same results as the clinical-grade micronutrient formulations used in Rucklidge's research.

Choose high-quality, practitioner-recommended brands that use bioavailable forms of nutrients and avoid harmful fillers. It's advisable to work with a qualified practitioner to find the right formulation and dosage for your child

While this is not a magic bullet, micronutrients are safe, well tolerated and backed by research. They provide the nutritional foundation on which other strategies (therapy, parenting tools, gut health or medication) work more effectively. Table 8.2 outlines some of the common supplements that can support ADHD symptoms.

Table 8.2 *Nutrient supplements for ADHD symptoms*

Nutrient	Role in ADHD	Food source	Supplement
Calcium	Supports bone development, nerve transmission and muscle function	Dairy, tofu, sardines with bones, leafy greens	Calcium citrate or hydroxyapatite (well absorbed)

Nutrient	Role in ADHD	Food source	Supplement
Choline	Supports brain development, memory and attention	Eggs, liver, salmon, chicken, soybeans	CDP-Choline or Alpha-GPC (brain active forms)
Copper	Works with zinc, imbalance affects mood and cognition	Liver, sesame seeds, cashews, lentils, mushrooms	Copper gluconate (use cautiously and only if needed)
Folate	Important for brain and nervous system development	Leafy greens, legumes, liver, avocado	Methylfolate (L-5-MTHF) active form
Iron	Supports dopamine production; low levels linked to inattention and fatigue	Red meat, liver, lentils, spinach, pumpkin seeds	Iron bisglycinate (gentle on stomach, highly absorbable)
Magnesium	Supports calming neurotransmitters, helps with sleep/anxiety	Dark, leafy greens, almonds, pumpkin seeds, black beans	Magnesium glycinate or citrate (calming and absorbable)
Omega-3 fatty acids	Essential for brain development, focus, mood and reducing inflammation	Oily fish (salmon, sardines), flaxseeds, chia seeds, walnuts	Triglyceride form fish oil or algal oil (for vegetarians)
Vitamin B6	Important for neurotransmitter synthesis (dopamine, serotonin)	Chicken, turkey, bananas, potatoes	Pyridoxal-5-phosphae (P5P; active form)
Vitamin B12	Essential for energy, memory and nervous system health	Animal liver, eggs, dairy, meat	Methycobalamin (active form)

(*continued*)

Table 8.2 *Nutrient supplements for ADHD symptoms (cont'd)*

Nutrient	Role in ADHD	Food source	Supplement
Vitamin C	Enhances iron absorption, supports immune and brain function	Citrus fruits, strawberries, capsicum, broccoli	Buffered vitamin C or liposomal form (gentle on stomach)
Vitamin D	Supports mood, immune function and overall brain health	Sunlight, egg yoks, fortified dairy or plant milks, salmon	Vitamin D3 (cholecalciferol) best absorbed
Zinc	Affects attention and behaviour, supports immune and brain function	Oysters, beef, pumpkin seeds, cashews, chickpeas	Zinc picolinate or zinc citrate (well absorbed)

Additional supplements

In addition to foundational nutrients, several herbal and adaptogenic supplements are gaining attention for their potential to support ADHD symptoms by enhancing focus, reducing anxiety and promoting cognitive resilience. These natural compounds often work by modulating neurotransmitters, reducing inflammation or supporting neuroplasticity. While research is still emerging, some notable examples are shown in Table 8.3.

Table 8.3 *Additional supportive supplements for ADHD symptoms*

Chaga mushroom[20]	May help reduce oxidative stress/inflammation, factors that impact cognitive health. Its neuroprotective properties make it a candidate for supporting overall brain function.
L-Theanine	Shown to improve sleep, calmness, attention without sedation.
Lion's mane mushroom[21]	Stimulates nerve growth factor, supporting brain plasticity and cognitive function. Research suggests it may enhance memory and focus, more studies needed to confirm its efficacy in ADHD.

Pycnogenol (French maritime pine bark extract)[22]	Reduces oxidative stress and inflammation, supports dopamine regulation, may improve blood flow to the brain, enhancing cognitive performance. Pycnogenol significantly reduced hyperactivity and improved attention, visual-motor coordination and concentration in children with ADHD after just one month of supplementation.
Saffron (Crocus sativus)[23]	Some studies found saffron useful for reducing ADHD symptoms, some found it as effective as methylphenidate (Ritalin) in managing inattention and hyperactivity by modulating dopamine and serotonin levels.

These supplements offer potential benefits, but it's essential to approach them with caution. Quality varies between products and individual responses differ. Consulting with a healthcare professional experienced in integrative or functional medicine will help determine the most appropriate and safe options tailored to your child's needs.

The importance of good gut health

Even the most nutritious diet and supplement protocol won't work effectively if your gut isn't functioning properly. Research increasingly supports the idea of the gut as our 'second brain', highlighting its powerful role in overall wellbeing. The foods you eat directly influence your gut microbiome, damaging it with poor nutrition or strengthening it with nourishing choices.

The gut-immune-brain axis

The gut-immune-brain axis describes the communication network between the digestive and immune systems and the brain. One of the key players in this gut-brain connection is the microbiome—the vast community of trillions of bacteria, microbes and around 70 per cent of the body's immune cells living in the digestive tract where they constantly interact with the microbiome and gut lining.

These microbes don't just help digest food, they also produce important neurotransmitters, which influence mood, focus and behaviour and send messages to the brain through the vagus nerve, immune system, hormones and neurotransmitters.

When the microbiome is out of balance (a state known as dysbiosis) due to poor diet, stress, infections or leaky gut, it triggers not only digestive issues but immune dysregulation and chronic low-grade inflammation. This inflammation may not cause obvious illness, but can quietly interfere with brain function, affect mood and intensify ADHD symptoms. For children with ADHD, who already experience differences in the way they produce and use these critical neurotransmitters, small fluctuations and imbalances can have a greater impact on them. Gut health is the foundation of nutrition and must be addressed alongside dietary changes for true, lasting results

Common gut issues for children with ADHD

Research shows what many parents have long suspected: gut health and neurodevelopmental conditions like ADHD and autism are closely connected. Altered gut microbiota and higher rates of gastrointestinal (GI) and bowel problems, including constipation, diarrhoea, bloating, abdominal pain, food intolerances and general digestive discomfort, are more likely to occur in 70 to 90 per cent of children with autism and 30 to 50 per cent of children with ADHD than their neurotypical peers.[24,25] Research also links these GI symptoms to behavioural challenges and the severity of ADHD and autism symptoms, such as gut inflammation, pointing to a shared mechanism.[26]

Intestinal permeability (leaky gut)

When the gut lining becomes too permeable (known medically as increased intestinal permeability and often referred to as 'leaky gut'), it allows partially digested food particles, toxins and bacteria to pass through the intestinal wall and enter the bloodstream. This can trigger an immune response and lead to systemic inflammation, including neuroinflammation (inflammation in the brain).[27] For children with ADHD, this inflammation can interfere with the production and function of neurotransmitters, contributing to ADHD symptoms. Leaky gut is often linked to food sensitivities, chronic stress, gut infections and an imbalanced microbiome.

Parasites

Parasitic gut infections, such as those caused by *Giardia, Blastocystis hominis, or Dientamoeba fragilis,* can significantly impact gut health and mental wellbeing.[28] These organisms can trigger chronic inflammation, disrupt the gut microbiome and damage the intestinal lining, leading to nutrient malabsorption and leaky gut. Parasites don't always cause obvious digestive symptoms, making them easy to overlook, but advanced stool testing will identify them. Addressing parasitic infections through appropriate treatment and gut repair can lead to meaningful symptom improvements.

Fungal overgrowth

Fungal overgrowth, particularly of *Candida albicans*, is a fungal imbalance in the gut that contributes to a range of physical and behavioural symptoms. While *Candida* is a normal part of your gut microbiome, problems arise when it grows unchecked due to factors like frequent antibiotic use, high-sugar diets, chronic stress or weakened immunity. Overgrowth leads to symptoms such as bloating, sugar cravings, brain fog, fatigue, mood swings, hyperactivity and even increased anxiety or aggression, all of which can overlap with or worsen ADHD symptoms.[29] *Candida* produces toxins damaging to the gut lining and contributes to leaky gut, fuelling inflammation and affecting the brain via the gut-brain axis. To address *Candida*, a multi-pronged approach is needed: reducing sugar and refined carbohydrates (which feed it), using antifungal herbs or supplements, and supporting the gut with probiotics, prebiotics and a healing diet. It's best done under the guidance of a practitioner, as die-off symptoms can occur during the initial phase of treatment.

Supporting gut health

As you can see, supporting gut health is an important part of a holistic ADHD support strategy. Let's explore how to start your journey.

Optimal gut health means having a diverse and well-balanced microbiome that supports digestion, immune function and brain health. When beginning to improve or maintain good gut health, the first step is to remove what harms the gut and add in what nourishes and supports it.

Meat stock

Meat stock is a gentle, nourishing liquid made by simmering meaty bones (chicken frames or beef shanks) for two to four hours. Rich in gelatine, collagen, amino acids (like glycine and proline) and minerals, meat stock is incredibly soothing for the gut lining and can help support the healing of leaky gut. Meat stock can be especially beneficial for children with food sensitivities, digestive issues or nutrient absorption problems, providing easy-to-digest nourishment—a foundational food in any gut-healing plan.

Bone broth

Bone broth is simmered for 12 to 48 hours using bare bones and vinegar to extract minerals and collagen peptides. While bone broth is deeply nourishing, it's higher in histamines and glutamates due to the long cooking time, which can be overstimulating or problematic for children with sensitive nervous systems. Meat stock is often the better choice when starting a gut-healing diet, with bone broth introduced later if tolerated.

Prebiotics and probiotics

Prebiotics and probiotics are crucial for a healthy microbiome. They play unique but complementary roles:

> ➤ Prebiotics are types of dietary fibre that feed beneficial gut bacteria, helping them thrive.
> ➤ Probiotics are live beneficial bacteria that add to the microbiome to help restore balance.

Research on *Lactobacillus rhamnosus* probiotic supplementation showed children with ADHD taking this supplement had better emotional, physical, social and school functioning and a higher health-related quality of life compared with the placebo group.[30]

The food-first approach to adding prebiotics and probiotics to your child's diet is the easiest and often most effective way to begin. Start small—a half teaspoon of kimchi, a small serving of kefir or live yoghurt is enough at the outset. Observe whether your child tolerates it before adding more. Some children may react at first due to the sudden shift in gut bacteria which may trigger temporary digestive or behavioural symptoms as the microbiome begins to rebalance and detoxify. If this happens and symptoms are mild and manageable, it's usually safe to continue with perhaps an even smaller dose. However, should symptoms be more severe or continue, it would be wise to stop and consult a qualified practitioner before continuing.

It's best to go the food-first route for these important reasons:

> Fermented foods additionally provide enzymes, vitamins and bioavailable nutrients further supporting digestion and gut health.
> Fermented foods typically contain smaller amounts of probiotics than high-dose capsules.
> Probiotics from foods survive stomach acid and reach the gut better than some supplements, so are better absorbed.
> Many children enjoy, or come to enjoy, the probiotic foods in their meals and associate them with gut-friendly eating.
> Including probiotic-rich foods allows children to understand the link between food and health, fostering better lifelong habits.

If you're working with a practitioner and have had a stool analysis, they'll advise you which strains to supplement. When supplementing, use high-quality, multi-strain probiotics containing at least five to ten billion colony-forming units. *Lactobacillus rhamnosus*, *Lactobacillus acidophilus* and *Bifidobacterium bifidum* have been studied for their impact on behaviour and mood.

Table 8.4 (overleaf) provides examples of prebiotic- and probiotic-rich foods you could include in your child's diet for good gut bacteria to thrive.

Caring for your child's gut is a holistic way to support their mental health and ease ADHD symptoms. By focusing on real, whole foods that nourish the microbiome and avoiding what harms it (highly processed foods, artificial additives, pesticides, frequent antibiotics, excess sugar and chronic stress), you create the ideal environment for healing and balance.

Table 8.4 *Beneficial prebiotic and probiotic foods*

Prebiotic-rich foods	Probiotic-rich foods
Inulin and fructooligosaccharides (FOS)	➤ Yoghurt with live cultures (check the label for 'live and active cultures'); can be dairy or coconut yoghurt
➤ Bananas	
➤ Onions	
➤ Garlic	
➤ Leeks	➤ Kefir (fermented milk or coconut water drink)
➤ Asparagus	
➤ Jerusalem artichoke	➤ Sauerkraut, kimchi (raw fermented vegetables, unpasteurised)
➤ Legumes (lentils, chickpeas, beans)	
Resistant starch	
➤ Cooked-and-cooled rice and potatoes	➤ Miso, tempeh (fermented soy products)
➤ Green banana flour	➤ Kombucha (fermented tea; low-sugar varieties are best) in moderation
Pectin	
➤ Apples	
➤ Citrus fruits	
➤ Carrots	
Polyphenols (prebiotic-like)	
➤ Berries	
➤ Green tea	
➤ Cocoa	
Partially hydrogenated guar gum (PHGG) is a gentle type of soluble fibre made from guar beans that dissolves easily in water.	

A healthy gut supports better nutrient absorption, reduced inflammation and more stable neurotransmitter production. Whether you're beginning a gut-healing journey or simply aiming to maintain good gut health, every small change in the right direction helps lay the foundation for a calmer, more resilient brain and a happier, more balanced child.

Bioindividuality

Every child is unique in how their body processes food, nutrients and environmental inputs. This concept, known as bioindividuality, reminds us there is no one-size-fits-all diet for ADHD. What works beautifully for one child may not help (or could even worsen) symptoms in another. Tracking your child's food, behaviour, mood and symptoms and working with a knowledgeable practitioner when needed is so valuable. Careful observation often reveals subtle patterns and responses that guide more personalised, effective nutrition and lifestyle choices for your individual child. The following section explains more about individual differences.

Nutrigenomics and epigenetics

When we talk about the heritability of ADHD, it means that research shows ADHD often runs in families. There isn't a single 'ADHD gene', but rather many small genetic differences that, combined, can affect how the brain develops and functions. These differences often include single nucleotide polymorphisms (SNPs)—tiny variations in genes that naturally occur when DNA is copied and passed down through generations. SNPs are a normal part of human diversity, but in some cases they may influence how a child produces brain chemicals, processes nutrients, detoxifies substances, or responds to stress and inflammation.

Epigenetics studies how genes are turned on or off by environmental factors, showing us that lifestyle (diet, stress, sleep and toxin exposure) plays a role in whether these genetic tendencies are expressed. As the saying goes: 'Genes load the gun, but the environment pulls the trigger.' Understanding your child's genetic makeup and supporting them with the right nutrition and environment can influence how their brain and body function.

With the foundations of gut health and nutrition in place, you may wish to delve deeper, because while food and lifestyle changes are impactful, some children may continue to struggle because of underlying SNPs. If your child's symptoms persist, or if your practitioner recommends a more individualised approach, exploring your child's genetic makeup can provide valuable insights.

In the context of ADHD, nutrigenomics explains why some children may need higher amounts of specific nutrients to support brain function and emotional regulation. It also helps identify which foods or environmental exposures may be more problematic for your child, allowing you to tailor your child's nutrition and supplementation in a more targeted, personalised approach.

Some of the more common SNPs linked with ADHD and the ways they may affect things like nutrition, gut health and brain function are outlined in Table 8.5. Don't worry if this looks technical at first glance; instead, focus on the bigger picture of how these variations might influence your child's health and where targeted supports (like nutrition or lifestyle changes) can make a difference. If you choose to have genetic testing done through a qualified practitioner, they will guide you through the results and explain what it means for your child in practical terms.

Table 8.5 *Common SNPs*

SNP	Characteristics
COMT (Catechol-O-Methyltransferase)	➤ Impacts how quickly dopamine, epinephrine, norepinephrine are broken down ➤ Fast vs slow variants influence stress tolerance and focus ➤ Nutrient considerations: magnesium, SAMe, adaptogens
DAO (Diamine oxidase)	➤ Involved in histamine breakdown ➤ Low activity may contribute to food intolerances, mood dysregulation, gut issues ➤ Consider low-histamine diet or DAO enzyme supplements or nutrients like vitamin C and B6. These are helpful, as they support the body's ability to break down histamine and reduce sensitivity reactions

SNP	Characteristics
FADS1/FADS2 (fatty acid desaturase genes)	➤ Involved in converting plant-based omega-3s (ALA) to usable DHA/EPA ➤ Some people may not convert efficiently ➤ Support: omega-3-rich diet or supplements
MAOA (Monoamine oxidase A)	➤ Breaks down serotonin, dopamine, norepinephrine ➤ Certain variants are linked to impulsivity and aggression in the context of trauma or environment ➤ Support: protein intake, gut health, mood regulation strategies
MTHFR[31] (Methylenetetrahydrofolate Reductase)	➤ Affects folate metabolism and methylation (important for neurotransmitter production) ➤ Can impact mood, attention and detoxification ➤ Nutrient considerations: methylfolate, B12 (methylcobalamin), B6 help the body's methylation process work more smoothly, which supports mood, energy and overall brain health in children with MTHFR variations
NQO1/GSTs (detoxification genes)	➤ Influence the body's ability to detoxify toxins, heavy metals, environmental chemicals ➤ Weak function may increase sensitivity to food additives or mould ➤ Support: cruciferous vegetables, glutathione, antioxidant support
PEMT (phosphatidylethanolamine N-methyltransferase)	➤ Affects choline metabolism (important for brain development, attention) ➤ Low function may increase need for dietary choline (eggs, liver, sunflower lecithin)

These SNPs highlight why everyone is biochemically unique and why one child may thrive on a particular diet or supplement while another sees little to no change or even reacts negatively. It reminds us there's no one-size-fits-all solution and personalised, targeted interventions informed by both observation and, where possible, testing, are key. Understanding bioindividuality moves away from trial-and-error approaches toward more effective, tailored care.

Many SNPs explored in nutrigenomics are involved in methylation and detoxification pathways, meaning genetic variations affect how well your child clears toxins and processes nutrients.

Methylation

Methylation is a crucial biochemical process affecting everything from detoxification and neurotransmitter production to immune function. When methylation isn't working optimally, it may contribute to neurological and behavioural challenges.

'Undermethylators' may experience low serotonin and dopamine levels, leading to anxiety, depression, inattention and irritability, while 'overmethylators' may experience mood swings, sensitivity to environmental triggers and hyperactivity. Methylation is influenced by both genetics and nutrient status, particularly levels of folate, B12, B6, zinc and magnesium.

Support involves identifying whether a child is over- or undermethylating (often via symptom patterns or functional testing) and then tailoring nutrient support accordingly. Improper methylation support can worsen symptoms so it's best addressed by a practitioner experienced in functional or integrative medicine.

Toxicity

Heavy metals such as aluminium, lead, mercury and cadmium can be toxic to the developing brain and have been linked to a range of neurological and behavioural issues, including ADHD symptoms, anxiety, irritability, learning difficulties and emotional dysregulation.[32] These metals can interfere with neurotransmitter function, increase oxidative stress and contribute to chronic inflammation. Children can be exposed through various environmental sources.

To assess whether heavy metals might be contributing to your child's symptoms, testing options include hair tissue mineral analysis (HTMA), urine challenge tests, or organic acids testing (OAT). If metals are present, gentle detoxification strategies, such as nutritional support for liver and gut function, increasing antioxidant intake or using binders under practitioner guidance help the body safely eliminate them over time.

Functional testing

If, despite your best efforts with dietary changes, your child continues to have ongoing or complex gut issues, food intolerances, mood, sleep or behavioural challenges, functional testing offers deeper insights. Tests can uncover hidden imbalances, such as gut dysbiosis, inflammation, nutrient deficiencies or detoxification issues. Table 8.6 describes common functional tests.

Table 8.6 *Common functional medicine tests*

Functional medical test	Purpose
Blood/nutrient panels	Uncover deficiencies in critical vitamins and minerals like zinc, magnesium, B12, and iron
Coeliac disease screening	Valuable, particularly with strong digestive symptoms, anxiety or a family history of autoimmune conditions
Comprehensive stool analysis	Reveals imbalances in the microbiome, inflammation, infections and how well nutrients are digested and absorbed
PCR-based stool analysis	Detects DNA of parasites and other microbes. Helps give a clearer picture of whether parasites may be contributing to symptoms
Food sensitivity testing (often IgG-based)	May help identify delayed immune reactions to common foods difficult to pinpoint through observation alone

(continued)

Table 8.6 *Common functional medicine tests (cont'd)*

Functional medical test	Purpose
Genetic testing	Helps personalise support by identifying how nutrients and neurotransmitters are processed, guiding more targeted and effective interventions
Hair tissue mineral analysis (HTMA)	Shows mineral imbalances or heavy metal exposure over time
Organic acids testing (OAT)	Offers a comprehensive view of metabolic function, gut bacteria by-products, neurotransmitter markers and detox pathways
Screening for pyroluria	Condition that depletes zinc and B6

Qualified naturopaths, integrative doctors or paediatricians who specialise in ADHD, gut health, nutrition and epigenetics can advise on and order any specific tests required and then accurately interpret the results to create an individualised protocol for your child. Testing isn't always necessary, but it can remove much of the guesswork and guide a more personalised, targeted approach to your child's nutritional support.

Lifestyle synergy

Nutrition doesn't work in isolation; it functions best when supported by a healthy lifestyle. This means sleep, movement and stress management all work together with nutrition to support the brain and nervous system. As you will discover in the following chapters, the most carefully planned diet can't fully support focus and emotional regulation if your child is chronically sleep deprived, overly sedentary or under constant stress. Regular movement helps balance blood sugar, improve mood and increase dopamine, while restful sleep allows the brain to reset and regulate. Managing stress through mindfulness, play and downtime supports digestion and nutrient absorption. When these elements are aligned, nutrition becomes even more powerful, and together, they create a stable foundation that helps your child thrive, both mentally and physically.

Chapter Nine

Sleep and circadian biology: Optimising your child's sleep

Sleep isn't just rest—it's regulation, repair and the reset button every ADHD brain relies on.

I've frequently mentioned the importance of quality sleep because sleep is a foundational pillar of mental and physical health and a lack of it exacerbates ADHD symptoms. In this chapter we'll explore why sleep is so important, and how to make sure you and your child get enough quality sleep to ensure you minimise ADHD symptoms and function at your best.

Unfortunately, for children with ADHD, getting quality sleep can often be one of their challenges, with some studies suggesting 25 to 55 per cent of individuals with ADHD experience significant sleep disturbances, including difficulty falling asleep, staying asleep or waking up feeling unrested.[1] Often this is exacerbated by some ADHD medications, a busy ADHD brain that's hard to switch off or, increasingly, screen use before bed.

The critical role of sleep and light in managing ADHD symptoms

Sleep is critical for your child with ADHD (and you) because poor-quality sleep has been shown to significantly worsen nearly every symptom associated with ADHD.[2] Let's see how sleep affects some of the most common ADHD systems.

Focus and attention

Impaired attention and focus is one of the most well-researched effects of poor-quality sleep. During sleep, our prefrontal cortex (the brain area responsible for executive functioning and attention) rests, allowing it time to recover, rebalance key neurotransmitters and consolidate neural pathways involved in learning and regulation. Even small sleep deficits have been found to make following directions, focusing on tasks or completing schoolwork more challenging.[3]

A lack of sleep also increases cortisol, the body's main stress hormone. Higher cortisol levels have been linked with increased anxiety, irritability and impaired memory — again worsening ADHD-related difficulties in self-regulation and focus.[4]

Impulse control

Research has shown significant increases in impulsive action following consecutive nights of insufficient sleep compared to nights of adequate, restful sleep. Lack of sleep can make it more challenging for children to pause before acting, and may result in more risk-taking behaviours, accidents, outbursts and social challenges.[5] Our prefrontal cortex regulates behaviour, manages emotions and allows us to use our logic and reason, so when sleep deprivation activates our amygdala instead, you can understand why we are more emotional than logical.[6,7]

Emotional regulation

We need sufficient quality sleep to restore balance in our emotional function, and when we are sleep deprived, we become less emotionally regulated and more sensitive to stressful stimuli and events. Sleep deprivation can cause our amygdala, which processes emotions, to become hyper-reactive. Paired with an underperforming prefrontal cortex, which calms the amygdala, people may experience greater emotional volatility, irritability and difficulty managing stress — symptoms already challenging for many young people with ADHD.[8]

Research also confirms that the relationship between emotion and sleep works both ways. When our daily stresses become too much, they may result in sleep disturbances and affect the quality and amount of sleep we are able to get.[9]

Learning and memory

Learning, memory consolidation and neuroplasticity are dependent on a well-functioning circadian rhythm (your body's sleep-wake cycle). For children with ADHD, who often struggle with processing, working memory and retaining information, poor-quality sleep can add another barrier to their learning. Research shows sleep deprivation causes significant impairments in these areas because our brain consolidates the integration of new knowledge while we sleep, meaning your child will find it harder to retain what they learn at school.[10]

When our brain's 'master clock', the suprachiasmatic nucleus (SCN), is not properly set by the natural rhythm of daylight and darkness, it struggles to keep the body and brain in sync. This can disrupt important processes that support learning and development, such as:

> ➤ strengthening brain connections (synaptic plasticity)
> ➤ consolidating memories during sleep
> ➤ releasing brain-supportive proteins like brain-derived neurotrophic factor (BDNF; which help neurons grow and communicate).

This is why getting outside in the morning light and keeping evenings darker (by reducing screens and bright lights) can help children learn better during the day and sleep more soundly at night.[11,12]

Mental health

Improving sleep is associated with better overall mental health, regardless of the severity of the mental health difficulty or the presence of comorbid health conditions. Poor sleep is causally related to mental health difficulties.[13]

When we're sleep deprived our neurotransmitter balance is altered, exacerbating low mood, anxiety and overthinking. In children with ADHD, co-occurring mental health conditions are common, so knowing poor sleep can worsen their emotional symptoms and increase the likelihood of developing a mood disorder is helpful. Sleep disturbances can be both a symptom and a factor in anxiety and depression.[14]

Blood sugar regulation

Sleep plays a critical role in regulating blood sugar, which, in turn, affects ADHD symptoms.[15] Sleep deprivation contributes to insulin resistance and unstable blood glucose levels, which can cause irritability, brain fog and energy crashes and can be problematic for those with ADHD. These fluctuations can mimic or amplify symptoms of inattention and impulsivity.[16]

What happens while we sleep?

Quality sleep promotes cognitive health by allowing the brain to repair, rebalance and replenish itself overnight.[17] While we sleep, the brain goes through a series of critical processes that support our physical, cognitive and emotional functioning (see Table 9.1).

During these stages, a number of key functions occur.

Waste clearance

Our glymphatic system primarily functions during sleep and is responsible for filtering out 'metabolic waste' like excess neurotransmitters and inflammatory proteins, and for facilitating the distribution of essential nutrients required for neuronal repair and function in the brain.

Table 9.1 *The stages of sleep*

Stage	Sleep type	What happens?	Key functions
Stage 1: Light sleep	Non-rapid eye movement (NREM)	Light sleep; transition from wakefulness; muscles relax	Prepares body and brain for deeper sleep
Stage 2: Light-moderate sleep	NREM	Heart rate slows, body temp drops; brain waves slow with bursts (sleep spindles)	Memory consolidation begins; protects sleep from disruption
Stage 3: Deep sleep/slow-wave sleep	NREM	Deepest sleep; slow delta waves dominate; hard to wake from	Glymphatic waste clearance, growth hormone release, immune repair, synaptic pruning
Stage 4: Rapid eye movement (REM)/dream sleep	REM	Brain becomes active; dreams occur; body is paralysed	Emotional processing, memory integration, mood regulation, creativity

A well-functioning glymphatic system supports increased cognitive performance, memory retention and executive function, while sleep deprivation decreases cognitive performance.[18]

Memory consolidation

During deep/slow-wave (stage 3) and REM sleep (stage 4), the brain sorts, strengthens and stores information learned during the day. Emotional memories are processed, problem-solving improves and learning is reinforced.

Hormonal balance

Sleep helps regulate hormones like cortisol (stress), melatonin (sleep-wake cycle), and growth hormone (cell repair and development). Disrupted sleep throws these off, affecting mood, focus, appetite and energy.

Emotional regulation

During REM sleep (stage 4), the amygdala (the brain's threat detection centre) becomes more active, while the prefrontal cortex (responsible for impulse control and regulation) shuts down. We also produce less noradrenaline (a stress-related neurotransmitter) during REM sleep. Together, this shift in our brain functioning allows the brain to surface and process emotional memories without triggering our fight-or-flight response.

The effects of light on sleep

One of the most important factors affecting sleep is light. To understand the effect of light on sleep, you first need to understand your circadian biology. Circadian rhythms (your body clock) are your body's natural 24-hour cycles, regulating normal biological processes like sleep and waking, digestion and hormone release.

Your circadian rhythms rely on natural light signals to know when it's time to be alert and time to wind down. During daytime light, your brain delays or stops the production of melatonin (the hormone that makes you sleepy) to ensure you stay alert and energised. Conversely, when it's dark, melatonin production ramps up to help you wind down for the night.

Disruptions to these rhythms can affect how well you sleep, but they can also affect your mood, focus and overall wellbeing, and this is especially so for children with ADHD. Think about how you feel when you're jetlagged—this is because your circadian rhythm is out of whack.

One of the biggest modern disruptions to our sleep cycle is blue light from screens (phones, tablets, TVs, computers) and artificial lighting. It's important to consider that, as a species, we've only had artificial light (apart from firelight) after dark for about 150 years. For most of human history, we've lived in sync with the sun—bright light during the day, darkness at night. Your body still expects this.

Blue light signals to your brain it's the middle of the day, even if it's 8 pm. Blue-light exposure after dark delays melatonin production by up to 90 minutes, pushing the sleep phase later and reducing the deep, slow-wave sleep essential for memory and learning.[19]

Chronic exposure to artificial light after dark disrupts melatonin signalling and potentially impacts sleep, thermoregulation, blood pressure and glucose homeostasis.[20] For children with ADHD, disruptions to their circadian rhythm caused by insufficient daylight exposure, excessive artificial light at night and poor light hygiene can worsen their ADHD symptoms.

Focus, attention and dopamine production

Dopamine, a key neurotransmitter involved in motivation, reward and attention, is already dysregulated in ADHD brains. What you may not realise is that dopamine production is tightly linked to circadian timing and light exposure. Disrupted circadian rhythms have been shown to impair dopamine signalling, which is critical in ADHD-related focus and reward processing.[21,22]

Mitochondrial researchers explain natural sunlight (particularly infrared, blue and red light) not only supports dopamine production but also energises mitochondria, increasing ATP (energy) production in brain cells.[23] This energy is essential for executive functioning, attention and working memory. Early-morning sunlight is especially powerful, as the mix of blue and red light acts like a natural 'on' switch for your child's brain, helping trigger dopamine production.[24] When your child misses out on morning sunlight and starts their day under artificial indoor lighting, dopamine signalling is reduced, leading to more distractibility and less focus.

In contrast, artificial blue light, LEDs and fluorescent light (particularly at night), which dominate our homes and schools, lack the full-spectrum wavelengths needed for optimal mitochondrial health and, instead, increase oxidative stress, contributing to fatigue, brain fog and poor motivation.

Electromagnetic frequencies (EMFs)

A factor not often brought up in relation to sleep is electromagnetic frequency (EMF) exposure. Studies have shown that EMFs reduce melatonin production, disrupt circadian rhythms and fragment sleep architecture.[25,26] If you're trying to optimise your child's sleep, exposure to wi-fi or mobile phones may worsen insomnia, restlessness and next-day symptoms.[27]

Tips to reduce wi-fi exposure

➤ Turn wi-fi routers off at night.
➤ Don't place wi-fi routers near bedrooms or where children spend a lot of time.
➤ Hardwire devices with ethernet cables.
➤ Keep devices out of bedrooms at night.
➤ Check Bluetooth devices are off or away from children.

The relationship between sleep, ADHD symptoms and mental health is profound. Poor sleep quality worsens nearly every single ADHD symptom as well as anxiety and depression. It also interferes with critical physiological processes like hormone regulation and blood sugar stability, further compounding the challenges.

In children with ADHD, sleep is not a nice to have, it's critical to their wellbeing. Supporting your child's sleep quality will be one of the most powerful and accessible ways to help improve their emotional, cognitive and physical functioning and wellbeing.

Let's look at ways to improve your child's sleep quality next.

Optimising sleep quality

Research consistently shows that people with ADHD are more likely to experience sleep difficulties, including trouble falling asleep, trouble staying asleep, restless sleep or waking too early. You may have experienced this with your child. Sometimes it can be as a result of a busy brain and sometimes it can be a medication side effect. Either way, sleep is of vital importance to your child, so finding ways to optimise sleep quality is critical.

I've headed this section 'Optimising sleep *quality*' because you want to achieve sleep 'quality' for your child, not just sleep duration.

What does good sleep hygiene look like?

For children with ADHD, good *sleep hygiene* (the habits, routines and environment that support healthy sleep) is especially important, since their busy brains and sensitivity to changes in routine can make winding down more challenging. Qualities of good sleep hygiene include:

➤ having a consistent sleep and wake time
➤ no screens 90 minutes before bed
➤ plenty of natural daytime light, especially in the morning
➤ a calming bedtime routine with sensory cues (baths, music, oils)
➤ a peaceful, supportive sleep environment (quiet, dark, comfortable temperature (18–20°C), comfortable mattress, pillow and bedding)
➤ balanced nutrition and gentle daytime movement
➤ nutrients such as magnesium via supplement or an Epsom salt bath (see Chapter 7)
➤ calming teas such as chamomile or lemon balm
➤ emotional support to ease stress and mental chatter.

Let's look at some practical ways to support good sleep hygiene.

Before bedtime

You may only start to think about sleep when your child is getting ready for bed, but you can do important things throughout the day to help them drop off more easily at night.

Support melatonin production naturally

If you're considering supplementing your child with melatonin, make sure you speak with a practitioner beforehand to ensure it's right for them. Here are some other ways you can increase their melatonin naturally.

➤ Get bright light exposure in the morning to kickstart melatonin production.
➤ Reduce blue-light screen exposure.

Balance blood sugar and nutrition

➤ Avoid sugar/processed carbohydrates before bed.
➤ Offer protein-rich snacks in the evening (e.g., nut butter, boiled egg, yoghurt).

Help clear busy brains

> ➤ Use a worry journal or draw feelings before bed.
> ➤ Try guided meditation or calming audio stories.
> ➤ Practice slow breathing techniques (e.g., 4-7-8 breathing; see Chapter 11).
> ➤ Allow time to talk through worries earlier, not at lights out.

Supporting circadian biology

To support your child's circadian biology, mitochondrial health and neurotransmitters through daily light-based lifestyle strategies, Table 9.2 provides some simple, natural strategies:

Table 9.2 *Strategies to support circadian biology*

Timing	Strategies	Why it helps
Morning sunlight	10–30 minutes within 30–60 minutes of waking See the sun rise if possible Go outside without sunglasses or lenses Open curtains/windows, eat breakfast outside, walk to school, play in the garden etc	Morning light sets the body's internal clock, supports serotonin/dopamine production and prepares the body to make melatonin later that night
Midday sunlight	Outdoor play or walks at midday, when UVB is strongest (ensuring you still practise sun-safe habits)	Supports energy, vitamin D production, mood and mitochondrial function
Sunset	Dim lights after sunset Keep lighting red/orange: no bright, blue-light/LED exposure	Prevents melatonin suppression and sleep-phase delay

Timing	Strategies	Why it helps
After sunset	Reduce screen time 90 minutes before bed	Minimises circadian disruption and eye strain
	Use blue-light-blocking glasses after dark	
	Swap overhead LED lights for red or amber bulbs in the evening	
	Try using tools that reduce blue light from screens, such as f.lux, Night Shift (on Apple devices), or Iris software.	
	You can also look for a daylight or warm-tone computer monitor to make screen time easier on the eyes and body's natural rhythms.	
	See Chapter 16 for more about managing light and screen exposure.	
Bedtime	Use blackout curtains and cover any lights emanating from electronics	Promotes deep, restorative sleep
	No nightlights: darkness supports melatonin release and deep sleep	
	If needed, use a red nightlight	
Sleep-wake schedule	Encourage a regular sleep and wake-up time, even on weekends	Reinforces natural circadian timing and hormone regulation

(continued)

Restoring a child's relationship with the sun through morning light exposure, minimising screens and artificial light after dark, and aligning routines with their body's internal clock is one of the most effective, non-invasive and empowering strategies for helping young people with ADHD thrive — mentally, emotionally and neurologically — for life! In this age of overstimulation and digital overload, reconnecting with natural rhythms may be one of the most healing, affordable and sustainable interventions available.

Calming bedtime routines

Integral to helping your child wind down for bed is a comforting bedtime routine that becomes a habit. Start limiting rough play and opt for calming activities instead.

Ideas include:

➤ Dim lighting and screen-free environment.
➤ Warm relaxing bath with Epsom salts (magnesium absorbed through the skin).
➤ Gentle stretching, breathwork or meditation.
➤ Reading, journaling or gratitude diary.
➤ Listening to low-stimulation music or an audiobook.
➤ Binaural beats/white noise can help calm busy brains.
➤ Diffuse essential oils like lavender, vetiver, cedarwood or frankincense for a sensory cue that it's time to wind down.
➤ Calming cues such as soft music, gentle stretching or reading.

Sleep-friendly environments

➤ Keep the bedroom cool, dark and quiet.
➤ Use blackout curtains or sleep masks.
➤ Remove electronic devices or anything emitting light.
➤ Limit clutter and make the space feel cosy and safe.
➤ Consider soft weighted blankets or white-noise machines.

Sleep disordered breathing

Some children may have breathing challenges such as enlarged adenoids, tonsils, asthma, sleep apnoea or allergies, which can have a significant impact on sleep quality and ADHD symptoms. These conditions cause interrupted sleep, leading to inadequate rest, which worsens attention, focus and emotional regulation.[28]

You may not be aware that your child has sleep disordered breathing, but if you notice them snoring or mouth breathing while they're asleep, this can be an indication and you might want to investigate further.

Sleep apnoea (where breathing repeatedly stops and starts during sleep) leads to oxygen deprivation, which disrupts the sleep cycle and affects cognitive function during the day. Likewise, allergies and chronic nasal congestion can make breathing difficult, especially during sleep, leading to restlessness and less restorative sleep.

Addressing these underlying breathing issues is crucial for improving sleep quality, which helps reduce the severity of ADHD symptoms and enhances overall wellbeing. Recognising and treating these health concerns can make a significant difference in ADHD symptoms.

When you prioritise sleep, everything gets easier for your child and for your family. Quality rest supports focus, emotional stability, growth, immunity and self-regulation. A few thoughtful changes to your child's day and bedtime routine can make sleep a strength rather than a struggle.

Chapter Ten

Moving the mind: How exercise supports children with ADHD

> Movement fuels the ADHD mind—unlocking focus, lifting mood and calming the chaos from the inside out.

Most people would agree exercise and movement is vital for health and wellbeing for all of us. You may see exercise as a way for your child to burn off some energy, have fun and support their growing body, but you may not realise exercise and movement are also essential regulatory tools for their brains.

Research shows physical activity has a significant positive impact on attention, behaviour, mood, learning, anxiety, sleep and emotional regulation in people with ADHD.[1] Movement should be an integral part of your child's daily life. Luckily, it's simple, often free and something you can easily organise.

Why movement helps ADHD brains

When your child moves their body, several important things happen in their brain:

> Dopamine and norepinephrine levels increase: these key neurotransmitters help with focus, motivation and emotional regulation.[2]

> Blood flow to the prefrontal cortex improves, helping with attention, impulse control and decision-making.

> Stress hormones like cortisol decrease, while feel-good endorphins and serotonin rise, helping your child feel calmer, happier and more balanced.

> Movement enhances neuroplasticity, the brain's ability to learn, grow and adapt, which is important for kids with learning differences or behavioural challenges.

Without enough movement, children with ADHD may experience:

> more hyperactivity, restlessness or emotional outbursts
> difficulty focusing or following instructions
> poorer sleep and greater difficulty settling
> increased anxiety, frustration or moodiness
> less ability to 'reset' and regulate after stress.

Movement helps regulate the nervous system, which is often in overdrive for children with ADHD.

What does the research say?

Each of the core symptoms of ADHD are positively impacted by movement, so regular exercise should be a non-negotiable part of your child's ADHD lifestyle protocol.

Focus and attention

People with ADHD tend to focus better when they're moving, something the brain does to help pay attention. Even fidgeting is a self-regulation strategy.

Physical exercise improves attention, motor skills and executive function in children with ADHD.[3] A 2012 study showed that just 20 minutes of moderate aerobic activity significantly improved attention and boosted math and reading performance in children with ADHD immediately afterward.[4] In another study, teachers and parents of children with ADHD reported that just 30 minutes of exercise before school improved ADHD symptoms, moodiness and peer functioning.[5]

A 2015 review and meta-analysis showed short-term aerobic exercise (over six to ten weeks) had a positive effect on inattention, hyperactivity, impulsivity, anxiety, executive function and social challenges. The longer the exercise program continued, the better the results. In other words, it has to become part of everyday life, it's not something you can do for a few weeks and then stop and still see the benefits.[6]

Even ten minutes of movement improves attention and mood, but daily movement has the most benefit, and if it can be outdoors in green spaces, even better. Nature and movement combined have a synergistic effect on ADHD symptoms and mental health.[7]

Exercise increases levels of dopamine, norepinephrine and serotonin.[8] We also know exercise improves blood flow to the brain's prefrontal cortex, enhancing information processing capacity and attention, decreasing impulsiveness, and increasing inhibitory control, thereby improving interpersonal relationships.[9]

Impulsivity and hyperactivity

Physical activity helps reduce impulsive behaviour and hyperactivity by engaging the parts of the brain responsible for executive function, especially the prefrontal cortex. One randomised controlled trial found children who engaged in regular physical activity showed significantly reduced impulsive decision-making and improved inhibitory control (that crucial ability to stop and think before acting).[10]

Emotional regulation

Exercise helps regulate emotions by reducing cortisol (the stress hormone) and boosting serotonin to promote calm and contentment. It also strengthens the amygdala, thereby improving the brain's ability to calm the emotions. A 2015 study showed children with ADHD who took part in regular movement programs reported better mood, fewer meltdowns and improved frustration tolerance.[11]

Learning and memory

Exercise stimulates brain-derived neurotrophic factor (BDNF), which supports learning and memory formation. It improves working memory, which is essential for following instructions, remembering routines and learning at school. A 2010 study found that children with higher aerobic fitness — measured by treadmill testing rather than just general activity — had larger hippocampal volumes generally linked to better memory, learning capacity and emotional regulation and performed better on memory tasks than their peers with lower fitness.[12]

Anxiety and depression

Children with ADHD are at higher risk of anxiety and depression, and exercise is a natural tool to help both. Children who move regularly tend to report lower levels of anxiety and depression and greater emotional resilience. A 2011 meta-analysis found exercise interventions significantly reduced depressive symptoms in children and teens.[13]

Mental health and self-esteem

When children engage in activities such as team sports, martial arts, dance and outdoor adventures, it helps build confidence and a sense of mastery, which children with ADHD often need after experiencing setbacks in school or social settings.[14]

For children with sensory processing challenges, rhythmic movement like bouncing, swinging or jumping can help them calm their nervous systems and improve body awareness.

Best movement for ADHD

The most helpful types of exercise for improving symptoms of ADHD are shown in Table 10.1.

Table 10.1 *Best types of movement for ADHD*

Type	Example	Result
Aerobic exercise	Running, skipping, swimming, dancing, cycling, brisk walking, trampolining	Raises the heart rate, boosts brain chemicals and improves mood
Movement and brain engagement	Martial arts, gymnastics, yoga, dance routines, ball games, obstacle courses	Builds coordination, rhythm, timing, attention and body awareness
Balance and cross-lateral movement	Crawling, climbing, crossing midline	Integrates left and right brain hemispheres, which is important for executive functioning
Strength/resistance and heavy work activities	Climbing, monkey bars, carrying heavy things	Helps ground the body and reduce anxiety through sensory input

Dual-task training

Movement that challenges the brain and body simultaneously can improve ADHD symptoms in children. Think martial arts, such as Taekwondo, gymnastics, obstacle courses, balance games — anything where your child has to coordinate their movements while focusing, remembering sequences and responding to cues. This is often called dual-task training, and it engages the brain's executive function systems.

One 18-month study looked at students with ADHD who took part in Taekwondo sessions twice a week for 50 minutes. The results showed large improvements in attention and inhibition.[15] Similarly, another study found children who participated in balance training three times a week for six months, while still taking their regular ADHD medication, experienced significantly greater improvements in their ADHD symptoms than those on medication alone.[16] Balance training doesn't have to be intense. Simple, fun activities like standing on one foot while tossing a beanbag, walking along a line or using a wobble board can do the trick.

Brain balance therapies

Programs like Brain Balance or Primitive Reflex Integration are designed to support brain-body integration. They often include balance and coordination movement patterns that strengthen body awareness and stimulate balance and regulation. While research is still emerging, many parents report improvements in attention, mood, sensory processing and behaviour after using movement-based brain therapies. But you don't need a formal program to include these elements — just make movement fun, varied and brain-engaging.

These types of movement activities are fun, accessible and incredibly supportive for ADHD brains. So whether it's a martial arts class, a home balance challenge or a playful movement game in the backyard, encouraging activities combining mental and physical coordination is a smart, research-backed way to help your child thrive.

How much movement?

The magic number is at least 60 minutes of physical activity per day. This can be broken into shorter chunks and doesn't have to be structured.

Some ideas to help you build movement into your child's everyday life are in Table 10.2.

Table 10.2 *Daily routine ideas*

Time of day	Movement ideas
Morning	Walk to school, mini yoga session, bounce on trampoline
After school	Park play, bike ride, martial arts, dance class
Before homework	Five-minute movement burst: trampoline, balance work or active game
Evening	Family walk, gentle stretching, backyard cricket or soccer
Weekends	Bushwalks, beach play, obstacle courses, climbing trees, swimming

Timing

Morning movement helps prime the brain for attention and reduces morning chaos. Movement breaks before homework or schoolwork improve productivity and focus. Evening movement should be calmer and rhythmic and not too stimulating before bed.

Keep it fun

> Keep it non-competitive and playful.
> Let your child choose the activity — autonomy boosts buy-in.
> Join in: co-regulation through shared movement builds connection.
> Start small: even ten minutes is better than none and builds momentum.
> Use music, games or timers to make it engaging.

Movement isn't just beneficial for ADHD symptoms — it's essential. It's one of the few things that supports every core symptom: attention, impulsivity, emotional regulation, learning, mood, sleep and overall mental health.

Whether it's structured sports, backyard play or a spontaneous dance break in the kitchen, regular, varied and joyful movement gives children with ADHD the brain and body support they need to thrive. It's natural, effective and helps your child feel strong, capable and more in control of their own minds and body.

Chapter Eleven

Nervous system and emotional regulation: From meltdowns to safety

When we calm the nervous system, we open the door to connection, safety and growth—for our child and ourselves.

At the heart of parenting your child with ADHD lies the need to understand what's happening beneath the surface beyond the outbursts, resistance or shutdowns that can leave you feeling helpless or overwhelmed. In this chapter, you'll explore how your child's nervous system holds the key to their behaviour and why creating emotional safety is a foundational need in my ADHD Parenting Hierarchy of Needs. You'll gain insights and tools to support emotional regulation—not just in your child, but in yourself as well—so you can both thrive in connection, not conflict.

Understanding the nervous system and emotional regulation

To understand your child's 'big feelings', you need to understand what's happening beneath the surface for them—and that's often a nervous system in distress.

There are two connected systems at play:

> ➤ the autonomic nervous system: how your body responds to stress
> ➤ the emotional regulation system: how your brain manages, interprets and expresses these feelings.

When your child's body feels threatened or unsafe—whether emotionally, physically, socially or from a trauma response—the autonomic nervous system reacts automatically. This helps explain why your child might suddenly melt down in seemingly safe situations: their nervous system has picked up on subtle cues (tone of voice, facial expression, lighting, noise) and reacted as if there's a threat, even if there is no actual threat.

This is their *survival response* kicking in. It's a primitive, hardwired system that evolved to keep us alive in moments of danger with four main survival responses:

> ➤ *Fight:* Your child may shout, hit or strongly push back. This isn't intentional misbehaviour—it's a protective response from a nervous system that feels overwhelmed or unsafe.
> ➤ *Flight:* This looks like running away, shutting down, hiding or avoiding—trying to escape the perceived threat, even if it's just their homework.
> ➤ *Freeze:* You might notice your child becoming zoned out, unable to answer questions or non-responsive, often mistaken for 'not listening' or being 'lazy'.
> ➤ *Fawn:* Some children become overly eager to please, abandoning their own needs to stay safe. This looks like perfectionism, people-pleasing or masking true feelings.

Your child's nervous system can't always tell the difference between a truly life-threatening situation and one that simply *feels* overwhelmed. They may have heightened sensitivity and a lower threshold for stress, making it more likely for their brain to switch from thinking to survival mode.

These behaviours aren't conscious choices. They're automatic, body-first reactions to survive a perceived threat. The more overwhelmed or unsafe a child feels, especially if they've experienced past emotional trauma, the more easily and often their nervous system will default to one of these states. Often these patterns were laid down in childhood to protect the child from abandonment, shame or emotional overwhelm. A lack of attunement, constant criticism or inconsistency can create a nervous system that's always bracing for danger.

What trauma means: Big 'T', little 't' and survival patterns

When you hear the word *trauma*, it's easy to think of extreme (big 'T') events: abuse, neglect, major accidents or disasters. However, many of the patterns shaping your child's nervous system (and your own) may stem from what's known as little 't' trauma, developmental wounding arising from repeated, subtle disruptions in emotional safety such as being yelled at, not being heard, emotional withdrawal, bullying or chronic stress at home. It's been estimated that children with ADHD hear 20 000 more negative comments than their neurotypical peers by the time they're 12, which, in itself, may create its own little 't' trauma.

Humans are incredibly sensitive, dependent mammals. We are biologically wired to seek safety through connection. Survival depends on caregivers feeding, sheltering, protecting and, hopefully, loving us. This intense dependency sees our nervous system become finely tuned to pick up even the slightest cues of disconnection, tension or threat — real or perceived.

If your child senses they're not safe, not seen, not enough or not loved, their body responds with adaptive survival responses. Over time, these responses become deeply embedded patterns such as people-pleasing, perfectionism, emotional shutdown, hypervigilance or even chronic illness. These are not personality flaws, but nervous system adaptations, created for our survival.

Polyvagal theory

According to polyvagal theory, we detect threats through an unconscious process called neuroception, facilitated by the vagus nerve. The vagus nerve is the longest nerve in the body and transfers sensory input from the body to the brain to help us determine whether we are safe or in danger.

In this way, cues are not only spoken words—your tone of voice, facial expressions, posture, breathing and energy all communicate safety or danger, even if you're saying all the 'right' things. Your child is constantly scanning their environment for cues: *Am I safe? Are you safe? Can I relax or do I need to brace myself?*

If you or anyone else in your child's environment is tense, anxious, frustrated or shut down, even if it's hidden well, your child will *feel* it. They may not understand it, but their nervous system will respond. Learning to regulate *your own* nervous system is one of the most powerful things you can do.

Dr Deb Dana developed the concept of the Polyvagal Ladder (see Figure 11.1) to illustrate the three main nervous system states we move between depending on our experiences and the cues we receive from the environment.

Ventral vagal: Social engagement (safe and calm)

This is the state you want to be in most of the time. When you're feeling safe and regulated, your vagus nerve is effectively regulating your heart rate, breathing and stress responses. This is the state where you can connect with others, engage socially and be calm. In this state, you're able to listen, learn and respond appropriately to social cues while calmly regulating your emotions.

Sympathetic: Fight or flight (stress response)

When your body perceives a threat, the sympathetic nervous system kicks in, triggering a fight-or-flight response. The vagus nerve is less active here as your body prepares to deal with the perceived danger. For your child, this might look like impulsivity, irritability or aggressive outbursts. In this state, they can feel overwhelmed or hyper-alert, and it can be difficult for them to regulate their emotions.

The Polyvagal Ladder

The nervous system is like a ladder that shows our response to stress in three distinct stages.

- The top rung (ventral vagal) is where we're calm and collected.
- The middle rung (sympathetic) is where we feel unsafe and shift into fight or flight.
- The bottom rung (dorsal vagal) is where we freeze or shut down (feel helpless).
- Depending on how safe we feel, we move up or down on the Polyvagal Ladder.

Ventral vagal (safe and social)
- Clear, open to others, able to solve problems
- Ability to talk, engage, self-regulate and remain calm
- Ready to learn and attend
- Normal heart rate, relaxed breathing, good eye contact

Sympathetic (mobilisation; fight or flight)
- Feeling anxious, restless or irritated
- The body is mobilised to fight or run away from danger
- Mind is filled with worry, focused on perceived threats
- Increased heart rate, shallow breathing, tense muscles

Dorsal vagal (immobilisation; freeze)
- Feeling numb, detached, overwhelmed
- Stuck, hopeless, hard to focus
- Shut off from the threat when you can't fight or flight
- Low energy, decreased heart rate, depressed, numb, shut down, dissociated

Figure 11.1 *Polyvagal Ladder*

Dorsal vagal: Freeze or collapse (shutdown)

When the body perceives a threat that's too overwhelming to fight or flee from, it enters a freeze or shutdown response. This is often seen in situations where a child may shut down emotionally, withdraw from social interactions or even become physically immobile. In this state, a child might display withdrawal, avoidance, or non-responsiveness. In adults, you might feel numb, disconnected, tired or like you want to disappear. It's a protective state that kicks in when fight/flight doesn't work.

Understanding your child's stress response

Support your child by helping them regulate their nervous system, build resilience and develop the skills to return to a state of calm and connection. The Polyvagal Ladder helps you recognise cues of dysregulation in your child and intervene early with supportive strategies to help them return to a more balanced, calm state.

Explore through questions

Approaching behaviours as clues rather than simply actions to be corrected enables a much deeper understanding of your child's emotional world. By exploring what's beneath the surface and addressing the root causes of difficult behaviours, you can offer the right support, build better emotional regulation and strengthen your relationship with them. When you see behaviour as a language of the body and learn to listen, you begin to parent from a place of compassion, not control. You don't need to be perfect, you just need to become a steady base your child can return to, which is a nervous system state that says, 'You're safe with me.'

You become more effective and compassionate when you get curious:

> ➤ What's underneath my child's behaviour?
> ➤ What might feel unsafe for my child right now?
> ➤ What might this behaviour be trying to tell me?

> Is my child overwhelmed by the environment? Could sensory input, like noise or bright lights, be a trigger?

> Is my child struggling with something they find difficult to express? Could it be anxiety about a task, schoolwork or social situations?

> Are there any physical needs not being met? Has my child had enough sleep, eaten enough or had time to move and play?

What's going on beneath the surface?

We discussed the iceberg metaphor in Chapter 5. Below the waterline (the largest part of the iceberg) lie the deeper causes of behaviours, which can include:

> sensory processing challenges
> overwhelm or anxiety
> hunger or fatigue
> fear or uncertainty
> medical or neurological factors.

Our bodies hold unresolved stress, which, when activated by the survival response again, can manifest as:

> emotional volatility
> sensory sensitivities
> digestive issues
> chronic tension or pain
> fatigue.

These are physiological expressions of a dysregulated nervous system. ADHD often coexists with sensory processing challenges so your child may also react strongly to noise, light, textures and transitions. Sensory overwhelm can *feel* like a threat to your child's sensitive nervous system. This isn't your child being 'dramatic', it's their nervous system sounding the alarm. Their body is doing exactly what it thinks it needs to do to stay safe.

The sensory-nervous system connection

Sensory processing and emotional regulation are two sides of the same coin. Both are governed by the nervous system. When your child has a dysregulated or overly sensitive nervous system, *every little thing* can feel overwhelming, uncomfortable or even threatening.

There's a good chance you've noticed your child is *extra sensitive* to the world around them. Maybe it's the seams in their socks, the buzzing of fluorescent lights, the scratch of a label or the chaos of a noisy classroom. Maybe they can't stand brushing their teeth or they *love* rough hugs or crashing into furniture. These aren't quirks or preferences. They're signs of sensory processing differences and they play a massive role in how your child experiences and responds to the world.

Their body is constantly scanning for sensory input: sounds, sights, smells, movement, textures, temperature. They are trying to decide:

> ➤ Is this safe?
> ➤ Is this too much?
> ➤ Can I handle this right now?

If their nervous system is already in a heightened state, maybe because of emotional stress, poor sleep or an earlier conflict, even mild sensory input can push them over the edge. Imagine feeling itchy, hot, overwhelmed by noise and then being asked to focus on schoolwork or get ready for bed. No wonder they explode or melt down as their window of tolerance for stress *shrinks*, and suddenly they're in fight, flight or freeze mode—not because they're being difficult, but because their brain-body system is screaming for relief.

Sensory overwhelm sometimes shows up as:

> ➤ avoidance (won't try new foods, refuses clothing with tags or loud places), e.g, discomfort with new foods, clothing tags, or busy/noisy environments
> ➤ hyperactivity (bouncing, crashing, non-stop movement to self-regulate)
> ➤ emotional outbursts (after holding it together all day at school)
> ➤ fatigue or zoning out (shutting down to avoid overwhelm)
> ➤ aggression (hitting or yelling when someone gets 'too close').

What looks like 'bad' behaviour might be a nervous system doing its best to cope.

Support your child's regulation

The vagus nerve is the longest nerve of the autonomic nervous system, running from the brain down through the body. It helps regulate heart rate, breathing, digestion and emotional responses, which means it plays a central role in how easily we move between stress and calm.

When the vagus nerve is working well, children (and adults) are better able to regulate emotions and return to calm after challenges. This is often described as having good *vagal tone*, which refers to how flexible and responsive the vagus nerve is.

Strong vagal tone supports resilience, emotional regulation and the ability to stay within the 'window of tolerance'. Lower vagal tone, on the other hand, can make it harder to self-soothe and more likely for the person to become overwhelmed by stress.

This connects directly to the Polyvagal Ladder: with healthy vagal tone, children can spend more time in the top 'safe and social' state, and move more easily back up the ladder if they slip into fight/flight or shutdown

The window of tolerance

Imagine your child has a 'window' in which they can manage stress, think clearly, learn and connect with others. Developed by Dan Siegel, a clinical professor of psychiatry, the window of tolerance describes the most desired nervous system state, where we're able to function and thrive in everyday life (see Figure 11.2, overleaf). When your child is within this window, they're regulated and calm enough to engage, problem-solve and function. When stress pushes them outside that window, they flip into the fight, flight, freeze or fawn mode and lose access to logic and emotional control.

Because of the way ADHD affects self-regulation, impulse control and sensitivity to stimuli, children with ADHD often have narrower windows of tolerance, meaning it takes less for them to become dysregulated and they may spend more of their time outside that window in survival mode (i.e., in hyperarousal (fight/flight) and hypoarousal (freeze/shutdown)).

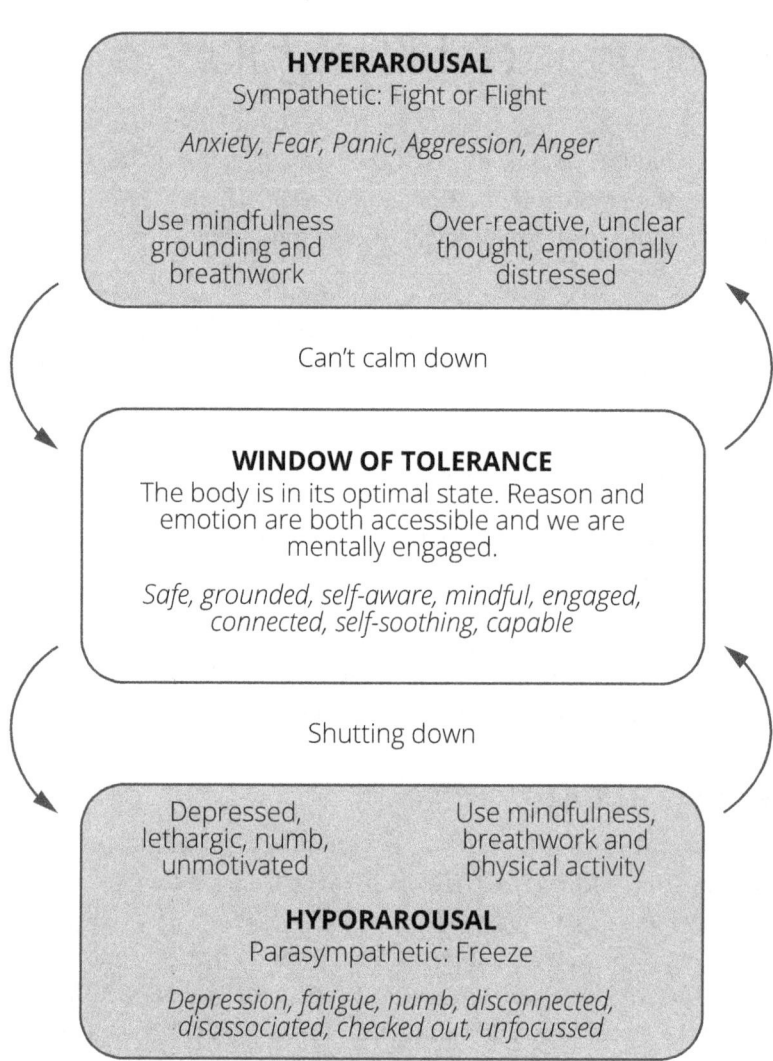

HYPERAROUSAL
Sympathetic: Fight or Flight

Anxiety, Fear, Panic, Aggression, Anger

Use mindfulness grounding and breathwork

Over-reactive, unclear thought, emotionally distressed

Can't calm down

WINDOW OF TOLERANCE
The body is in its optimal state. Reason and emotion are both accessible and we are mentally engaged.

Safe, grounded, self-aware, mindful, engaged, connected, self-soothing, capable

Shutting down

Depressed, lethargic, numb, unmotivated

Use mindfulness, breathwork and physical activity

HYPOAROUSAL
Parasympathetic: Freeze

Depression, fatigue, numb, disconnected, disassociated, checked out, unfocussed

Figure 11.2 *Window of tolerance*

In my Parenting Hierarchy of Needs from Chapter 4, emotional safety and nervous system regulation sit near the base—right alongside physiological needs like food, sleep and connection. Because until your child *feels safe*, they can't access the parts of their brain responsible for reasoning, learning or self-control. That's not poor parenting, or a misbehaving child— that's neurobiology.

With consistency and support, your child's window of tolerance can grow. So can yours. Essential to fostering emotional regulation for your child is supporting their vagal tone and improving their autonomic regulation. Let's look at some strategies to help you do this.

Create a safe environment

If your child feels safe, they're more likely to act calmly and express themselves in a healthy way. To improve your child's vagal tone, create an environment that feels safe and predictable for your child, where they feel heard, understood and supported. This might mean removing them from overwhelming situations or offering a quiet, calming space. When they feel safe in their environment they're more likely to remain emotionally regulated.

Safe environments have:

> ➤ clear, consistent routines offering predictability and structure
> ➤ reduced sensory inputs (e.g., light, noise) to avoid overwhelm
> ➤ safe spaces where your child can retreat if they feel overstimulated.

Calming strategies

Work with your child to explore what helps them feel calm. They may benefit from deep breathing, counting to ten or using a fidget tool. Others may find comfort in visualisation (imagining a peaceful place) or gentle movement (stretching or walking).

Teach emotional awareness

Help your child develop emotional intelligence by teaching them to identify and label their feelings. Say, 'It looks like you're feeling frustrated right now. What do you think would help you feel calmer?' This helps your child become more aware of their emotions and gives them tools for managing them.

Validate and empathise

Sometimes, your child just needs to know their feelings are valid. Rather than immediately jumping to discipline, say, 'I can see you're upset, and that's okay. Let's take a deep breath and work through this together.' Your empathy fosters a sense of connection and encourages your child to express themselves more openly.

Create predictable routines

Children with ADHD or sensory sensitivities often do best in an environment offering predictability and routine. Knowing what comes next in the day reduces anxiety and provides structure, helping your child feel more secure and less likely to act out. This doesn't mean your days must run like a military schedule, but simple routines, visual charts and consistent responses from you can help lower their baseline stress.

Tip: Visual schedules or a 'what to expect today' chat in the morning can work wonders, even for older children and teens.

Encourage social connection and positive engagement

Your vagus nerve becomes activated when you engage in social bonding and positive connections. To capitalise on this, create a socially engaging environment where your child feels connected, heard and validated.

> Encourage interactions using games, reading together or shared hobbies.
> Use eye contact, a soothing voice and calm physical touch (when appropriate) to help your child feel safe and regulated.
> Model calm, slow breathing and emotional regulation when your child is upset to co-regulate and help them regulate their nervous system.

Movement and physical activity

Vagal tone can also be supported by physical movement. Physical activity helps activate the parasympathetic nervous system, calming the mind and body. Think playing outside, walks or activities requiring balance or coordination to engage both the body and brain. See Chapter 10 for more tips on the benefits of movement.

Sensory integration techniques

Another way to boost vagal health and soothe your child's nervous system is through sensory integration — simple, grounding experiences such as weighted blankets, gentle rhythmic movement, calming essential oils or other forms of comforting touch and sensory input that help the body feel safe and settled.

Sleep and rest

Sleep is critical for restoring your body's nervous system and supporting vagal tone. Your child's autonomic nervous system can reset and prepare their body to handle stress the next day after a good night's sleep. I cover this more in depth in Chapter 9.

Supporting sensory needs

Sensory sensitivities are a key part of ADHD and trauma-related dysregulation.

> Sensory overwhelm = nervous system overload = meltdown risk.

Supporting sensory needs is not spoiling, it's *preventing shutdown*. Your goal isn't to eliminate all sensory stress but to understand and support it, so your child feels *safe and seen*.

Notice patterns

Keep a sensory journal or mentally track when meltdowns or shutdowns happen. Is it noisy environments? Scratchy clothes? Transitions? Mealtimes? Being hungry? Awareness is the first step.

Create a sensory toolkit

Depending on whether your child is sensory-avoiding or sensory-seeking (or both!), have calming tools on hand, such as:

- ➤ noise-cancelling headphones
- ➤ chewable jewellery
- ➤ fidget toys

- ➤ weighted blankets
- ➤ soft fabrics or sensory-friendly clothes
- ➤ movement break or trampoline.

Adjust the environment

Sometimes, small tweaks make a big difference—dim the lights, lower your voice, create a quiet corner or let them sit on an exercise ball for homework. Think of yourself as their *sensory interpreter*, tuning the world to help them stay in their window of tolerance.

Validate, don't dismiss

Even if you can't *see* the discomfort, trust your child's experience. Say:

- ➤ 'That noise bothers you.'
- ➤ 'You need quiet right now. I get that.'
- ➤ 'Let's find something that helps your body feel better.'

Sensory needs in your Parenting Hierarchy of Needs

Sensory regulation is a *biological need*. Just like food, sleep and connection, it forms the *foundation* of your ADHD Parenting Hierarchy of Needs because your child can't regulate emotions in a body that feels under attack. When you support their sensory system, you expand their capacity to stay regulated, connected and engaged with the world around them. When you stop seeing sensory behaviours as misbehaviour and start seeing them as communication, you become a partner in your child's regulation journey, not an adversary.

Managing meltdowns with co-regulation

We've all been there—your child suddenly flips their lid over something seemingly small. Maybe it's the wrong colour plate. Maybe it's putting on shoes. Maybe it's a full-blown storm over homework or leaving the house. You feel your own body tense, your heart racing, maybe the pressure to 'get it under control'.

This is the make-or-break moment—not for your authority but for your connection. The question isn't 'How do I stop this?' it's 'How do I become the safe base my child needs right now?'

Here's how to respond in a way that calms rather than escalates.

Step 1: Regulate you first

Your child is constantly reading you—your tone, posture, facial expressions. This is neuroception at work. We all move through the three main nervous system states during the day—it's natural. The key is having flexibility and awareness so you notice when you're leaving that safe and social space, and gently bringing yourself back.

Your ability to stay in the ventral vagal state (see page 198 for a reminder) helps your child feel safe enough to regulate their own system. Your regulation is not a luxury, it's a lifeline. When you're dysregulated, even if your words are kind, your child will feel the stress in your body. When you learn to notice your own state, you can better support your child through theirs.

Your child borrows your nervous system when they can't access their own regulation. Your calm presence is the medicine they need.

Of course, this is much easier said than done. When your child is escalating or pushing back on something that seems simple for the fiftieth time, your own stress response can kick in. You may go straight into fight (yelling), flight (leaving the room) or freeze (shutting down emotionally). That's normal. It doesn't mean you're a bad parent, it means you're human.

The goal isn't to be perfectly regulated all the time. The goal is to become aware of your nervous system state, and build the tools to come back to a place of safety and connection, both for yourself and your child.

Before you even attempt to help your child, check in with yourself. Are you in fight, flight, freeze, or fawn? Is your voice sharp? Are your shoulders tight? Is your breath shallow?

Ask yourself:

> ➤ What's happening in my body?
> ➤ Am I safe right now? (Hint: Yes, you are.)
> ➤ Can I slow down and lead with calm?

Sometimes that means stepping into another room for 30 seconds. Sometimes it means placing your hand on your heart and taking a few deep breaths before responding. Your energy will shape theirs.

How to support your own regulation

Support your nervous system with a few simple, science-backed ways:

> ➤ *Breathe low and slow.* Deep-belly breathing activates the vagus nerve and shifts you toward calm. Try inhaling for four counts, exhaling for six.
> ➤ *Use grounding.* Place your feet on the floor and notice the contact. Wiggle your fingers or touch something with texture. Sensory input helps bring you back to the present.
> ➤ *Soften your body.* Relax your jaw, drop your shoulders, unclench your fists. Your child reads these subtle signals.
> ➤ *Make eye contact with someone safe.* Connection with another regulated nervous system (even over the phone or through a pet!) helps co-regulate you.
> ➤ *Name your state.* Saying to yourself 'I feel activated' or 'I'm shutting down' is powerful. Awareness begins the shift.

Your goal isn't perfection. You're not expected to be a calm, centred guru every minute of every day. You're allowed to be real. What your child needs most is a safe base, someone who returns to connection and repair. Someone who models what it looks like to feel big feelings and come back to calm.

So when you feel your child's behaviour starting to pull you into your own survival mode, pause. Breathe. Soften. Step away if needed. You're not abandoning them, you're protecting the connection by taking care of your own nervous system first. Because when you regulate you, you regulate them too.

Step 2: Say less, soften more

When your child is in overwhelmed (screaming, crying, running, resisting), they're not choosing that state. Their brain is busy trying to protect them from perceived danger and they're flooded with stress hormones like cortisol and adrenaline. Their thinking brain (prefrontal cortex) is offline. They're not in a place to listen, reason or 'behave better'. Talking at them, giving consequences or demanding explanations will likely escalate things. What they need is calm, not control. That means:

> - slowing your speech
> - lowering your voice
> - sometimes saying nothing at all
> - softening your tone and your face
> - reducing stimulation (turning off bright lights, moving to a quieter space)
> - just being there, regulating yourself so they can borrow your calm.

Your job in these moments is to become the safe harbour not the storm. Say:

> - 'I'm right here with you.'
> - 'You're safe. We'll get through this together.'
> - 'I can see this is hard right now.'

No fixing or explaining—just your safe presence in their emotional storm.

Step 3: Offer co-regulation (but don't force it)

Co-regulation is crucial since children with ADHD often struggle with self-regulation and they need help calming down. This doesn't mean fixing the problem or talking them out of their feelings, but staying present, modelling calm, being emotionally available and offering comfort while they ride the wave of emotions.

Some children want a hug or physical closeness. Others need space. Let your child's cues guide you, not your own need to 'make it better'. If your child pushes you away, respect that boundary but stay nearby so they don't feel abandoned. Your presence still matters.

This might look like:

> ➤ sitting nearby in silence
> ➤ sitting next to them instead of in front of them
> ➤ offering a sensory tool (squishy ball, chewy, weighted item)
> ➤ humming softly or breathing visibly
> ➤ gently saying 'It's a big feeling. I'm staying close.'
> ➤ offering a hand to hold
> ➤ speaking in a calm voice
> ➤ gently guiding them through breathing exercises
> ➤ using rhythm: gentle rocking, breathing together, walking side by side.

You become the external nervous system helping guide your child back to safety. Over time, this helps expand their window of tolerance and builds the wiring in their brain for future self-regulation.

Step 4: Wait for the storm to pass

Remember: all meltdowns end. It may feel like forever in the moment, but your child will come back to regulation, especially if you've stayed regulated yourself.

Once their body starts to calm, you'll often notice a deep sigh, eye contact or a softening in their tone or posture. That's your cue that they're re-entering their window of tolerance. This is not the moment to bring up consequences, lectures or logic. That comes later, if needed.

Step 5: Repair and reflect (when calm returns)

You're not always going to respond the right way. You're human. You have your own nervous system, your own histories and your own limits. What matters most is repair. Later, sometimes hours later, come back to the moment together. Keep it brief and connection-focused.

If you've lost your cool (and you will), the healing happens when you come back and say: 'I'm sorry I yelled. I was feeling overwhelmed, but it's not your fault. You didn't deserve that. Let's try again.'

Every repair moment helps rewire the belief: I'm safe. I'm loved. Even when things go wrong, I'm not alone. Say:

➤ 'That was a tough moment for both of us.'
➤ 'You were really upset. I stayed close because I care.'
➤ 'Next time, what could help you feel safe sooner?'
➤ 'I got frustrated too. I'm sorry I raised my voice. Let's figure it out together.'

Over time, these repair moments build trust and resilience. Your child learns: I'm allowed to fall apart, and love doesn't go away when I do.

What this looks like in real life

Let's say your eight-year-old is screaming because device time is over. They're thrashing, throwing things, shouting they hate you.

You feel triggered. Every fibre in your body wants to yell, punish or walk away.

But instead, you pause.

You breathe. You remind yourself: My child is in survival mode. This is not personal.

You crouch down nearby. Soften your voice:

'I know it's hard to stop. You wanted more time. I'm here.'

You sit in silence, offering presence, maybe gently rubbing their back if they allow it.

The meltdown runs its course. Later that evening, when the moment has passed, you say:

'You were really upset earlier. I get it. It's hard when fun things end. Let's talk about ways we can make transitions feel a bit easier.'

That's nervous system–aware parenting. And no, it won't work every single time, but over time, it builds safety, regulation and connection.

Mindfulness and relaxation techniques

Mindfulness and relaxation are closely linked but not quite the same. Relaxation techniques, such as deep breathing or progressive muscle relaxation, focus on calming the body and lowering stress levels. Mindfulness, on the other hand, is about paying attention to the present moment without judgement.

Both practises support vagal tone and help you or your child stay in a calm, regulated state. When used together, they're especially powerful: relaxation soothes the nervous system, while mindfulness trains the mind to notice thoughts and feelings without being swept away by them.

Practises like deep breathing, body scans or meditation often serve both purposes at once, helping to relax the body and strengthen mindful awareness. This combination improves attention, emotional regulation, impulsivity and even sleep.

I've shared a couple of easy techniques here, but you can find more at adhdsupportaustralia.com.au/resources. 🌐

Body scan

A body scan is a simple mindfulness exercise that helps focus awareness to the sensations in your body, allowing you to relax, release tension and improve emotional regulation.

> ➤ Lie or sit down comfortably with your eyes closed.
> ➤ Focus on your toes first, paying attention to any sensations, such as feelings of warmth, tightness or relaxation.
> ➤ Gradually move your attention up your body to your feet, calves, knees, thighs, abdomen, chest, hands, arms, neck and, finally, your head.
> ➤ Breathe into any areas of tension or discomfort to release it.
> ➤ If your mind starts to wander, gently bring your attention back to the part of your body you're focusing on.

Mindful listening

Another exercise that helps improve attention and focus encourages you to pay close attention to the sounds in your environment, fostering greater awareness of the present moment.

> ➤ Find a quiet place to sit comfortably with your eyes closed or gazing softly at the floor.
> ➤ Focus on the sounds around you such as the ticking of a clock, birds chirping or even the sound of your own breathing.
> ➤ Listen attentively to the sounds, noticing the pitch, volume and any other details.
> ➤ Gradually expand your focus to other sounds in the environment, without labelling or judging them.
> ➤ When your mind wanders, gently bring it back to the sounds you can hear.

Mindful walking

This exercise brings awareness to how your body moves through space and is an effective way to reduce stress, improve concentration and connect with your body in the present moment.

> ➤ Find a quiet space to walk undisturbed, preferably outside in nature.
> ➤ Pay attention to the sensation of each footstep and how your feet feel when they make contact with the ground.
> ➤ Focus on the movement of your legs, your arms swinging and your breath as you walk.
> ➤ Notice what you see, hear and smell as you walk. Stay present and aware of your surroundings.
> ➤ If your mind begins to wander, gently bring your focus back to the sensations around you as you walk.

The 5-4-3-2-1 grounding exercise

This is a great exercise to help distract you from overwhelming thoughts or emotions, regain focus or reduce anxiety when feeling disconnected or stressed. It works by engaging your five senses with your surroundings.

> Find a quiet space and sit comfortably.
> Name 5 things you can see (e.g., trees, sky).
> Identify 4 things you can feel (e.g., the texture of the chair).
> Listen for 3 things you can hear (e.g., birds singing).
> Notice 2 things you can smell (e.g. cooking or food).
> Focus on 1 thing you can taste (or recall your favourite taste).

The safe and sound protocol

The safe and sound protocol (SSP), developed by Dr Stephen Porges, is an evidence-based therapeutic listening program utilising specially filtered music to stimulate the vagus nerve and the auditory pathways involved in emotional processing. This is designed to allow people to achieve greater emotional regulation by calming the nervous system and promoting feelings of safety.

SSP can enhance focus and reduce anxiety by stabilising their emotional and physiological state. It can also be of benefit to you by supporting your emotional wellbeing and enhancing your capacity to remain calm and regulated. The SSP can be accessed via various therapists.

Bottom-up healing

Talk therapies and parenting books (even this one!) are *top-down* approaches. They help you understand what's happening, but healing happens from the bottom up—in the body.

Co-regulation, breathwork, bodywork, movement, play, safe touch, sensory tools and rhythm are powerful tools for helping your child (and yourself) release stored survival energy.

> Top down = logic, story, reasoning
> Bottom up = sensation, rhythm, movement, connection

For true healing, the nervous system must *feel* safe, not just *think* safe.

By focusing on creating safety, connection and regulation, you can support the development of a resilient, emotionally regulated child who feels empowered to navigate their emotions and behaviours with growing confidence.

Retained primitive reflexes

Retained primitive reflexes are automatic movements developed in the womb and early infancy that typically integrate as a child's nervous system matures. When these reflexes don't fully integrate, as can happen in some children, they interfere with motor coordination, posture, attention and emotional regulation. This can leave a child feeling constantly on edge or dysregulated, as their body is reacting to stimuli in ways they can't control.

In the context of nervous system regulation, retained reflexes can act like static in the system, making it harder for a child to stay calm, focus or transition smoothly. Identifying and working to integrate retained reflexes can be a key part of supporting emotional and nervous system regulation. A chiropractor specialising in this area will be the most likely professional to assist.

From dysregulation to safety

By now, I hope you can see what often looks like 'bad' behaviour is just a stress response—a signal from your child's body and brain saying, *'I'm not okay. I need help.'*

And that's the heart of this chapter—understanding that regulation comes before responsibility, that safety comes before strategy. Your job isn't to control your child, it's to create the conditions so they can learn to control themselves.

In my Parenting Hierarchy of Needs framework, the foundational levels of *physiological regulation* and *emotional safety* are essential to address before expecting cooperation, listening or problem-solving. This means supporting your child's nervous system, addressing sensory and regulation needs, and providing unconditional connection within a predictable, safe environment. When these needs are met, your child feels secure enough to access higher-level skills like reasoning and problem-solving.

When you:

> take into account trauma (whether it's a big, obvious event or the quieter wounds of rejection, shame or chronic overwhelm), you'll stop asking, 'What's wrong with my child?' and start asking, 'What happened to their nervous system?'
> learn to recognise your child's survival responses — fight, flight, freeze, fawn — you'll begin to respond with compassion and understanding, not frustration and punishment
> support your child's sensory needs and stop seeing them as just 'quirks' or 'drama', you empower your child to feel safe in their own skin
> regulate yourself first, you give your children the gift of *borrowing your calm* until they learn to find their own.

This isn't easy work; it takes time, courage, patience and a whole lot of grace. You won't do it perfectly (and that's okay); you're not supposed to. But this compassionate, neuroscience-informed approach is the ultimate game-changer — it not only leads to more positive behavioural outcomes, but also fosters deeper connections and a more supportive, empathetic environment for your child to flourish in. It has the potential to improve long-term outcomes for you and your child. Children who have their emotional, sensory and neurobiological needs met, instead of just focusing on modifying behaviours, are more likely to develop strong self-regulation skills, better relationships with others and higher levels of self-esteem. They're also more likely to thrive in school, social settings and, eventually, adulthood, as they learn to navigate their feelings and reactions.

This approach represents a paradigm shift in how you view and respond to the needs of your child with ADHD. It allows you to stop blaming your child for concerning behaviours and, instead, look for solutions by focusing on their biological, emotional and sensory needs.

Every time you pause instead of punish, offer safety instead of shame, co-regulate instead of control, you're rewiring not just your child's brain but possibly your own. You're breaking cycles and creating safety where there was once stress. You're parenting with both your heart *and* your nervous system—and that's where real change begins.

So keep going, one meltdown, one deep breath, one repair moment at a time.

You're not just raising a child, you're raising a nervous system. And you're doing an incredible job.

Nervous system checklist

When things get hard remember:

- [ ] *My child isn't giving me a hard time — they're having a hard time.* Behaviour is communication. Meltdowns are signals, not manipulation.
- [ ] *Connection comes before correction.* My child needs to feel safe before they can think clearly or cooperate.
- [ ] *If my child is dysregulated, I will regulate myself first.* My calm is more powerful than any consequence. Breathe. Soften. Slow down.
- [ ] *I will look beneath the behaviour to see what's going on underneath.* Use the iceberg metaphor: What sensory, emotional or unmet needs are driving this?
- [ ] *I won't try to 'teach' during a meltdown.* I'll save explanations, lessons and problem-solving for when we're both calm.
- [ ] *I'll validate what my child is feeling even if I don't understand it.* 'You're having big feelings. I'm right here.' That's co-regulation.
- [ ] *I'll create a calming environment where possible.* Dim lights. Reduce noise. Offer sensory tools. Make space for calm.
- [ ] *I'll respect my child's sensory profile.* Whether they need movement, quiet, pressure or space, it's not 'extra', it's necessary.
- [ ] *I'll be flexible, not perfect.* It's okay to mess up. What matters most is repair and reconnection.
- [ ] *I am my child's safe base.* When I respond with safety and love, I help build their capacity to thrive.

Quiz: How well do you understand your child's sensory and emotional needs?

Answer yes or no to each question.

Does my child	Yes	No
Get easily overwhelmed in loud or crowded places?		
Struggle with certain textures in food, clothing or materials?		
Have a hard time transitioning between activities?		
Seem to have stronger emotional reactions than their peers?		
Need a lot of movement breaks throughout the day?		
Benefit from structure and routine?		
Respond well to visual schedules or timers?		
Seem to focus better when engaged in a hands-on task?		
Struggle to express their emotions verbally?		
Do well with deep pressure (hugs, weighted blankets, etc.)?		

Reflect on which of these needs you already accommodate and where you could make small adjustments to better support your child's sensory and emotional regulation.

Chapter Twelve

Confidence pathways: How to build self-esteem and resilience in your child

> When a child sees themselves through your eyes
> with love, belief and encouragement, they begin to
> believe in their own worth too.

One of your main goals for your child must be for them to have great self-worth. There's nothing more important. High self-esteem is linked to healthy development in children in the following ways[1]:

> greater confidence in their abilities
> form more secure and supportive relationships
> maintain motivation in learning environments and when faced with challenges.

These factors play an important role in supporting academic performance, emotional wellbeing and overall life satisfaction. Self-esteem is also a protective factor against mental health issues such as anxiety and depression, especially during adolescence when identity development is front and centre.[2]

Self-esteem is closely linked to emotional regulation. When your child feels secure and valued, they're more likely to feel able to express their emotions appropriately and tolerate more frustration or stress. By contrast, low self-esteem can contribute to more emotional reactivity where your child may struggle to moderate feelings of anger, shame and anxiety. In relationships, low self-worth can lead to difficulties with trust and setting boundaries, and is often a risk factor for falling prey to peer pressure and bullying.[3]

Children with ADHD experience more frequent criticism, social rejection and academic challenges, which can lead them to internalise negative feedback as a reflection of their worth, character and abilities, even though it's often simply a reflection of the limitations of their neurotypical environments.[4]

Rejection sensitivity dysphoria (RSD)

Children with ADHD are also more likely to experience RSD, perhaps due to the frequency with which they experience situations that may undermine their self-esteem. People with RSD experience intense emotional distress in response to perceived rejection, criticism or failure, even where this may seem subtle or unintended to another person. Supportive environments that help children feel validated and understood can help reduce the likelihood of RSD and build self-esteem overall.

Promoting self-esteem is not just about making your child feel good, it's about building a strong foundation of self-worth and self-compassion to support lifelong wellbeing and connection, and help prevent the development of ongoing emotional issues.

Building blocks of self-esteem and resilience

Self-esteem and resilience are closely intertwined concepts. Self-esteem is your overall sense of self-worth or personal value. Resilience is the ability to adapt to and overcome setbacks, challenges, stress or uncertainty—to keep moving forward despite difficulties.

Resilience involves maintaining your self-esteem and optimism even in the face of obstacles, whether it's struggling with schoolwork, coping with big emotions or struggling with relationships.

The best way to encourage your child to believe in themselves and keep trying when things get tough is through fostering a growth mindset. This is the idea that we can learn and improve with effort and is seen as a way to build self-esteem and resilience. Encourage your child to embrace challenges rather than avoid them and to maintain their self-esteem and optimism even in the face of real-world challenges.

For neurodivergent children, it's essential we consider the concepts of 'resilience' and 'growth' in the context of their unique brain wiring. The mantra of 'you can do anything if you just try hard enough' can lead to feelings of failure or shame when challenges persist, or if you fail to acknowledge it can be much harder for them to bounce back when they face more setbacks and negative feedback more often than neurotypical children.

What we can take from the idea of a growth mindset is an understanding that, yes, effort and learning from mistakes can help you master new skills and overcome challenges, but everyone learns differently and progress can be personal and unique to each person. Instead of focusing on outcomes, we should praise effort alongside strategy, self-advocacy, creativity and perseverance.

Nurturing self-esteem

The importance of self-esteem and resilience for your child may seem obvious, but it can often feel like an abstract concept. This section provides some practical strategies to nurture self-esteem in your child.

Celebrate the small stuff

Receiving higher rates of negative feedback or rejection than their neurotypical peers makes finding opportunities to recognise and celebrate your child's strengths and achievements one of the best ways to build your child's self-esteem. By acknowledging and celebrating their wins—no matter how big or small—and focusing on their strengths, you'll help foster a sense of accomplishment and encouragement that's important in developing their positive self-image.[5]

Focus on effort over outcome

It's often second nature to celebrate outcomes (the exam result, the netball trophy etc.), but it's equally if not more important to praise the effort your child puts into a task. Acknowledging their hard work makes it more likely they'll keep trying, even when it feels difficult. It reinforces the idea that giving things a go, trying hard and being persistent is often just as important as the outcome itself. Improvement is as noble a goal as perfection.

It's also important to note different definitions of 'effort' and 'hard work'. For children with ADHD who may have difficulty focusing for long periods of time or finding motivation to complete a particular task, praise their approach to the task or activity.

For example, instead of saying, 'You'll get better at reading if you keep trying', you might say, 'I noticed how you used your coloured overlay to make reading easier—what a smart tool!' or 'I love how you took a break and came back when you were ready. That shows you know how to take care of your brain.'

Celebrating smaller milestones along the way can help you meet your child at their level and pace. For example, if your child struggles with getting homework done, celebrate when they complete the first ten minutes of work or when they stay focused for 20 minutes.

Celebrate small victories as a family

Whether it's finishing homework, sticking to a routine or practising self-regulation in challenging situations, hold family celebrations that are personal and meaningful to your child when they achieve their goals or progress toward their goals. Celebrating as a family with an outing or small treat shared with everyone, can strengthen bonds and create a positive environment that values shared success.

Offer genuine praise

Praise helps your child internalise positive self-beliefs about their worth and capability. Regularly praising their strengths, efforts and progress can help silence that nasty inner critic. For example, 'I'm proud of you for trying your best' or 'I love how you think outside the box!' Show them (as always) that your love and respect are unconditional, no matter what they achieve.

Reinforce positive behaviours

Positive reinforcement can be an effective way to support your child's development and motivation. Acknowledge efforts like staying focused for a set period or showing kindness to others. Here are some examples of rewards systems.

- ➤ *Sticker charts:* Add a sticker for every task completed or whenever progress is made. Once your child has collected a certain number of stickers, they can exchange them for a reward of their choosing.
- ➤ *Praise jars:* Add a token or affirmation to a jar every time your child accomplishes something. Once the jar is full, celebrate with a family activity.
- ➤ *Victory wall or achievement board:* Use a pinboard or poster to create a visual representation of your child's progress and achievements. Each time they complete a task or reach a goal, they can add a new item to the board so they can see their progress in a tangible way.

> ➤ *Success journal:* Keep a success journal where your child can write down or draw about their small victories, which helps them focus on the positive rather than the challenges. For example, each day or week, ask your child to write down one or two accomplishments, no matter how small. You could also encourage them to use a journal to document any challenges they overcame. Provide a small reward for a certain number of journal entries.

Model positive self-talk

Your own expressions of self-esteem and self-image and your approach to challenging moments play a significant role in shaping your child's self-esteem. It's essential to model positive self-talk, self-compassion and healthy coping mechanisms to encourage your child to adopt these practices themselves.

This is definitely not always easy (as we explored in Chapter 4). We all have experiences, trauma and emotions that shape how we view ourselves and how we react to situations.

Consider this an opportunity to reframe your relationship with yourself. Show your child how to be kind to themselves when things don't go as planned, and that mistakes are part of learning and don't define their worth. For example, if you make a mistake, say something like, 'I made a mistake, but I can learn from it and do better next time.'

Foster independence

You're likely often walking a delicate tightrope between letting your child learn from their mistakes and stepping in to avoid letting them fail. I know this challenge all too well, both personally and from the many parents I've worked with.

Research in neuroscience shows the ADHD brain develops more slowly in areas related to executive function, such as planning, organisation and time awareness. One study[6] found an eight-year-old with ADHD may function similarly to a neurotypical five-year-old in some of these areas. Knowing our child's brain is wired differently and may be two to three years behind their peers socially and emotionally means we naturally want to support, scaffold, remind and anticipate consequences for them.

Advice from your well-meaning friends or professionals rings in your ears: 'Just let them fail. They'll learn from their mistakes!' Deep down you know there's truth in that, but it also makes your heart skip a beat. You want to catch them before they fall, because you know the fall for them may often be harder than for their neurotypical peers. You know how fragile their motivation and self-esteem is, and the idea of letting them fail when they're already struggling can feel too risky, even irresponsible. So what do you do? You step in, rescue, manage, do it for them—not out of control but out of love.

Many parents (myself included) jump in to become their child's executive function, managing their morning routine, backpack, homework, appointments and so on. Things run smoother in the moment for you and your child. However, what is the effect of this on your child over the longer term? Are you serving them? Or are you hindering them?

Consider what would happen if, when your child was learning to tie their shoelaces, they were struggling, getting frustrated, crying, saying 'I'll never get the hang of this', and you stepped in and tied their shoelaces for them every time. Are they ever going to learn to tie their shoelaces? Are they ever going to be independent? Are they ever going to feel the sense of achievement that they have mastered a difficult task? Of course, the answer is a definite 'No!'

It seems obvious from this example, but this is exactly how you're hindering your child's growth and development, self-esteem and independence when you step in and do things for them instead of helping them figure out how to do it for themselves. You just don't see this at the time. You believe you need to step in and get them through the difficult situations.

Being an overhelpful parent ends up creating learned helplessness in your child and, eventually, young adult. When your child doesn't get the chance to believe they can do something by doing it (because you step in), over time this sends a quiet message—'I don't think you can handle this'—and your child begins to internalise this. They end up second-guessing themselves, doubting their abilities and continuing to turn to you or others to help them.

So what's the answer? How do you find that balance you're looking for?

We've talked about the coach approach to parenting, and the key here is to become a coach, not a crutch. In the coach model, you scaffold—not by doing it all—but by guiding, breaking things down, asking how you can help and then stepping back just enough for them to try and try again. Encourage your child and help them to see any failure they experience as just a temporary setback and a learning opportunity, not a failure!

Using the coach approach, support your child in developing independence without leaving them to flounder. Just like a coach on the sidelines, you guide them, cheer them on, and step in *only when truly needed*. That means giving them space to try, to mess up, to problem-solve and to fail. It's not failure that harms your child, it's not having the chance to learn from it. When you stay calm, regulated and encouraging, you become a safe base they can return to as they navigate life's inevitable bumps.

In a talk I hosted with Dr Craig Sidol, he explained that if we constantly jump in and do the hard thing for our child, their brains don't get the chance to form the neural pathways they need. Growth mostly happens through effort. Those neural connections are built when our child does the hard thing, not when we do it for them. It's not about throwing them into overwhelm with no assistance, but about stretching them just enough outside their comfort zone to build confidence and competence. It's a tricky balance, but it's worth it!

Research highlights that the brains of children with ADHD can change over time when they focus on problem-solving and skill-building. A longitudinal study by Philip Shaw provided evidence that these types of interventions could lead to measurable brain growth in regions associated with executive function and self-regulation.[7]

This research highlights how our brain's neuroplasticity is able to change and grow with repeated practice of difficult skills. Even though children with ADHD find things like planning, managing emotions or completing multi-step tasks more challenging than their neurotypical peers, it doesn't mean progress isn't possible. When you support your child in doing the hard things instead of stepping in, they begin to strengthen the very neural pathways they need to succeed. It's not going to be easy, but these facts just might give you the motivation to persevere, knowing that using this approach, your child's life will get easier in the long run.

They're going to make mistakes, but in doing so, they learn that effort matters more than perfection, and they'll begin to trust in their ability to figure things out for themselves even when it's hard. This is how your child builds resilience and independence.

How does this look in practice?

> We ask: 'What would make this easier for you?'
> We say: 'I'll be nearby if you need help.'
> We remind them: 'It's okay if it's hard. You're learning.'

It's not your role to remove every obstacle for your child. Your role is to allow them to struggle but not abandon them in their struggle. You support their effort without doing it for them and encourage from the sidelines—and you're there for them when they fall. Supporting your child to build self-esteem isn't about completely protecting them from their challenges, it's about guiding and scaffolding them as they discover what they're capable of.

Encourage independence through responsibility

Having age-appropriate responsibilities that increase over time can help your child build their confidence by seeing themselves as capable individuals. Learning how to take responsibility for their actions supports their emotional and social development, and teaches valuable life skills. In addition, working as a team can contribute to a sense of belonging and contribution within the family.

Taking responsibility can range from:

> Letting your child make decisions about their life, from schoolwork to social activities. Small decisions (e.g., what to wear or eat) can gradually progress to bigger decisions as they get older.

➤ Helping them develop problem-solving skills by encouraging them to think critically about how to approach challenges. For example, if they're struggling with homework, ask questions like, 'What might help you stay focused?' or 'What strategies have worked before?'

➤ Encouraging them to take responsibility for their actions and decisions, even when they don't work out. Have open conversations about what they could have done differently.

Encourage responsibility through household chores

Research suggests that children who have regular household chores tend to have higher self-esteem through the development of a sense of competence and accomplishment. These children showed a greater capacity to cope with stress and navigate responsibilities.[8]

Examples of age-appropriate chores:

➤ Younger children (ages 5–8): Setting the table, putting away toys, feeding pets or watering plants.

➤ Older children (ages 9–12): Helping with laundry, vacuuming, washing dishes, taking out the bins or organising their room.

➤ Teens (ages 13+): Doing their own laundry, meal preparation, mowing the lawn, cleaning common areas, managing their own schedule or assisting with family errands.

Children and teens who regularly contribute to household chores are more likely to grow up with strong values of collaboration, self-sufficiency and empathy. When they see their parents sharing responsibilities, they learn that household work is a collective effort. This creates a healthy family dynamic, where everyone works together to maintain the home, and no one is left feeling like they have to do it all alone.

The best way to foster independence in your child is by being a steady, supportive guide who believes in your child's ability to grow and succeed and gives them the chance to try and stay calm when they don't get things quite right. Because children with ADHD often feel like they're falling short, when you shift your focus from compliance to capability, and from control to connection, you help them discover they *can* do hard things, with support, encouragement and space to grow. Letting your child stumble a little now and then is part of the process. It's not a failure, it's practice. Every small step toward independence today is an investment in their future confidence, resilience and success.

Set realistic expectations and goals

We build self-esteem through a sense of accomplishment and achievement but these don't have to be big accomplishments! Self-efficacy (the belief you're able to successfully complete and perform tasks) is built through mastery experiences (small everyday accomplishments that reinforce a sense of capability).

Setting small, achievable goals, ideally aligned to your child's unique strengths, helps your child build their self-esteem little by little, and keep them motivated toward task completion.

This might look like:

> ➤ Helping your child to lean on their individual strengths, such as creative thinking, sports or communication, to help them feel confident in their abilities.
> ➤ Breaking larger tasks or projects into manageable steps, which can help to reduce anxiety and make it easier for them to succeed. Imagine the small confidence boost they receive as they complete each step. This also helps avoid procrastination and frustration and sustain the motivation to continue.
> ➤ Seeking to understand and accommodate their limitations while encouraging them to push themselves, where appropriate. While

it's important to challenge your child, make sure the tasks are not so overwhelming that they cause anxiety or feelings of failure.

➤ Tracking (and celebrating) progress using clear milestones so your child can see how they're advancing over time and reinforce a sense of achievement. For example, milestones might be 'I'll finish this assignment by 3pm', or 'I'll read two chapters tonight'. When the goal is met, celebrate it!

➤ Providing emotional support as needed. Listen without judgement to their frustrations or uncertainties and validate their feelings. Make sure they know they can come to you for practical support at any time, and that you love them regardless of whether they complete the task or not.

➤ Being flexible in your approach and understanding. There will be moments of difficulty, and that's okay. Progress isn't always linear, and sometimes the journey takes unexpected turns. When things don't go as planned, remind your child that setbacks are a natural part of the process and encourage them to keep going.

Perfectionism in children and teens with ADHD

Perfectionism is a surprisingly common trait in children with ADHD,[9] even though it may seem at odds with the stereotype of forgetfulness or disorganisation. Many young people with ADHD experience a deep fear of failure, criticism or not being 'good enough', often fuelled by years of struggling to meet expectations, receiving negative feedback or comparing themselves to their peers.

This can lead to anxiety, procrastination, emotional meltdowns or avoidance, not because they don't care, but because they care too much and are terrified of getting it wrong. Some children set impossibly high standards for themselves, and when they fall short (as we all do), it can trigger intense frustration or self-blame.

Parents can support perfectionistic children by reframing mistakes as learning opportunities, emphasising effort over outcome, modelling self-compassion and creating an environment where 'good enough' is truly enough. Helping your child develop a growth mindset (the belief that ability grows through practice and persistence, not perfection) is one of the greatest gifts you can offer.

Encourage well-rounded interests and relationships

Evidence has linked participation in extracurricular activities to higher self-esteem when compared to peers who were not involved.[10] Hobbies, extracurricular activities and meaningful peer relationships all present opportunities to build self-efficacy in their day-to-day lives. Engaging in activities of their choice enables children to explore their interests, form a sense of identity and provides opportunities for skill-building and a sense of mastery in contexts that are meaningful to them.[11]

Encourage your child to pursue activities that engage their creativity, physical activity or social interaction, such as drawing, playing an instrument, sports, writing or cooking. Help them set time aside each week to engage in these activities. These tools will help support your child's growth, build their self-esteem and track their progress toward meaningful goals.

Empower them to speak up for their needs

Children with ADHD often feel misunderstood or experience criticism or 'othering' in neurotypical environments. Teaching your child to advocate for themselves and their needs can help counteract these experiences through a greater sense of agency and empowerment.

Self-advocacy involves understanding and expressing their own needs, asking for support and actively participating in decisions that affect them. This process can help children feel seen and heard and reinforce that their voice and needs matter.

What does this look like in practice?

> Support your child to build self-understanding, a critical ingredient to self-compassion, self-esteem and in effectively advocating for themselves. Make sure to use simple language focusing on their unique strengths, while acknowledging any challenges or differences they may need to communicate; for example, 'Your brain is good at noticing lots of things at once. That can make focusing on one thing harder sometimes.'

> Practice identifying needs in general and in the moment. The better your child is able to identify and name their emotions and needs, the easier it will be for them to express those to others in a constructive way. Where possible, work with them to link emotions to strategies; for example, 'What helps you calm down when you feel frustrated?'

> Practice common scenarios where they may need to ask for help, such as with teachers, peers and family members. This might include asking for instructions to be repeated or to be moved to a quieter area. You may want to note down simple, respectful scripts for scenarios they feel particularly anxious about; for example, 'I'm trying, but I need help to get started' or 'Can I move to the reading corner so I can concentrate better?'

> Offer choices and meaningful opportunities to collaborate when challenges arise to encourage problem-solving and show them their voice matters; for example, 'Would you rather do your homework at the kitchen table or your desk?' or 'Let's plan together; how can we make this task easier for you?'

> ➤ Acknowledge and celebrate your child's efforts to speak up for themselves. It can be scary (even for adults) to set boundaries and express our needs; for example, 'I liked that you told me what you needed when things got tricky.'

For children with ADHD, celebrating small wins, nurturing their self-image and fostering independence are essential steps toward emotional wellbeing and academic success. By focusing on strengths, praising efforts and encouraging hobbies outside of technology, you help your child build resilience, confidence and a growth mindset. These habits not only help your child succeed in the short-term but also provide the foundation for their future success and happiness.

Chapter Thirteen

Understanding ADHD medications: A practical guide for parents

Choosing whether to medicate your child is a deeply personal decision—one that deserves time, support and careful consideration.

This chapter aims to help you understand how medications for ADHD may be able to support your child, but before we dive in, I want to be clear—I'm not a doctor and nothing in this chapter is intended as medical advice. Always speak to a qualified health professional about your child's individual needs and circumstances. What I *can* offer you here is an overview of the ADHD medication landscape. I won't be covering every nuance of ADHD medications, but will give you a general understanding of what medication can and can't do. This will help you feel more informed, confident and equipped to make decisions for you and your child as well as to have meaningful conversations with your child's doctor, teachers and care team.

To medicate or not?

When most parents first receive an ADHD diagnosis for their child, one of the most immediate and often overwhelming questions is: *Should we try medication?*

According to global clinical guidelines, including those from the American Academy of Pediatrics and the Australian guidelines for ADHD,[1] medication is considered a first-line treatment for children with moderate to severe ADHD. Research shows that, for many children, stimulant medications can significantly reduce some of the core ADHD symptoms such as inattention, hyperactivity and impulsivity, allowing them to function more successfully at school, at home and in social situations.[2]

However, not every child will respond in the same way, and medication will not treat all the symptoms of ADHD. If this was the case, there would be little reason for supportive professionals, organisations or this book. Medication is part of the solution for treating ADHD, not the whole solution. For some children, they will trial an ADHD medication and immediately have a life-changing result, enabling them to improve their academic performance and behaviour and need no other support. For the majority of children, medications play an important role, but they also most often require a variety of other supports, as I've covered in this book.

For some parents, it can be a lengthy trial-and-error process to find the right type of medication, at the right dose, at the right time of day. Some children experience side effects such as appetite suppression, mood swings or sleep issues. Sometimes, after trying several options, families may decide that medication isn't helping or the right fit after all.

Creating strong foundations

As you'll have seen throughout this book, my philosophy is that the most sustainable approach to supporting your child is to get the foundations right first so you have a clear baseline to work from. Supporting your child's nutrition, sleep, movement, nervous system regulation and emotional wellbeing can all have powerful effects on your child's day-to-day functioning. Once those are in place, it gives a more accurate starting point to assess whether and how much medication is required.

The role of neurotransmitters

Neurotransmitters are chemical messengers that transmit signals between nerve cells in the brain, allowing different parts of the brain and body to communicate with each other. They play a key role in regulating everything from mood and motivation to attention, movement and emotional responses.

In ADHD, the brain's neurotransmitter systems, especially those involving *dopamine* and *norepinephrine*, don't work in the usual way. These chemicals act like messengers that help brain cells communicate. Dopamine plays a key role in motivation, reward and focus, while norepinephrine helps regulate alertness, attention and the ability to stay on task. In ADHD, it's not always that there is 'too few' of these messengers, but rather that the brain struggles with how they are produced, transported or received in areas such as the *prefrontal cortex* (the part of the brain responsible for planning, self-control and decision-making). This miscommunication means messages aren't passed efficiently between neurons, which can lead to the hallmark ADHD symptoms of distractibility, impulsivity, inattention and difficulties with executive functioning.

What ADHD medications do

Stimulant medications for ADHD like methylphenidate (e.g., Ritalin, Concerta) and dexamphetamine (e.g., Dexamphetamine, Vyvanse) work by modulating neurotransmitters in the brain, primarily dopamine and norepinephrine. They work by helping to increase the availability of these neurotransmitters or by making them more effective in the brain, improving communication between brain cells with the aim of helping children focus, regulate their emotions and stay on task.

The medications don't increase the total amount of these neurotransmitters in the brain. They recycle and preserve what is already present in the synaptic gap, allowing the brain to use these neurotransmitters more efficiently. This differs from some holistic approaches, which aim to increase the natural production or availability of neurotransmitters through diet, gut health, lifestyle or supplementation.

Improving neurotransmitter availability in key brain areas can enhance focus, reduce hyperactivity and support children in developing stronger impulse-control skills.

What ADHD medication can't do

Despite their benefits, medications are not a silver bullet. They can't teach your child emotional regulation skills, help them build self-awareness, understand social cues, create consistent daily routines or gain problem-solving skills. These are skills that still need to be intentionally taught and supported, and that's where the rest of this book comes in.

Even if your child is taking medication, you'll still need to support them with compassionate parenting strategies, structured routines, environmental accommodations and emotional safety.

Medication types

Two main classes of ADHD medication exist: stimulants and non-stimulants. Stimulants are the most commonly prescribed type, and typically the first-line option. Non-stimulants are often prescribed when stimulant medications are not effective or well tolerated. Occasionally, antidepressants or other off-label[3] medications may be used in complex cases.

Table 13.1 takes a closer look at the most common medications. It's important to remember that any medications should be administered by a doctor, and you should also consult with them prior to making changes to the type of medication or dose, or if you intend to wean your child off the medication.

Table 13.1 Common medication types for ADHD

Medication	Starts working	Duration	Potential benefits	Common side effects	Notes
Stimulant medications: work by increasing the availability of certain neurotransmitters					
Methylphenidate					
Ritalin (short acting)	20–30 mins	3–4 hrs	Improved focus and attention	Decreased appetite (especially around mealtimes)	Does not build up in the body, can generally be stopped immediately without tapering
Ritalin LA (long acting)	30–60 mins	6–8 hrs	Reduced impulsivity and hyperactivity	Difficulty falling asleep	
Concerta (extended release)	45–60 mins	10–12 hrs	Better task completion and emotional regulation	Headaches or stomachaches	Always make changes in consultation with your prescribing doctor
			Improved classroom participation and social interactions	Rebound irritability or moodiness as the medication wears off	
				Mild increase in anxiety or emotional sensitivity in some children	

(continued)

Table 13.1 *Common medication types for ADHD (cont'd)*

Dexamphetamine: simpler compound for some children who don't tolerate methylphenidate

Medication	Starts working	Duration	Potential benefits	Common side effects	Notes
Dexamphetamine (short acting)	30–60 mins	4–6 hrs	Improved focus, attention, and task follow-through Reduced hyperactivity and impulsivity May provide smoother coverage (especially Vyvanse) Convenient once-daily dosing (Vyvanse)	Reduced appetite (especially breakfast/lunch) Trouble falling asleep (less common with Vyvanse than short acting Dexamphetatmine) Irritability/mood changes, especially as medication wears off Headaches or stomachaches Emotional sensitivity or tearfulness in some children	Does not build up in the body, can generally be stopped immediately without tapering (speak to your doctor first)
Vyvanse (Lisdexamfetamine)	1–2 hrs	10–14 hrs			Has a gradual, smoother release resulting in fewer peaks and crashes compared to other stimulants; helpful for children who experience emotional rebound or irritability with other medications

Medication	Starts working	Duration	Potential benefits	Common side effects	Notes
Non-stimulants					
Strattera (Atomoxetine)	2–4 weeks benefits build gradually 6–8 weeks for full effects	24 hrs	Provides all-day symptom control Doesn't suppress appetite as strongly as stimulants No risk of abuse or dependency Can be helpful for children with co-existing anxiety May help regulate sleep, emotional reactivity and impulsivity over time. Less likely to worsen tics or cause emotional rebound	Nausea, especially when first starting (often improves over time or with food) Sleepiness or fatigue Mood swings or irritability (less common, but important to monitor) Appetite loss (milder than stimulants) Dry mouth, dizziness or increased heart rate in some children	Consider when stimulants are not well tolerated or if concerns about sleep, anxiety, tics or appetite suppression, when there is co-occurring anxiety or emotional sensitivity or if parents prefer a non-stimulant Must take consistently; missed doses reduce effectiveness Should not be stopped abruptly, needs to be weaned off slowly under medical supervision

(continued)

Table 13.1 *Common medication types for ADHD (cont'd)*

Medication	Starts working	Duration	Potential benefits	Common side effects	Notes
Intuniv (Guanfacine extended release)	1–3 weeks; benefits build gradually	24 hrs	May improve impulsivity, hyperactivity, emotional regulation and sleep Can reduce tics or nervous system overstimulation No risk of abuse or dependency Often used when stimulants aren't effective or well tolerated Can be combined with stimulant medication for a more balanced effect	Sleepiness or fatigue (especially at first) Low blood pressure or dizziness Irritability or moodiness in some children Headaches Dry mouth Heart rate changes (rare)	Has calming and sedating effect so useful if child has trouble falling or staying asleep, is highly sensitive, reactive or emotionally dysregulated, experiences tics, has co-occurring anxiety, doesn't respond or tolerate stimulants Can be used alongside a stimulant to smooth out emotional ups and downs or extend symptom coverage into the evenings

Medication	Starts working	Duration	Potential benefits	Common side effects	Notes
			Has a calming / sedating effect so can support sleep and overnight regulation		Should never be stopped abruptly, doctor will taper the dose slowly
Clonidine IR (immediate release)	2–4 weeks for full benefits; builds gradually	6–8 hours	May improve impulsivity, hyperactivity, emotional regulation and sleep	Drowsiness or fatigue (most common)	May be helpful if child has sleep difficulties, struggles with anger or emotional meltdowns or has co-occurring anxiety or sensory overload, experiences tics or other nervous system overstimulation, has not responded well or tolerates stimulants
Clonidine (extended release)		Close to 24 hrs		Dry mouth	
			Can reduce tics or nervous system overstimulation	Low blood pressure or dizziness	
			No risk of abuse or dependency	Irritability or mood swings	
			Often used when stimulants aren't effective or well tolerated	Headaches or constipation in some cases	
			Can be combined with stimulant medication for a more balanced effect	Because of its sedating effects, some children may feel too sleepy or sluggish during the day and may benefit from taking it only at night or adjusting the dose.	

(continued)

Table 13.1 Common medication types for ADHD (cont'd)

Medication	Starts working	Duration	Potential benefits	Common side effects	Notes
					Can be used in combination with stimulants to reduce 'rebound' effects or support smoother regulation through day/night
					Never stop it suddenly, must be tapered off gradually under medical supervision

The importance of monitoring medications

One of the most important things you can do when your child starts any new medication is to closely monitor how things go—both the potential benefits and any side effects.

Sometimes a medication that's supposed to help can unexpectedly make things worse because of unwanted side effects. Ensure that, before you give your child medication, you're aware of any potential side effects. A medication package insert will list all possible side effects ever reported, which can seem scary as it may include serious side effects such as suicidal ideation. While rare, you want to be aware, just in case your child's mood suddenly changes for the worse. Knowing the possible side effects means you're able to take immediate action in contacting your prescribing professional to let them know the issue immediately and ask for an urgent call back. If you don't know what side effects to look for (some common ones are increased anxiety, headaches, loss of appetite or sleep disruption), you might not connect the dots. Being well-informed and observant is key.

Keep a simple log or journal to note changes in mood, focus, appetite, sleep, behaviour and general wellbeing. This record will be invaluable when you speak with your prescribing doctor at follow-up appointments. Our memories tend to fade in our busy lives, and without clear notes, it's easy to forget what your child's symptoms were just a few weeks ago.

Asking for input from your child's teachers or school support staff is also essential. They're the ones seeing your child in a structured environment where attentional and behavioural challenges become most apparent, and, for the majority of the time, the medication is active. Their perspective can offer important clues about whether the medication is having a meaningful impact.

Gluten or lactose in ADHD medications

Some ADHD medications may contain inactive ingredients such as gluten, lactose, artificial dyes or fillers, which can be problematic for children with food sensitivities, coeliac disease or intolerances. While many mainstream formulations are now gluten-free, it's important to check each brand specifically, as ingredients can vary between manufacturers and even between different strengths of the same medication.

If your child reacts to certain additives or cannot tolerate specific ingredients, talk to your prescribing doctor about using a compounding pharmacy. These specialised pharmacists can custom-make medication without gluten, lactose, dyes or other unwanted excipients, tailored exactly to your child's needs.

Pharmacogenetics

Pharmacogenetics studies how a person's genes affect their response to medications. For children with ADHD, this can be an important piece of the puzzle. Some children metabolise medications very quickly or slowly due to genetic differences, which can affect how well they work, or how likely they are to experience side effects. For example, a child who is a slow metaboliser may be more sensitive to certain stimulant medications and experience stronger or increased side effects at lower doses.

Pharmacogenetic testing can provide insight into how your child's body may process different medications, helping guide more personalised and effective treatment choices. While it's not routinely done for all children, it can be helpful if your child has had unusual reactions to medications or if finding the right fit has been challenging.

Gut health and medication effectiveness

The health of your child's gut plays a surprisingly important role in how well ADHD medications work. Most medications are absorbed through the gastrointestinal (GI) tract, so if your child has gut issues (constipation, diarrhoea, inflammation or dysbiosis (an imbalance of gut bacteria) etc), this can affect how quickly or slowly the medication is absorbed.

If gut transit is too fast, the medication may pass through the system before it can be properly absorbed, reducing its effectiveness. If it's too slow, your child might absorb too much at once or over a longer period than intended, which could lead to stronger side effects. A healthy gut supports more predictable absorption, steadier effects and better outcomes overall (see Chapter 8 for more on gut health).

Medication is an individual choice

Choosing whether to medicate your child is a deeply personal decision—one that deserves time, support and careful consideration. Medication is not a cure but, for many children, it can be a powerful tool that opens the door to learning, connection and emotional regulation. For others, it may not be the right path, or only part of a broader support plan.

What matters most is that your decision is informed, collaborative and centred on your child's unique needs, not pressure from others. Keep the lines of communication open with your child, your prescriber and the school. Track what's working, what's not and always trust your instincts. You know your child best. Whether you choose medication or not, the philosophy and principles in this book should still form the main base of support for your child.

Part IV

Helping your child thrive

Thriving isn't about fixing your child—it's about giving them the tools, support and belief they need to flourish in their own way.

This section is about helping your child step into the world with confidence. Thriving isn't about being perfect, it's about feeling capable, connected and supported in real-life situations. We'll explore how to nurture your child's social skills, support their learning at school, navigate the digital world mindfully, and guide them through everyday transitions and life changes. These chapters are about bridging the gap between home and the wider world so your child feels safe enough to grow, resilient enough to adapt and empowered enough to shine.

Chapter Fourteen

School strategies: From overwhelmed to empowered

School success isn't about fitting the mould, it's about creating an environment where your ADHD child can shine as they are.

Children with ADHD often face unique challenges in school and social environments, where the expectations for attention, organisation and behaviour are high. However, with the right strategies, support and mindset, these challenges can be transformed into opportunities for growth and success.

Reframing school success: A strengths-based approach

When your child has ADHD, one of the first places the challenges show up (or become most visible) is at school. Whether it's difficulty sitting still, forgetting homework, being easily distracted, struggling to follow instructions or experiencing social setbacks, school can quickly become a pressure cooker of expectations for your child *and* for you.

It's easy to fall into the trap of comparing your child's school performance to their peers or to your own educational experience. You might feel anxious when your child is falling behind, getting in trouble or not keeping up in the way others seem to. You may worry about the future—what this means for high school, university or even just getting through next week. It's only natural. We've been conditioned to believe that academic achievement is the ultimate indicator of success.

But success at school is not about grades, gold stars or being the 'good kid' who never gets into trouble. For children with ADHD, school success looks different. It's about helping them feel emotionally safe, supported, understood and capable. It's about nurturing their confidence and strengths, not just managing their challenges. It's about playing the long game, where wellbeing and self-worth come first, and everything else follows.

Your child is not a problem to be fixed. They're a person to be understood. When we shift the lens from 'How do I make my child behave or perform like other kids?' to 'How can we create an environment where my child can truly thrive?', we begin to see school through a more compassionate, realistic and empowering lens.

Instead of asking:
- ➤ Why can't they just do their work?
- ➤ Why are they always getting into trouble?
- ➤ Will they ever catch up?

Try asking:
- ➤ What support do they need to feel successful?
- ➤ How can I help the school see their potential?
- ➤ What does *their* version of progress look like?

Every child's school journey is different. Some children take a winding path to school success, some succeed in unexpected ways, while, sadly, some just do what they have to do to get through the experience, and come out of the other end wondering where they go from there. What matters most isn't ticking boxes or keeping up, it's that your child is supported to develop in their own time, in their own way and move through their school years with their confidence intact.

This isn't about forcing your child to fit into a system that wasn't designed for them. It's about shifting that system — or stepping outside it if needed — so your child has the chance to thrive, exactly as they are.

Understanding ADHD in the classroom

It's easy to see the surface-level behaviours of a child with ADHD in the classroom: fidgeting, interrupting, daydreaming, forgetting instructions, being 'off-task' or even being disruptive. But these visible behaviours are just the tip of the iceberg.

Beneath the surface, your child might be grappling with intense internal challenges: difficulty regulating their attention, struggling to initiate tasks, feeling overwhelmed by sensory input, or desperately trying to keep up, but not knowing how. They may be anxious, frustrated, masking to fit in or feeling ashamed when they can't meet expectations despite trying very hard.

ADHD in the classroom doesn't look the same for every child. Some are hyperactive and impulsive, constantly moving, blurting out or unable to wait their turn. Others are inattentive and quiet, drifting off into daydreams, missing instructions and often going unnoticed. Many are a combination of both. For those with co-occurring conditions, such as anxiety, learning disorders, sensory sensitivities or autism, the picture becomes even more complex.

To understand more about common co-occurring conditions and how they interact with ADHD, see Chapter 3.

Common classroom challenges

Children with ADHD often face unique hurdles in the classroom, where the demands for focus, organisation and self-regulation can highlight their difficulties and sometimes overshadow their strengths. In this section, we'll explore some of the most common classroom challenges and look at the kinds of support that can make a real difference in helping children with ADHD succeed.

> *Difficulty sustaining attention:* particularly with repetitive, boring or not immediately rewarding tasks
> *Impulsivity:* blurting out, interrupting, acting without thinking
> *Hyperactivity:* talking excessively, needing to move or fidget
> *Working memory challenges:* trouble with long instructions, not sure what they're meant to be doing
> *Slow processing speed:* taking longer to complete tasks
> *Emotional regulation:* overreacting to criticism, becoming easily frustrated or shutting down
> *Executive function challenges:* difficulties with planning, organisation or time management or procrastination.

These challenges can often be mistaken for laziness or wilful misbehaviour, but they're simply signs your child's brain processes information and stimuli differently. Although they struggle with these challenges, they *can* thrive in the classroom with the right support, understanding and accommodations, and when education staff shift their focus from punishment and compliance to connection and support.

You'll likely need to help your child's teacher understand ADHD beyond the stereotypes. Many educators still believe ADHD is just about being 'hyper' or needing to 'try harder'. Your role as an informed, calm advocate is key.

Positive school environment

Ensuring a positive school environment means working collaboratively with teachers and support staff to create a setting where your child feels understood, supported and empowered to learn in ways that work for their unique brain.

Choosing the right school for your child

I've personally explored—and lived—a wide spectrum of school settings in Australia: selective, co-ed and single-sex schools, Catholic, Steiner, private and public and home schooled for three years! I've seen the pros and cons of each, what works in theory versus what works in real life, for my children.

Beyond my personal experience, I'm a qualified teacher with a Master of Teaching, and I've completed teaching placements in both public and private schools. That background has given me a broader view of how different school systems operate, the kinds of support they typically offer and where the gaps often lie for children with ADHD.

One thing I've learned? There's no 'perfect' school. But with the right questions and a willingness to advocate, you can find a school that fits your child's needs more closely.

Choosing a school can feel daunting. You want to find somewhere your child feels safe, supported and has the chance to thrive (both academically and emotionally) so you don't want to get it wrong. But remember: there's no one 'right' school. There is only the school that's right for *your* child.

Because every child is unique, with their own strengths, interests, sensitivities and social-emotional needs, what works brilliantly for one ADHD child might be unsuitable for another. Your decision should be guided not by reputation, rankings or pressure from others but by your child's unique profile.

As you make your choice, ask yourself whether your child will:

> - be seen for who they are, not just how they perform
> - feel accepted, not constantly corrected
> - have the opportunity to shine, not just survive?

Factors to consider when choosing a school

Choosing the right school for your child with ADHD can feel overwhelming, as every environment will have different strengths and challenges. In this section, we'll look at the key factors to consider so you can feel more confident in finding a school that supports your child's learning, wellbeing and growth.

Staff attitude and training:

> ➤ Are the teachers and leadership team knowledgeable about neurodivergence and trauma-informed practice?
> ➤ Do they focus on regulation and support or compliance and punishment?
> ➤ Are they willing to implement adjustments without defensiveness?

Size and environment:

> ➤ Would your child benefit from a smaller, quieter school or do they thrive on activity and energy?

Are class sizes manageable?:

> ➤ Is there access to quiet spaces or learning support rooms?

Curriculum and strength-based opportunities:

> ➤ Does the school offer programs aligned with your child's strengths, interests and passions, whether in sports, music, creative and performing arts, nature, hands-on learning or academic subjects such as maths, science or literacy
> ➤ Are students encouraged to pursue strengths as part of their identity?

Flexibility and inclusion:

> ➤ Are learning plans and adjustments genuinely followed or just ticked off?
> ➤ How are behaviour and learning differences responded to?
> ➤ Is there flexibility in how students can show their knowledge?

Support structures:

> ➤ Is there a learning and support teacher?
> ➤ Are there social skills programs or peer support groups?
> ➤ What mental health or counselling services are offered?
> ➤ Is the student community mostly local, making it easier for your child to build and maintain friendships?

Types of schools to explore

In this section, we'll look at the different types of schools you might explore, so you can better understand the options available and how they may support your child's needs.

> ➤ *Mainstream public schools:* These schools often have policies that encourage inclusion and access to support services, but the actual experience can vary widely depending on leadership, staff training and available resources. Some schools are highly supportive of neurodiverse learners, while others may struggle to meet individual needs.
> ➤ *Private/independent schools:* These schools often have more facilities and resources, but their level of ADHD support depends heavily on staff attitudes and leadership. Some place a strong emphasis on academic results and rankings, which can make them less flexible for children with ADHD, while others adopt a more inclusive approach that values diverse learning styles and encourages each pupil to reach their potential.
> ➤ *Catholic schools:* Values-based with varied support. Ask detailed questions about inclusion and behaviour policies.
> ➤ *Steiner/Waldorf schools:* Emphasise creativity, rhythm and hands-on learning, but may not offer structured support for ADHD.

- ➤ *Montessori schools:* Hands-on, self-paced learning can work well for some children with ADHD but independence expectations may be too high for others.
- ➤ *Selective schools:* Academically rigorous; can suit gifted or twice exceptional (2e) students, but may be high-pressure and lack pastoral care.
- ➤ *Alternative schools:* Focus on individualised learning and wellbeing, often with flexible or therapeutic models.
- ➤ *Homeschooling:* Offers complete flexibility for your child. Ideal if your child has past trauma, chronic school distress or is burnt out by school, needs time to heal or thrives in a calmer environment. This is a significant commitment for you.
- ➤ *Distance education:* A hybrid option with structured curriculum delivered remotely, often with support from teachers and learning advisors.

This isn't about finding the best school, it's about finding the best fit, so visit schools in advance and trust your gut. Talking to other parents of neurodivergent children can give you different insights. Ask clear, practical questions of the prospective school, such as:

- ➤ How do you support students with ADHD?
- ➤ What adjustments are typical in your classrooms?
- ➤ How do you handle behavioural challenges?
- ➤ What wellbeing supports are available?

You can change your mind

Sometimes, the school that looked perfect on paper just doesn't work out in practice. That's not a failure, it's a course correction. You can change schools, start homeschooling or advocate for change within your current school. The goal isn't to force your child to fit the system, it's to find (or shape) a system that fits your child.

In the next section, we'll look at what to do when school isn't working, whether that's due to chronic school can't, anxiety, burnout or exclusion, and how to reset when your child needs something different.

Establish a collaborative relationship

Working with your child's school can feel like walking a tightrope, balancing your child's needs, the teacher's capacity and your own emotions. When collaboration works well, it can be one of the most powerful tools in helping your child thrive at school.

The key is building a respectful, ongoing partnership, one where your voice is heard, your child's needs are central and everyone is on the same team.

It helps to approach the school as a partner not an opponent. Assume goodwill, but also be clear, calm and assertive. Most teachers genuinely want to help, but they may not have the training, time or understanding to know how best to support your child with ADHD. That's where your insight becomes vital.

Try saying:

> ➤ I know my child can be tricky to understand sometimes, but I'm here to work with you so we can support them together.
> ➤ You see them in one way at school; I see them differently at home. Let's compare notes.

Set the tone early

The way you begin your relationship with a school can set the stage for how well your child is supported. Starting with clear communication, realistic expectations and a collaborative mindset helps establish a positive foundation from the outset.

> ➤ *Introduce yourself early in the school year.* Send a short email outlining your child's strengths, challenges and what strategies have worked in the past.

➤ *Keep it brief and constructive.* Teachers are busy and the more solution-focused you are, the more receptive they'll likely be.

➤ *Provide a simple one-pager about your child.* Highlight their needs, triggers, motivators and calming strategies. 🌐

➤ *Get in early.* Request a meeting early in the year or when you first notice challenges—don't wait until the wheels are falling off!

Successful school meetings

School meetings can feel daunting, but when approached with preparation and collaboration, they become powerful opportunities to ensure your child's needs are understood and supported. In the section below, we'll look at practical strategies to help you approach these meetings with confidence and clarity.

Before you meet with your child's teacher, ensure you're fully prepared with:

➤ concerns and goals related to your child

➤ specific examples of your child's challenges and effective past solutions

➤ paperwork: diagnosis reports, past individual education plans (IEPs), clinicians letters and recommendations

➤ a collaborative, calm mindset.

Have a clear idea of your child's needs and some possible solutions to help guide the conversation. You don't have to have all the answers, and nor do the education staff, but this is your chance to co-create a plan with them.

During the meeting, there are some strategies you can employ to ensure you get the most out of your time together:

➤ Stay solution-focused and ask open questions, such as:
  • What are you noticing in class?
  • What's working well so far?
  • Where do you think we could provide more support?

➤ Acknowledge their perspective, while still advocating for your child; for example, you could say: 'That must be difficult to manage in a busy classroom; here's what's helped at home.'
➤ Ensure the focus isn't on blaming your child by explaining reasons for behaviour; for example: 'That behaviour often happens when they're overwhelmed or confused. Can we look at the task setup or timing?'

It's important that the conversation doesn't end with the meeting. You should look at this as an ongoing partnership with your child's teacher.

➤ Follow up. Send a brief email summarising what was discussed and agreed upon.
➤ Keep a paper trail of any decisions, supports and next steps you agreed on.
➤ Check in regularly (via email or brief chats) to see if strategies are working, if they need changing, continuing or stopping.
➤ Use positive reinforcement to build trust with the teacher by acknowledging wins.

Tips for effective collaboration:

➤ Be proactive, not reactive.
➤ Focus on shared goals: helping your child feel safe, successful and understood.
➤ Speak up early; don't wait until things spiral.
➤ Praise the school when they get it right—it goes a long way.
➤ Keep your cool, even when you feel emotional (vent later in a safe space).
➤ You're not being a 'difficult' parent, you're being a loving advocate.

Collaborating with the school isn't always easy, especially if you have to fight to be heard. But showing up, staying informed and keeping the lines of communication open can transform your school experience, not just for your child, but for others who come after.

Know your rights

When your child has ADHD, it's not just about hoping for a kind teacher or a flexible school, it's about knowing your legal rights and the school's responsibilities to provide appropriate support. Too often, parents are left to advocate without clear guidance, or they're told 'We don't do that here'.

The truth is: they must. ADHD is recognised as a disability under Australian law. Even though it may be 'invisible', and not every child with ADHD looks the same, ADHD falls under the *Disability Discrimination Act 1992* and is also supported by the Disability Standards for Education 2005.

These laws protect your child from discrimination and ensure they have the same educational opportunities as their peers, including access to reasonable adjustments and support.

Key terms and what they mean

In this section, I'll unpack some of the key terms you're likely to hear when navigating school systems, policies and supports, so you can feel confident about what they mean and how they apply to your child with ADHD.

> ➤ *Disability Discrimination Act:* Makes it unlawful for schools to treat a student unfairly or exclude them due to their disability, which includes behavioural challenges related to ADHD.
> ➤ Disability Standards for Education: Clarifies what schools must do to ensure students with disabilities can access and participate in education to the same degree as other students. This includes adjustments to curriculum, communication, assessments and behaviour policies.
> ➤ Reasonable adjustments: Changes or supports made to help your child succeed at school. These might include extra time on tasks, movement breaks, simplified instructions or reduced homework. If the school says an adjustment is 'unreasonable', they must explain why and consider alternatives.

> Nationally Consistent Collection of Data (NCCD) on school students with disability: Schools are required to include students who receive adjustments for ADHD in their annual NCCD reporting, even if they don't have formal diagnoses or funding. This helps track support levels and shape national policy.

Important: ADHD does not currently attract individual funding through the NDIS or all school systems, but that doesn't mean schools can avoid providing support.

What can you ask for?

You have the right to request:

> a formal student support group meeting
> adjustments to homework, classroom tasks or assessments
> additional supervision during transitions or unstructured times
> calming tools or sensory supports (e.g., movement cushions, noise-cancelling headphones)
> a copy of your child's IEP or behaviour support plan (BSP)
> a review meeting if things aren't working.
> an individual education plan (IEP)

Request your child's diagnosis and needs be communicated respectfully to all relevant staff, not just their classroom teacher.

Common types of school support

When it comes to supporting your child at school, understanding the most common types of available support can help you advocate more effectively for your child's needs and ensure they have the tools to thrive in the classroom.

> Individual education plan (IEP): This is a document outlining your child's specific learning goals and the strategies in place to help them. You have a right to be involved in this process.

- ➤ Behaviour support plan (BSP): For children who experience behavioural challenges, a BSP can identify triggers, outline calming strategies and help school staff respond consistently.
- ➤ Learning and support teacher (LaST): Many schools have a LaST who works with students needing extra help. Ask your school what support is available and how your child can access it.
- ➤ School counsellor or psychologist: School counsellors or school psychologists can provide in-school support and also help with behaviour plans or emotional regulation strategies.

When things go wrong

Sometimes, despite your best efforts, your child may be misunderstood, excluded or even suspended for behaviour related to their ADHD. This can be deeply distressing, but it's also where your understanding of the law matters most.

If you feel your child is being discriminated against:

- ➤ document everything: emails, meetings, incidents
- ➤ request a formal meeting with the school principal
- ➤ bring a support person or advocate to meetings
- ➤ refer to the DDA and Disability Standards: these are not optional requirements
- ➤ lodge a complaint through your state's Department of Education or Human Rights Commission, if necessary.

Later in this chapter we'll explore how to handle school can't, suspensions and advocating through crisis points.

Quick checklist: Your rights

Understanding your rights gives you the confidence to speak up, ask for support and help shape a more inclusive learning experience for your child. The school may be the expert in curriculum, but you're the expert in your child.

☐ I understand the laws that protect my child's right to education.
☐ I've asked for a student support group meeting.
☐ My child has an IEP or is on the NCCD.
☐ I've requested reasonable adjustments in writing.
☐ I've kept records of communication with the school.
☐ I know who to contact if I need to escalate concerns.

In this chapter, we'll bring the focus to how you can build a strong connection between home and school and help your child succeed academically and emotionally, even when the system isn't perfect.

Strategies to support your child's school experience

In this section, we'll look at practical strategies you can use to make your child's school experience more positive, supportive and successful.

Behaviour and emotional regulation

For many children with ADHD, *behaviour* is the thing that gets them noticed at school—and often not in the way we'd hope. They might be labelled 'defiant', 'disruptive', 'lazy', 'aggressive' or 'disrespectful', but these labels ignore the fact that behaviour is communication. It's not always about choice, it's about capacity.

Most ADHD-related behaviours come from a combination of executive function challenges, emotional dysregulation, sensory overload, unmet needs or simply a nervous system on high alert. In Chapter 5, we explored the ADHD iceberg, where behaviour is just the visible tip and emotional regulation difficulties often hide beneath the surface.

ADHD affects your child's ability to pause, reflect and respond calmly. When your child is overwhelmed or overstimulated, their fight-flight-freeze response kicks in faster and more intensely than their peers. Add in rejection sensitivity, poor impulse control and difficulty understanding others' perspectives and it's no wonder they might lash out, shut down or run off.

This isn't 'bad' behaviour, it's a sign your child is still learning how to navigate big feelings. Common triggers for these behaviours include:

> unstructured times (recess, transitions, assemblies)
> social stress/feeling excluded
> tasks that feel too hard, boring or overwhelming
> sensory overload (noise, lights, crowds)
> feeling misunderstood, criticised or micromanaged
> fatigue or hunger
> sudden changes in routine/relief teachers.

These aren't excuses, they're clues. When we decode the triggers, we can better support our children before things spiral.

Traditional discipline, such as detentions, suspensions or losing privileges, often does more harm than good. Your child usually already knows the rules, their brain just struggles to apply them in the moment. Instead, they need:

> connection before correction
> clear boundaries, delivered calmly
> logical consequences that help them repair, not feel ashamed
> a chance to reset without blame.

What you can do

> Ask for a functional behaviour assessment to understand what's driving challenging behaviours.

- Ensure your child has access to calming tools (fidget, movement pass, quiet space).
- Advocate for predictable routines and clear visual cues.
- Share what works at home; your insights are valuable.
- Help your child build a toolkit of regulation strategies (deep breathing, movement, sensory play).
- Debrief at home with compassion, not shame; for example: 'That sounds like it was a hard day. Let's figure out what happened together.'

What the school might do

If your child's behaviour is impacting their learning or that of others, the school should work with you to create a positive behaviour support plan (PBSP), not just rely on punishment or exclusion. A good PBSP includes:

- the function of the behaviour (what's really going on)
- known triggers and early warning signs
- strategies to prevent escalation
- calming tools or sensory supports
- consistent responses from all staff
- focus on teaching skills, not just managing symptoms.

When behaviour leads to exclusion or suspension

If your child is sent home, suspended or excluded for behaviour that stems from their ADHD, this may be discrimination under the *Disability Discrimination Act*, especially if no reasonable adjustments or support plans were in place. If this happens to your child, there are a number of things you can do:

- Request a copy of the incident report and behaviour policy.
- Ask for a review meeting to discuss alternatives and support.
- Involve a support person or advocate in future meetings.
- Escalate to the school principal or department if your child's rights are being breached.

What are reasonable adjustments?

Most children with ADHD want to do well at school. Many learning challenges in ADHD stem from weak executive functioning. These skills include:

> planning and organising
> starting tasks
> managing time
> remembering instructions
> staying focused
> regulating effort and emotions.

But, often, they don't have the tools or support they need to keep up, stay focused or show what they know. It's not that they *won't* do the work, it's that they *can't*, consistently, without the right scaffolding.

When schools provide learning support tailored to your child's unique needs (and when you reinforce those strategies at home), it can make a world of difference to their confidence, motivation and progress.

Under the Disability Standards for Education, schools are required to make reasonable adjustments to help students with disability (including ADHD) access and participate in learning. These aren't about giving your child an unfair advantage, they're about levelling the playing field. These adjustments could include:

> classroom accommodations, such as:
  - seating: near the teacher and away from distractions such as doors or windows can support focus; flexible options, like stability balls, wobble cushions, standing desks or movement-friendly workstations, can help children channel energy and stay engaged
  - movement breaks
  - breaking up long activities using timers or task strips
  - oral/written instructions
  - use of assistive tools/technology (audiobooks, speech-to-text, timers)

- use of headphones/fidgets
- simplified/chunked instructions
- extra time or reduced volume of work
- quiet spaces for work or tests
- alternatives to written work (oral reports, drawings, video responses)

➤ supporting executive functioning skills (planners, checklists, scaffolding tasks)
➤ recognising and supporting giftedness or twice exceptional (2e) learners
➤ using positive reinforcement charts tapping into child's motivators
➤ reduced/differentiated homework.

Your child doesn't need to have a learning disorder diagnosis to access these supports. ADHD is enough.

Reducing homework stress

Homework is so often a battleground for families of children with ADHD. If your child's homework is causing daily tears, meltdowns or shutdowns, it's time to rethink whether the homework is right for them or if they should be doing it at all.

Tips for managing homework

➤ Ask the teacher for reduced or modified homework.
➤ Implement a ten-minute rule (or whatever time is age-appropriate); if it takes longer than that, let it go and inform their teacher.
➤ Focus on your connection over homework compliance (your relationship matters more than incomplete homework).
➤ Choose a time of day that works for your child, perhaps after a break/snack, not immediately after school.
➤ Use body doubling: sit with your child while they complete their homework (even while doing your own tasks). See page 111 for more on this.

- ➤ Create a consistent, calm space for homework.
- ➤ Organise a homework planner with parent-teacher communication space.
- ➤ Use reward systems to incentivise short bursts of effort followed by breaks.
- ➤ Chunk tasks down into smaller pieces with clear, simple instructions.
- ➤ Use visual timers or countdown clocks to support focus.
- ➤ Use colour-coded folders or labels for different subjects.
- ➤ Help your child review feedback in a way that builds (not breaks) their confidence.
- ➤ Let teachers know if your child is struggling or unable to do the homework.
- ➤ Don't complete it for them!

Sometimes it helps to have external support, such as:

- ➤ tutoring or coaches who understand ADHD and executive function challenges, and who can teach 'how' to learn, e.g., how to write an essay/revise for a test
- ➤ speech or occupational therapists for learning or sensory needs
- ➤ learning support teachers within the school (find out how your child can access them).

Remember:

- ➤ Success in learning is not about achieving top marks, it's about confidence, engagement and progress.
- ➤ Ask how learning can be made easier for your child: are there any barriers that can be removed?
- ➤ Don't be fobbed off with cookie-cutter strategies; ensure they work for your child.
- ➤ Adjustments can be made on observable needs, you don't need to wait for a full academic assessment.
- ➤ Celebrate your child's effort more than outcomes; it builds long-term resilience.

Fostering a sense of belonging

Amidst all the reports, meetings, behaviour plans and curriculum goals, it's easy to lose sight of the most important question:

Is my child happy at school?

If your child doesn't feel emotionally safe, seen and valued at school, no amount of academic support will help them thrive.

Children with ADHD are more likely to experience school-related anxiety, shame and exclusion. They often internalise messages (spoken or unspoken) that they're *too much*, *not enough* or somehow fundamentally *wrong*. Over time, this can damage their self-esteem and love of learning.

Your child might appear 'fine' at school, only to fall apart at home, withdraw, mask their struggles or become the class clown to avoid embarrassment. It's so important to look beyond the academic report and ask yourself:

- ➤ Does my child feel *liked* and *accepted* by their teachers and peers?
- ➤ Do they look forward to going to school most days?
- ➤ Do come home emotionally drained or energised?
- ➤ Are they showing signs of stress (headaches, tummy aches, sleep problems)?

The importance of belonging

Research consistently shows a sense of belonging at school—feeling connected, included and valued—predicts better academic outcomes, mental health and motivation for all children, and this is especially true for those with ADHD.[1,2]

Belonging doesn't mean being the most popular child or getting awards. It means:

- ➤ being greeted warmly in the morning
- ➤ having at least one friend or trusted adult who *gets* them

> having space to move, fidget or decompress without being punished
> time each day when they feel competent and successful
> connection with others who share their interests or experiences
> feeling safe to make mistakes knowing that you matter, even when you mess up.

For many children with ADHD, making and keeping friends can be just as challenging as the academic side of things—or even more so. Social struggles are often the hidden heartache of school life. When children feel rejected, excluded or constantly misunderstood by their peers, it chips away at their confidence and sense of belonging. Unlike reading or maths, social skills aren't usually formally taught, although they can be, yet they're expected to be mastered (see Chapter 15).

Why social skills can be difficult for children with ADHD

ADHD affects more than attention and behaviour. It also impacts the way a child perceives, processes and responds in social situations. They may experience challenges with:

> impulsivity (blurting out, interrupting, acting before thinking)
> navigating big feelings (especially during teasing or perceived rejection)
> reading body language or facial expressions
> following the flow of conversation
> taking turns or playing cooperatively
> rejection sensitivity, sometimes called *rejection sensitive dysphoria (RSD)*, where even small social setbacks can feel overwhelming.

As a result, many children with ADHD feel isolated or cycle through friendships quickly. This can look like:

> not being invited to parties or playdates
> being teased, bossed around or ignored

> big emotional reactions to losing a game or making a mistake
> misunderstanding social rules or personal boundaries
> taking the lead in play or group activities more often than others
> concerns from teachers or other adults about how your child interacts socially
> overwhelm after school due to social load or sensory exhaustion.

Chapter 15 explores more strategies to support your child with social challenges.

Work with the school

Supporting your child's social world at school is just as important as supporting their learning. Below are some practical ways you can partner with the school to help your child build friendships, feel included and experience positive social connection.

> Ask teachers for honest, compassionate feedback on your child's peer interactions.
> Advocate for structured social supports like:
>   • a designated buddy
>   • supervised lunch clubs
>   • small group work with supportive peers
>   • social goals included in their IEP.
> Involve the school counsellor or psychologist if social exclusion or bullying is a concern.
> Ask whether your school runs social learning programs such as PEERS (secondary) or Zones of Regulation (primary). These programs help children recognise emotions, navigate impulses and respond to social situations in ways that feel supportive and successful.

Dealing with bullying or social exclusion

If your child is being excluded or bullied, it's important to respond promptly. Children with ADHD may be more vulnerable to bullying because they can have big feelings, act impulsively or have fewer close friendships to buffer them. Some steps you could take include:

> documenting what your child tells you
> asking the school for a clear plan of action
> requesting increased adult supervision during unstructured times
> involving the school wellbeing team or principal, if needed
> making sure our child feels heard and supported at home
> empowering them to name bullying behaviour and seek help.

For more tips on responding to bullying, see Chapter 15.

Celebrate who they are

More than social success, what truly matters is that your child feels emotionally safe, welcomed and understood — by peers and by the school community. Chapter 12 explored ways to build self-esteem and resilience, which can be especially important in schools that are often designed with neurotypical learners in mind. In a school setting, key strategies include:

> *asking open-ended questions* about your child's day to show interest in their experience, not just their behaviour or grades
> *focusing on strengths and interests*, especially outside traditional academics, such as creativity, social insight or problem-solving
> *prioritising emotional safety over performance*: school success should never come at the cost of anxiety or burnout.

When things aren't working

You've done all the 'right' things (collaborated with the school, sought assessments, attended meetings, advocated for adjustments, tried strategies at home and maybe even changed schools), but your child is still struggling—or worse, they're miserable.

If that's where you are right now, I want to say clearly: it's not because you haven't done enough. It's because the system wasn't built with your child in mind. Many schools still operate on a one-size-fits-all model. While some teachers and schools go above and beyond to make it work for neurodivergent children, others simply don't have the training, time or flexibility.

Sometimes, despite everyone's best efforts, school just doesn't work. Maybe your child dreads going each day. Maybe you're getting constant calls from the office. Maybe they're overwhelmed the moment they walk in the door or the moment they get home. Maybe they've stopped learning, become emotionally shut down, or are avoiding school altogether. If you're in this place right now—it's not your fault. Many parents, unfortunately, reach this point.

School can't

Sometimes, children with ADHD reach a point where school feels impossible. This is often described as *'school can't'*, a term that shifts the focus away from blaming the child and toward recognising the barriers that make school attendance so difficult. Unlike truancy, children experiencing school can't usually want to attend but feel unable to due to factors like social anxiety, fear or overwhelming stress.

Closely related is *school burnout*, which develops when ongoing challenges, such as masking (see page 287), struggling to keep up or feeling excluded leave a child emotionally depleted. Burnout may look like apathy or disengagement, but underneath is a child who is overwhelmed and needing support, not lazy or defiant.

Together, both school can't and school burnout signal that something isn't working and that your child needs understanding, support and changes to their environment, not punishment.

Signs of school can't or school burnout

Watch for these signs that your child's nervous system is overwhelmed and they are finding school hard to cope with:

> ➤ ongoing tummy aches, headaches or sleep difficulties (often linked to anxiety or stress about school)
> ➤ intense emotional outbursts before or after school, such as meltdowns or shutdowns
> ➤ repeated suspensions or discipline issues, often masking underlying distress
> ➤ a sudden drop in academic performance, motivation or willingness to try
> ➤ social withdrawal: avoiding peers, even close friends
> ➤ verbal expressions of dread, fear or hopelessness about school
> ➤ statements of self-harm or self-hatred, such as saying they hate themselves or wish they didn't have to be here
> ➤ seeming apathetic, disengaged or 'checked out', which may actually be signs of burnout rather than lack of effort

If any of these sound familiar, it's time to step back and reassess.

> ➤ *Pause and breathe:* It's okay to step off the treadmill. Your child's wellbeing is more important than perfect attendance. Take a day or a week if you need to.
> ➤ *Seek professional support*: Talk to your GP, psychologist or paediatrician, and get a mental healthcare plan, if needed. Ask for support letters or documentation for school adjustments.
> ➤ *Request a support meeting*: Bring your concerns to the school gently but firmly. Ask: 'What can we do together to make school feel safe and manageable for my child right now?' If needed, request adjustments such as a reduced or flexible timetable, modified expectations, or a short reset period at home.
> ➤ *Document everything*: Keep a log of your child's symptoms or incidents as well as all communication. Put your requests in writing and keep any responses for clarity and accountability.

When you need to try something different

If your child is consistently unhappy, anxious or dreading school, it's a sign something in their environment isn't working. You're allowed to:

> ask the school to make changes
> consider moving class, teacher, school
> pause, reassess and make your child's mental health the priority.

While it can be confronting to step away from what's familiar, it can also be liberating to finally stop trying to squeeze your child into a system that doesn't fit and, instead, start creating a learning life that *does*. There's no single roadmap to follow, you're the expert on your child and they're more than enough—just as they are.

By now, you've likely realised your child doesn't need fixing, they just need more freedom, understanding and space to learn and develop in a way that works for *them*. That may mean shifting your view of success or even stepping outside the traditional system altogether.

It may mean:

> redefining education as life skills, curiosity and meaningful learning
> prioritising mental health above academic performance
> exploring alternative schooling options
> rebuilding self-worth through interests, creativity and play
> recognising that learning happens through everyday life.

Remember, you're not failing by stepping away from traditional schooling, you're allowed to pivot, pause or rebuild.

If your child's distress continues despite reasonable efforts to support them at school—or if the school environment itself is contributing to their overwhelm—it may be time to explore alternative pathways.

Options to consider:

> *Changing schools*: A fresh environment with a different culture or leadership can make a world of difference.

- > *Flexible or part-time schooling*: Some schools allow reduced hours or a staged return.
- > *Distance education*: Offers structure and teacher support while learning from home.
- > *Home schooling*: Provides full flexibility, ideal for recovery and customisation.
- > *Therapeutic support programs*: Some regions offer re-engagement or wellbeing-focused programs.

Changing direction is not giving up; it's advocating for your child with courage.

Creating a healing plan

After a tough school experience, some children need a reset, a break to calm their nervous system, rebuild trust and reconnect with their strengths.

During this time, focus on:

- > mental health support (e.g., therapy, OT)
- > low-pressure, interest-led learning at home
- > strong connection and co-regulation with trusted adults
- > gently reintroducing structure when they're ready.

Healing takes time, but it is possible.

Navigating school when your child has ADHD is rarely straightforward; it's a journey filled with twists and turns, highs and lows. You'll likely find yourself juggling advocacy, frustration and collaboration, all while trying to protect your child's self-esteem; nurture their strengths, interests, and unique talents; and worry over their friendship struggles. No school is perfect, but with the right support, environment and your supportive presence, your child *can* thrive.

Chapter Fifteen

Navigating friendships: Helping your child build social confidence

> Every child deserves to be themselves and to learn
> the skills that help them connect, belong and thrive.

Most people agree social skills are vital to success and happiness in life—but why is that? Social skills are the foundations of interpersonal communication, friendships, communication, cooperation and emotional intelligence.

Friendships are a vital part of childhood and adolescence for social and emotional development, providing an all-important sense of belonging, fun, joy, mutual emotional support and the opportunity to learn and practice social and communication skills.

For some children, especially those with ADHD, the subtleties of social interactions can feel confusing. Impulsivity, distractibility, emotional regulation, taking turns in conversations, resolving conflicts and difficulty reading social cues all make it harder to connect with their peers, so making and maintaining friendships and navigating group dynamics becomes tricky, leading to misunderstandings.

Social connection is an essential part of your child's long-term wellbeing. Feeling connected to others supports friendships, strengthens self-esteem and resilience and helps children develop emotional regulation. It plays a vital role in mental health and in feeling a sense of belonging in the world.

Building and maintaining relationships can take extra support for children with ADHD. With connection, practice and gentle guidance, they can grow their confidence and learn to navigate their social world in ways that feel authentic and supportive.

The importance of friendships

Research shows that having just one or two close friends predicts how confident and secure someone will feel later in life and is protective against the impact of stressful life events. It's also correlated with greater self-esteem and independence and fewer negative mental health outcomes such as anxiety or depression, because you simply feel more accepted and supported. Having supportive friends in your life means you're less likely to feel lonely or experience as much anxiety or depression and are, therefore, better able to weather life's inevitable ups and downs.[1]

With this in mind, children who have fewer opportunities for close friendships may be more vulnerable to later anxiety or depression. Supportive friendships provide an emotional safety net, so when those connections are harder to build, it can affect wellbeing over time.

You need to look at the quality of your child's friendships: do they have close friendships or just acquaintances? Acquaintances may chat during lunchbreak or play online games but that's as far as it goes and they don't know each other on a deeper level.

To form stronger friendships, your child needs to engage in conversations beyond the surface level: finding out more about friends (or potential friends), their likes and dislikes and so on, so they're able to invite them to hang out outside of school or structured activities. Once they start to do this, others can get to know them better and their relationships will deepen over time. Gently helping your child learn how to take turns in conversations and share interests can open the door to deeper, more connected friendships.

Common social challenges

It's widely recognised that autistic children may face social challenges, but what's less understood is that many children with ADHD can also find social interactions difficult. Because many children with ADHD appear outgoing or chatty, their difficulties with making or keeping friends are often overlooked. These struggles may be more subtle, such as missing social cues, interrupting, or finding conflict difficult to navigate, but they can have just as big an impact on relationships.

As a PEERS® Certified Provider, I often see two distinct groups join the program: the socially misunderstood and the socially cautious.

Children who are socially misunderstood

Socially misunderstood children truly want to connect and often seek out friendships. However, differences in reading social cues or navigating conversational flow can sometimes lead to misunderstandings or exclusion, even when their intentions are positive.

They may appear charismatic, chatty and as good conversationalists who confidently start or join conversations. They may also make plenty of new friends but, sadly, those friendships often don't last and it can be difficult to discern why. Their confidence can sometimes make it seem as though everything is going well socially, but they may find it hard to notice subtle cues—such as when someone is interested in talking, when it's a good moment to join a conversation or whether the other person is still engaged in the topic.

Some children use humour to connect with others and be liked, and may even become known as the 'class clown.' But when it's hard to tell whether others are enjoying the joke or want to shift the conversation, this approach can sometimes create misunderstandings instead of connection. In addition, when children overuse humour—making a joke about everything—it inhibits deeper conversations and doesn't allow people to get to know them better.

Picking up on social cues and perspectives is something many of us do without thinking, but for some children, that doesn't come naturally. Many children find perspective-taking—understanding how someone else might think, feel or react—challenging. Sometimes the social world needs to be made explicit, with cues and expectations explained openly so interactions become clearer and easier to navigate..

ADHD traits can also influence social interactions. Impulsivity may make it harder for your child to wait their turn in conversation, stay on one topic or notice when others want to contribute. Emotional dysregulation can lead to big reactions in the moment, which can sometimes affect how social interactions unfold.

Socially misunderstood children can be more vulnerable to teasing and to reputations that are difficult to change, often because their intentions are misunderstood.

Children who are socially cautious

Socially cautious children may hang back from social interactions and participate less in group activities. This can look like shyness or social anxiety or simply preferring to observe before engaging. They may rarely initiate conversations or may stay quiet in groups, which can make them appear withdrawn—but this is often a way of protecting themselves when social situations feel overwhelming or uncertain. Some children are naturally more introverted and prefer smaller, quieter interactions—and that is completely okay. We're all different.

However, often what appears to be low social motivation is not what's going on. Many children are very motivated—they want more friends and social connection but they just don't yet know how to start or join in. Without clear tools for how to approach others, conversations and friendships can feel out of reach.

They may share enthusiastically about the things they care about, but not notice when others are ready to speak or shift the topic. Without that natural rhythm of turn-taking, friendships can be harder to build and maintain.

When children withdraw from social activities, they get less practice. The more isolated they become, the harder it is to re-engage. Some children gravitate to online friendships, but these don't build the same real-world practice with social cues.

Sometimes, social withdrawal may also be a sign of anxiety or depression. If you suspect this, it's important to seek professional support.

The good news? Social skills can be taught, and we'll explore how to help your child build them.

Consequences of social challenges

Watching your child struggle socially or face rejection from peers can be heartbreaking, and its effects can extend beyond friendships alone. Ongoing social isolation and challenges with social skills are associated with an increased risk of anxiety, depression, lower self-esteem and school avoidance. This is why supporting social confidence and connection early on can be so protective.

Friendship difficulties aren't just a childhood issue, they often persist across the lifespan. Without support, children who struggle to make or maintain friendships early on may grow into adults with few meaningful, reciprocal relationships, leading to greater loneliness and disconnection.

We hope, as our children grow towards adulthood, things will improve, that our child will overcome their shyness or that leaving school for university or work will bring new social opportunities. Sometimes it does if they're lucky enough to find their tribe but, for many, the transition to adulthood brings even more isolation. Social activities become fewer, less structured and are no longer organised by you. They need the skills and confidence to take the lead and run their own social life, but without targeted support to build those skills and the confidence to seek out connections, many struggle to form the friendships they deeply need and deserve.

Why online friendships aren't the same

Don't allow yourself or your child to be complacent thinking they have plenty of 'online' friends! Online friends can often lead to young people feeling a sense of comfort that they're having social interactions but without ever leaving the house. Online communications just aren't the same as interactions in real life and this can also be a destructive cycle. The more your child stays home, the more they want to stay home. They get comfortable in their own space and going out starts to feel like more effort!

Leaving the comfort zone

It's understandable that your child may prefer to stay home—it feels safe and predictable. New situations can feel uncomfortable at first. But if they remain in that comfort zone, they may have fewer chances to practise skills and build the confidence they'll need for relationships, work and daily life as they grow.

Impact on employment

Poorly supported social skills can affect opportunities even as early as university. Difficulties connecting with peers or lecturers may contribute to feeling isolated or disengaged. Later, during job hunting, challenges with things like eye contact, reading social cues or building rapport in interviews can make it harder to secure a position—even when a young person is highly capable and well-qualified.

Even once employed, day-to-day challenges such as teamwork, handling feedback, managing misunderstandings or navigating workplace dynamics can make it difficult to thrive or maintain a role. Recognising these challenges early and putting the right supports and skill-building opportunities in place is essential, ensuring young people have the social tools they need not only to get a job but also to succeed and flourish in the workplace.

Impact on parents

Nothing hurts more than seeing your child excluded, teased or left out. You know how much they have to offer as a friend, yet they struggle to connect—and it's heartbreaking. They want to be invited, to join in, to belong and it's painful to watch them miss out on birthday parties, playdates or weekend plans simply because others don't see how wonderful they are. It feels unfair—and it is.

The good news is, whether your child is socially misunderstood or socially cautious, social skills can be taught. There's so much we can do to help.

Supporting children with social skills

With the right support, practice and guidance, your child can improve their social skills and confidence, and develop strong, meaningful friendships that enrich their lives and boost their self-esteem. You can play a key role in nurturing your child's social development, creating opportunities for connection and helping them navigate the ups and downs of social life.

A word about masking

Masking involves consciously or unconsciously hiding natural behaviours to fit in or meet social expectations. Many in the neurodivergent community express concern about the emotional impact of masking, emphasising the importance of supporting children to be themselves. Some worry that social skills teaching could unintentionally reinforce the pressure to conform.

It's an important perspective to keep in mind. Every child deserves to feel accepted and valued for who they truly are.

Masking involves consciously or unconsciously hiding natural behaviours to fit in or meet social expectations. Many in the neurodivergent community express concern about the emotional impact of masking, emphasising the importance of supporting children to be themselves. Some worry that social skills teaching could unintentionally reinforce the pressure to conform.

The reality is, we use social skills every day, whether we realise it or not. Teaching children clearly and compassionately isn't about changing who a child is, it's about giving them the tools to connect, feel more confident and navigate the world on their terms.

I love teaching social skills because it's a strengths-based and practical way to support wellbeing. For many young people, anxiety and low mood are deeply linked to feeling disconnected or unsure socially. Watching their confidence grow — and seeing how that transforms their daily life — is incredibly rewarding.

Evidence-based socials skills

You can use your parent-coach approach to support your child's social growth, and structured social skills programs can build on this. When considering a program, it's helpful to look for ones that measure progress, so you can be confident that the strategies are effective and making a difference.

Early intervention is important for younger children, but the social skills your child requires will change over their lifespan. The skills they need as a preschooler are different from those they will need in the teen years and adulthood, so they need to learn age-appropriate skills.

Evidence-based programs such as PEERS (Program for the Education and Enrichment of Relational Skills) are specifically designed to support teens and young adults in developing social confidence in a structured and supportive way. Through guided skill practice, role-play, parent coaching and real-world application, PEERS provides practical tools that help young people build and maintain meaningful friendships.

Structured social skills programs have several benefits over coaching your child yourself:

> Your child can benefit from learning from their peers in a group situation.
> Many young people respond better to learning social strategies from a neutral adult and peers, rather than from parents, because it feels less personal and more collaborative.
> Learning alongside peers in a structured group setting can reinforce skills naturally. Seeing others model the same strategies and practise them together helps young people feel supported, increases confidence and makes the skills easier to use in real-world situations.
> Where perspective-taking is covered, they hear their peers explain how they would feel in given situations.
> The programs can give them a feeling of solidarity with peers.
> Programs that also upskill caregivers allow for more effective coaching at home during and post-program.

Tips for teaching social skills

Whether or not your child participates in a formal program, you can do a lot to support their social development at home. Let's look at some practical, everyday strategies for teaching foundational social skills.

Be an encouraging social skills coach

These are skills your child is still learning and practising. They won't get it right every time—and that's okay. Try to offer encouragement rather than correction, even when things feel tricky. Be gentle in your coaching:

> Practice in short bursts, using visual cues or role-play—don't forget to praise their efforts!
> Employ a 'praise sandwich': praise them for what they've done well, give constructive feedback to make it a learning opportunity and then finish with more praise; for example:
> • 'Well done for starting a conversation with Jo.' (praise)
> • 'Next time you talk to them, try asking what games they like, so you can find out more about them.' (feedback)
> • 'What you said about Minecraft was great at letting Jo know what you're interested in.' (praise)

> If they're worried a social interaction didn't go quite as well as they hoped, say: 'You're learning! That's a great start; we'll keep practising together.'

> Reflect, ask questions and brainstorm with them on their real-world social interactions:
  - 'What did you learn about your friend in your conversation today?'
  - 'If some parts were tricky or awkward, what could you do differently next time?'
  - 'If the conversation went well, what was it that made it flow so well?'

> Celebrate small improvements, such as starting a conversation with someone new or remembering to ask a follow-up question. You're looking for effort and incremental improvements, not perfection. Each time they try out their skills with others, they're building their social confidence and emotional regulation over time.

> Let your child see you enjoying spending time with them. Comment on what you love about your time together, for example: 'I love how creative your ideas are' or 'Your jokes always make me laugh' (only if they do!).

> Model positive social behaviour through play rather than correcting: 'Great idea to build a tower. Let's add a car to each level. Pick your favourite!'

> Link their actions to natural outcomes: 'Thanks for sharing your toys; I had so much fun playing with you!'

When you offer calm, consistent guidance, your child will feel safe enough to try again, enabling them to continue learning and improving.

Teach your child what makes a good friend

I often work with young people who *feel* they have lots of friends, while their parents describe something different—for example, few invitations, limited contact outside school, or difficulty naming close friends. It's important not to dismiss your child's experience. Instead, gently explore together what friendship means to them and support them in understanding what healthy, mutual friendships look and feel like, and what it means to have or be a good friend. Discuss different types of friendships: acquaintances, online friends, work friends, casual friends, close friends and best friends. Help your child identify qualities they should expect from their friends and what their friend might expect from them.

Encourage your child to talk about their friendships: Do they feel safe, fun and respectful? Help them recognise red flags like teasing, exclusion or one-sided dynamics. Once they understand what a healthy friendship looks like, remind them it's not just about playing together, it's about kindness, flexibility, listening and having fun.

Break social skills into teachable parts

For some children, social skills don't come naturally, and just like learning to read, they may need more explicit teaching. Social interactions have many hidden rules and steps that aren't always obvious. To avoid overwhelm, focus on one area at a time, such as:

> conversational skills: taking turns and showing interest in others
> starting/joining conversations
> asking questions and follow-up questions
> letting others finish their thought before sharing yours
> assessing the interest in a conversation
> being a good sport
> using humour appropriately
> respecting other people's boundaries
> resolving conflicts.

Taking turns

Turn-taking isn't just for games, it's a key part of conversations too. Children with ADHD can struggle with this due to impulsivity and the fear of forgetting what they want to say (and sometimes they really do!). But it's important they learn how constant interruptions can feel to others: rude, dismissive or like they're not listening. Social skills always come back to understanding the other person's perspective.

Practise turn-taking by:

> using board games, card games or shared storytelling
> talking through the process: 'Now it's your turn ... now it's mine'
> giving plenty of praise: 'You waited so patiently while I had my turn—thank you'
> using visual timers or verbal cues to help children understand the two-way rhythm of conversations.

Reading social cues

Children with ADHD often struggle to pick up on social cues, such as eye contact, body language and tone of voice, which are key to understanding how others feel. Teaching perspective-taking helps them recognise what someone might be thinking or feeling during an interaction, like whether they want to keep talking or need space. While social cues can seem like a mystery at first, you can help your child learn to spot clear, concrete signs in everyday situations.

Eye contact (or looking at someone's face)

Many neurodivergent children find eye contact uncomfortable—and that's okay. Rather than forcing it, a helpful compromise is to look at someone's nose, chin or temple, which gives the impression of eye contact while allowing your child to pick up on important social cues.

Help your child understand that avoiding eye contact or not looking at someone's face can lead to missing key nonverbal signals and may be interpreted as disinterest, making others less likely to engage.

Practise what natural eye contact looks like—it's not staring into someone's eyes the whole time (that would feel awkward for anyone!). It's about glancing at someone's face, then looking away briefly and finding a comfortable rhythm. Encourage your child to self-advocate by letting others know. They might simply say, 'I'm listening, I just find it easier when I'm not looking directly at you.'

Assessing interest

It's important your child learns how to gauge whether someone is interested in the conversation, rather than continuing to talk when the other person has clearly checked out. This is especially true when your child wants to talk at length about a favourite topic, which might not interest everyone.

Help them learn to spot positive and negative social cues by asking whether the other person is:

> looking at me
> talking to me in a friendly tone
> smiling at me
> asking me questions
> giving short or one-word answers
> looking distracted, tired, irritated or uncomfortable

Once they can recognise these cues, coach them to adjust their approach based on how the other person is responding by:

> role-playing social interactions and asking them to name your facial expressions, body language and tone of voice to identify when you're interested or uninterested in the conversation
> take turns practising looking interested or uninterested; remind them how the other person might feel if they don't show signs of interest in the conversation (i.e., they may think they're not interested and leave the conversation or not bother speaking to them another time)
> observe other people in public or on TV together and ask: 'What do you think that person is feeling?' or 'Does that person look interested in talking to that person? How can you tell?'
> teach your child to look for signs in real-life conversations indicating whether someone is bored, interested or uncomfortable
> have them watch for signs of interest when starting conversations with others.

If your child has low self-esteem or has had previous negative experiences, they may interpret social cues more negatively than others or assume peers are being unkind even when they're not. Encourage them to approach each interaction with a fresh perspective and judge it on its own merits.

Not overstaying in conversations

Once you've discussed assessing interest, explain that if someone isn't engaged, it's best to stop and politely exit the conversation.

Empathy and perspective-taking

We've mentioned perspective-taking (your child's ability to consider how others think or feel in a situation). Often, they're so focused on what they're saying or doing, they forget to think about the other person's experience. Gently remind them to reflect on others' perspectives. When they better understand how it feels to be on the receiving end of certain ways of communicating, they're able to reflect and course-correct when necessary.

Help them practice by asking:

> ➤ 'How might your friend feel if you do all the talking?'
> ➤ 'How would you feel if that happened to you?'
> ➤ 'What do you think your friend needed then?'

Use books, stories or real-life moments to explore different points of view and praise positive social behaviour when you see it, such as turn-taking, asking questions or showing kindness, for example, 'That was really thoughtful—did you see how your friend smiled when you helped?'

Practising new skills and building social confidence

Social skills are best learned in the real world, in the everyday moments of life. Everyday situations and role-play are two useful (and underused) tools you can use to support social learning and build social confidence.

Role-playing provides a safe, low-pressure way to practise new behaviours before using them in real situations. It helps reduce anxiety, boost readiness and reinforce what to say or do in common social scenarios.

Try role-playing the following:

> ➤ starting or joining single or group conversations
> ➤ ending conversations politely
> ➤ taking turns in two-way conversations
> ➤ using follow-up questions to learn about the other person

- handling teasing or exclusion
- giving/receiving compliments
- asking to share or take a turn
- saying 'no' politely
- recognising if someone is bored or annoyed.

Take turns: let your child be the adult or friend, and you play the child. Switching roles makes it fun and also builds their perspective-taking skills!

Practise in low-pressure, real-life situations first

Once you've practised at home, encourage your child to try their social skills in real life, starting with low-pressure situations, like extended family or younger/older kids. These settings offer a gentler space to build confidence before stepping into higher-stakes moments, like talking to same-age peers or potential new friends. Surrounding your child with people who 'get' them creates a safe, supportive space to practise while feeling good about themselves.

Coach social skills before and after play

Set your child up for success by talking through a social skill before their social interactions; for instance:

- 'What could you ask your friend to show your interest?'
- 'What can you do if you feel frustrated during the game?'

Afterwards, reflect together on what went well and what could be improved to build awareness and confidence, such as:

- 'What went well today?'
- 'Did anything feel tricky?'
- 'What could you try next time?'
- 'How did your friend react?'
- 'How did you feel when that happened?'

These short check-ins help your child grow their social skills with support and intention.

Use everyday situations as teaching moments

Everyday life is full of opportunities to build social skills if we use them intentionally. These common scenarios can provide opportunities to practise.

> ➤ *At the dinner table or in the car:* Practise turn-taking, asking questions and sharing about your day.
> ➤ *During outings:* Practise greetings, waiting patiently, asking for help or using manners with staff.
> ➤ *While watching TV or reading:* Pause to talk about characters' feelings, social missteps or kind moments:
>   • 'What would you have done there?'
>   • 'How do you think they felt?'
> ➤ *At school:* Encourage simple, low-pressure gestures like saying 'hi' to a friend, sharing something or starting a game.

Help your child recognise social boundaries

Your child may struggle to recognise social boundaries, and when these are crossed, it can make others feel uncomfortable or avoid future interaction. Help your child reflect by asking what might make *them* feel uncomfortable, and how it would feel if someone crossed their boundaries. Remind them that everyone's comfort levels are different. What feels fine to them might not feel okay to someone else. Learning this helps build empathy and respectful relationships.

Personal space and physical contact

Everyone has different comfort levels with physical touch: some children love hugs and cuddles, while others prefer more space. Neurodivergent children may also have sensory differences that make them seek or avoid physical contact more than others.

It's important to teach your child that all bodies deserve respect. It's okay to enjoy hugs and it's okay not to, but we always ask first and accept the answer without pressure or hurt feelings.

Help your child understand what appropriate physical contact looks like in different situations, like high fives with friends, hugs with close family (if both are comfortable) or a handshake when meeting someone new. Explain the idea of personal space and that getting too close—especially to someone we don't know well—can feel uncomfortable. A good rule of thumb is keeping about an arm's length distance. Practise together so it feels natural.

Don't get too personal or overshare

Even if your child is comfortable sharing personal information, others might not be. Oversharing or asking personal questions can make people uncomfortable. Teach your child to wait until they know someone better before sharing more personal details, and even then, to go slowly and pay attention to how the other person is reacting before continuing.

Create opportunities for connection

Social skills improve with practice, so it's important to create regular, low-pressure chances for your child to connect with others. When they're younger, it's easier to organise playdates and guide interactions. As they grow older, especially in the teen years, you'll need to step back but the same principles still apply.

Younger children

Practising with you (through shared play, games and conversations) builds confidence for peer interactions. Talk about what makes play fun or uncomfortable, and practise speaking up if needed (e.g., 'That's too rough' or 'Can I have a turn?'). Here are some other things you can do to support your child at this stage:

> Follow your child's lead; they may prefer one or two close friends or enjoy a wider mix.
> Focus on quality over quantity; support up to three solid friendships.
> Set up relaxed playdates with one or two children at a time.
> Choose calm times and low-stimulation environments.
> Discuss what makes play enjoyable for both them and their friend.
> Encourage regular contact through shared activities or short, simple playdates.
> Stay nearby to support and coach if needed.
> Before playdates, agree on two or three simple reminders like:
  • use your words
  • share your ideas
  • take turns choosing the game.

For all ages

As your child gets older, you can support their growing autonomy with some of the following:

> Coach *before* the interaction (what to try).
> Observe during the get-together (without hovering).
> Reflect afterwards (what went well, what could improve).
> Look for social opportunities based on your child's interests, such as coding, Lego clubs, scouts, sport or art, especially those with regular meetups and unstructured time for socialising.
> Choose collaborative activities over competitive ones; for example, baking, building or imaginative play.
> Friendships can also grow through cousins, neighbours or family friends.
> Take an interest in their friendships, connect with the other parents where possible.
> Always celebrate the little social wins—they really do add up.

Help your child have successful get-togethers

Spending time together is key to building stronger friendships. Hanging out, having fun and making memories helps deepen connections—and the more often it happens, the better.

If your child has a get-together planned, support them to make it a success. A fun, conflict-free hangout makes it more likely their friend will want to come back.

Tips for hosting a great get-together include:

> planning activities based on shared interests
> having backup options ready to avoid boredom
> giving them one-on-one time (without siblings, if possible)
> encouraging your child to prepare their space beforehand
> practising polite greetings and goodbyes
> reminding them to be flexible if plans change
> letting their friend choose some activities too
> providing snacks for them to offer
> keeping it short and sweet to start
> reminding them about turn-taking and being a good sport
> role-playing conversations beforehand for extra confidence.

Supporting friendships in the high school years

Once your child starts high school, you may not know their friends or their parents but you can still support them from the sidelines. Your role now is to gently scaffold and encourage them to reach out and organise catchups themselves.

This can be tricky if they're unsure of how to go about it or don't yet feel close enough to someone to make plans outside of school. It's a delicate balance—don't push them to ask too soon, but do encourage them when the time feels right. Confidence in these moments often builds with support and small wins.

Help your child build new friendships by:

> meeting them where they're at — they may not be ready to invite someone over yet, and that's okay
> encouraging mini conversations with more people to break the ice
> role-playing how to start a casual chat, and praise their efforts
> demonstrating that mini conversations can start with a compliment, question or comment, such as: 'I like your bag — where did you get it?' or 'You like Percy Jackson books? Me too!'
> reminding them to assess interest, and that it's normal if someone doesn't want to chat — it's not personal
> reinforcing that these small moments open the door for future conversations and help grow their social network over time
> enrolling them in group activities where new connections can form naturally.

Once they've had a few positive interactions and discovered shared interests, they'll have an easy reason to invite someone to hang out; for example:

> 'Have you seen the new XYZ movie? Want to go together?'
> 'I'm going surfing this weekend — want to come?'
> 'What are you up to this weekend? Want to come over and shoot hoops?'

Understanding responses to invitations

Explain to your child that people often have busy schedules or need to check with their parents, so a 'not this time' isn't always a rejection. That said, help them learn to gauge genuine interest so they know when it's worth asking again and when to move on.

Some cues that might help your child assess interest include the following:

> Are they smiling and nodding?
> Are they agreeing and sounding enthusiastic?
> Are they saying they'd like to, but can't on that day?
> Do they seem unsure?
> Are they saying 'no', or 'I don't think so'?
> Are they making excuses and not offering another time?

Maintaining friendships

Does your child seem to cycle through friends quickly, always talking about a new one, while the last quietly disappears? It's normal for kids to try out different friendships, but if connections never stick, they may be struggling to maintain them.

Making friends is one thing, keeping them takes skill and practice. Many children need guidance on how to strengthen friendships over time by:

> using conversation skills to get to know friends better
> following up after hangouts with a simple message, such as: 'That was fun yesterday. Want to hang out again soon?' or 'I still want to see that movie. Want to go?'
> following up on conversations during a get-together: 'Did you end up going surfing?' or 'How did your game go?'
> resolving conflicts effectively
> resolving conflicts with words instead of walking away
> being a caring, supportive friend who listens and shows up.

Resolving conflict

Arguments happen in all relationships—including friendships—but if your child doesn't know how to resolve them, even small conflicts can end a friendship. If they have only a few connections, losing one can feel huge.

Teaching conflict resolution skills helps your child navigate disagreements in a healthy way, strengthening their current friendships and building a skill they'll use throughout life with family, classmates, co-workers and future partners too.

Handling social disappointment

Children with ADHD often face social disappointment more often than their neurotypical peers. These experiences can be deeply painful, especially when your child may already be sensitive to perceived rejection or struggles with self-esteem.

While we can take steps to reduce how often it happens, it's just as important to support them when it *does* happen by:

> *Validating their feelings* without jumping in to fix it: 'That sounds really hurtful; I'm so sorry that happened.'
> *Exploring possible reasons* for the rejection that aren't personal.
> *Helping them reflect on the situation:* 'Do you think your friend might have been having a tough day?' or 'Why do you think they reacted that way?'
> *Discussing their friendship:* Is this a good choice of friend; for example, 'Is this friend kind and respectful to you most of the time?'
> *Teaching social resilience:* Not everyone will be their person and that's okay: 'Let's keep trying. The right people will appreciate you for who you are.'

Handling bullying

If your child is being teased or bullied, they need tools to respond effectively and a safe space to talk. Let them know they can come to you with anything, big or small. When they feel safe sharing the little things, they're more likely to open up about the big ones. From there, you can decide whether they need to handle it themselves or if it's time for an adult to step in.

Teasing

What some children call 'banter' (a friendly form of teasing) can sometimes cross the line into hurtful behaviour. Children with ADHD may struggle to tell the difference and might try to join in, only to upset someone or get upset themselves. Because banter can easily go wrong, it's safer to guide your child toward genuine conversations and shared interests instead.

Help your child understand why people tease, such as to:

> feel better about themselves
> show off or get attention
> create drama or alleviate boredom
> knock someone's confidence.

Discuss what the teaser wants — a big reaction such as:

> crying
> anger
> embarrassment
> starting an argument
> teasing back.

Teach your child how to stay regulated and respond calmly by:

> not teasing back
> shrugging, rolling their eyes or giving a short response like 'whatever' or 'do I look like I care?'
> avoiding debating or arguing
> walking away.

These responses make teasing less rewarding and less likely to continue. If the teasing becomes frequent or hurtful, don't hesitate to step in or contact the school for support.

Physical bullying

Teasing can sometimes escalate into physical bullying, so practising teasing responses and staying calm can help prevent things from progressing. Children who feel less confident socially or who have fewer supportive friendships can sometimes be more vulnerable to bullying. Strengthening your child's social confidence and helping them build even one or two supportive friendships can make a meaningful difference.

Bullying is *never* your child's fault. They can't control others' behaviour, but they *can* learn to respond in ways that protect them and reduce risk.

If your child is having friendship issues, they're already vulnerable because they don't have those supportive friends around them (yet), so encourage the following:

> assertive body language: stand tall, speak clearly, make eye contact (or look at the face)
> avoiding the bully when possible
> never teasing back, arguing or provoking
> staying near adults or in groups when the bully is nearby

- reporting incidents discreetly
- sharing any bullying with you so you can support them or step in when needed
- asking a trusted adult for help when necessary (without broadcasting it)
- using calm, clear phrases like 'That's not okay', 'Please stop' or 'I don't like that'.

With the right tools and support, your child can feel safer, more empowered, and less alone

Be your child's social coach

All children face social ups and downs because friendship is a choice, and not everyone will click. That's a normal part of growing up. For neurodivergent children, social struggles can be more frequent and discouraging, especially alongside the other challenges they're already navigating.

Social confidence isn't something your child either has or doesn't, it's a skill they can build, step by step. Use everyday moments to help them grow these skills in a way that feels light, fun, safe and free of judgement.

Take on the role of a gentle coach. Help them learn how to connect and communicate with peers through encouragement, practice and support. That might mean setting up playdates, guiding a teen to reach out to a friend or enrolling them in a social learning program. Meet them where they're at; support without taking over.

It may take time to build their skills and confidence, and they will require practice and patience. Children with ADHD may require slightly more coaching and repetition, but they're just as capable of learning the social skills they need to create meaningful, lasting friendships.

Chapter Sixteen

Digital parenting: Creating healthier screen habits

> Digital habits shape developing brains. When we guide them with care, we protect our children's wellbeing, connection and future.

In today's digital world, managing screen use has become one of the greatest parenting challenges, especially for families with children with ADHD. Throughout my years working with parents and young people with ADHD, screen use has consistently been a key driver of unwanted or aggressive behaviours, dysregulation and family conflict.

While digital environments can offer valuable learning opportunities, entertainment and social connection, overuse can amplify ADHD symptoms and contribute to overstimulation, dysregulation and difficulty transitioning to other activities. For children struggling to find their place among their peers, online social connections can be a lifeline, but over-reliance on these can, in turn, result in withdrawal from real-life pursuits and activities that could help grow their community. The addictive nature and rapid pace of the online world makes it hard to stay focused, maintain healthy routines and engage in face-to-face relationships and activities.[1]

We likely also struggle with our own screen use. Being hooked to our devices is not a youth issue, nor an ADHD one—we could all benefit from a little bit less time spent online.

The impact of screens on the ADHD brain

The use of screens, social media and gaming can have significant effects on a developing brain, particularly for children with ADHD.[2] According to research, excessive screen time, especially when focused on highly stimulating activities, like gaming or social media, can impact attention span, impulse control and emotional regulation.[3,4] The constant barrage of fast-paced images, notifications and social feedback can overload the brain's reward system, leading to dopamine dysregulation.[5] As a result, the brain becomes accustomed to quick bursts of pleasure or excitement, which then makes it harder for children to focus on tasks where sustained attention and delayed gratification is required. Children may then experience increased distractibility, hyperactivity and impulsivity as the brain becomes conditioned to seek constant stimulation and novelty, which are freely available in digital media.

Additionally, excessive screen use, especially social media, can negatively affect children's social skills and mental health.[6] Social media platforms often present an idealised view of life, which can lead to feelings of inadequacy, anxiety or depression in children and teens who struggle in comparing themselves to others.[7]

This can be particularly detrimental to developing brains, as social interactions are key to emotional development. Prolonged gaming sessions or social media use can also interfere with sleep patterns, disrupting the production of melatonin and leading to sleep deprivation, which exacerbates attention and behavioural problems.[8] See chapter 9 for more information on sleep.

Furthermore, screen time replaces opportunities for physical activity, which is essential for healthy brain development and emotional wellbeing.[9] Balancing screen time with offline activities, such as physical exercise, face-to-face social interactions and creative play, is crucial for supporting healthy brain growth and emotional regulation in children and teens.

Setting digital boundaries

Setting healthy boundaries around screen time is essential to a balanced digital diet for all children, but it becomes even more crucial for children with ADHD. The nature of ADHD can make it harder for children to pause before acting, stay focused and shift between tasks.

Creating a more balanced relationship with technology should be a whole-of-family discussion. In my Digital Parenting Program, we work through the process of developing a 'family contract' as a tool to establish a healthier balance between screen use and the real world. It's designed to provide clear expectations and guidelines about screen use in collaboration with your children. This section gives an overview of the steps involved.

Discuss technology as a family

Firstly, it's important for the whole family to have a shared understanding of the potential challenges that technology poses. Acknowledge that, while it can be a wonderful resource, it also has dangers and drawbacks. Be open about how difficult it can be to stay on top of the amount of our time and attention technology takes up in this digital age.

Use the facts outlined in this book as a resource to start the conversation. You may want to share with them some of the science in this chapter—whatever resonates most with your experience as a family or your observations of your child's relationship with technology. Use the concept of 'digital veggies and treats' (see page 311), or other metaphors that help to explain the relationship between excessive screen time and negative effects on our health and relationships.

Sit down together and discuss your goals and concerns around technology use. Involve everyone in the discussion, including children, as it helps them feel ownership over the rules and encourages responsibility.

In this conversation, ask each other:

> ➤ Why is technology important in our day-to-day lives? What do we use it for and what value does it add for that purpose (e.g., learning, socialising, entertainment)?
> ➤ What are the potential challenges (e.g., distractions, screen addiction)?
> ➤ What specific issues or problems related to technology use do we have (if any)? Are we noticing excessive screen time, difficulty focusing or emotional impacts? Have your children noticed this themselves?
> ➤ What do we want to achieve by reshaping our relationship with technology (e.g., better balance between screen time and offline activities, improved family connection or fewer tech-related arguments)?

The family contract is not just a metaphor—make it concrete and visible! Once specific rules, time limits, consequences and planned offline activities have been discussed and agreed upon by everyone, write them down. Post them in a visible place, such as the fridge or family bulletin board, so everyone can refer to it as needed. Set a time to review the agreement as a family, especially if your child's screen habits change or as they outgrow certain rules.

Consistency reinforces boundaries

As discussed in Part II, consistency is key for children with ADHD, and boundaries can create a sense of safety and routine that, over time, help them regulate. Once your goals around technology use are clear and agreed, you'll need to translate them into clear boundaries that are easy for your whole family to understand and follow.

These should include some of the following.

Daily or weekly limits

Determine how much screen time is reasonable for your child, taking into account their age, maturity and the purpose of screen use (e.g., one hour per day for recreational screen time).

A daily schedule

Set specific times for screen time (such as after homework or in the evening) and make sure both you and your child knows when the 'screen time window' begins and ends. Account for schoolwork and learning in this schedule—if your child uses screens for educational purposes, make a distinction between recreational and educational screen time.

Screen-free zones

Identify areas in your home (e.g., dining table, bedrooms) where screens aren't allowed in order to promote better communication, rest and family time.

Rewards and consequences

Decide what happens if your child exceeds their screen time limit or engages in inappropriate activities (e.g., a loss of screen privileges, extra chores). Create rewards for sticking to the digital agreement, such as engaging in a special family activity, for positive reinforcement. Avoid using extra screen time as a reward.

While it will help to work collaboratively to decide on your family's new technology boundaries, there will inevitably be some that your children disagree with or that you worry will be a source of conflict when it comes time to enforce them. I understand why you may feel apprehensive—one of the major sources of conflict amongst parents I work with is excessive screen use. (See Chapter 7 for more on rewards and consequences.)

Try some of the strategies here to help with implementing new boundaries, or to better enforce existing ones.

Be firm, but compassionate

It's normal for children to push boundaries, but it's important to maintain consistency. Gently remind your child why limits are necessary for their health and wellbeing. Be curious: what is it that screen time is providing for them, and how can you replace or mitigate it?

Use timers to signal when screen time starts and ends

Timers offers a clear visual and auditory cue that helps children with ADHD navigate transitions.

Use parental monitoring and control tools to help to implement these boundaries

Apps that assist in limiting screen time and filtering inappropriate content on your children's devices are available and these are covered in more depth on page 324.

Monitor usage together

Periodically review your child's device usage and talk about what they're doing online. Encourage open conversations about their digital experiences, focusing on safety and responsibility.

Consider prevention as part of the digital boundaries for your family

The longer you delay the use of screens, the more chance your child's brain has to develop, and the more their prefrontal cortex can develop better executive function. So delay, delay, delay the use of screens with young people where possible.

Establishing a balanced digital environment

Just as vegetables are essential for a balanced diet, digital veggies are the types of online content and activities that promote positive development for our children—those that support learning, creativity, critical thinking and socio-emotional development, including how to be a responsible digital citizen (see page 319). Examples may include educational content and collaborative or social tools that children and young people can engage with in a way that builds their confidence and self-esteem (see Figure 16.1).

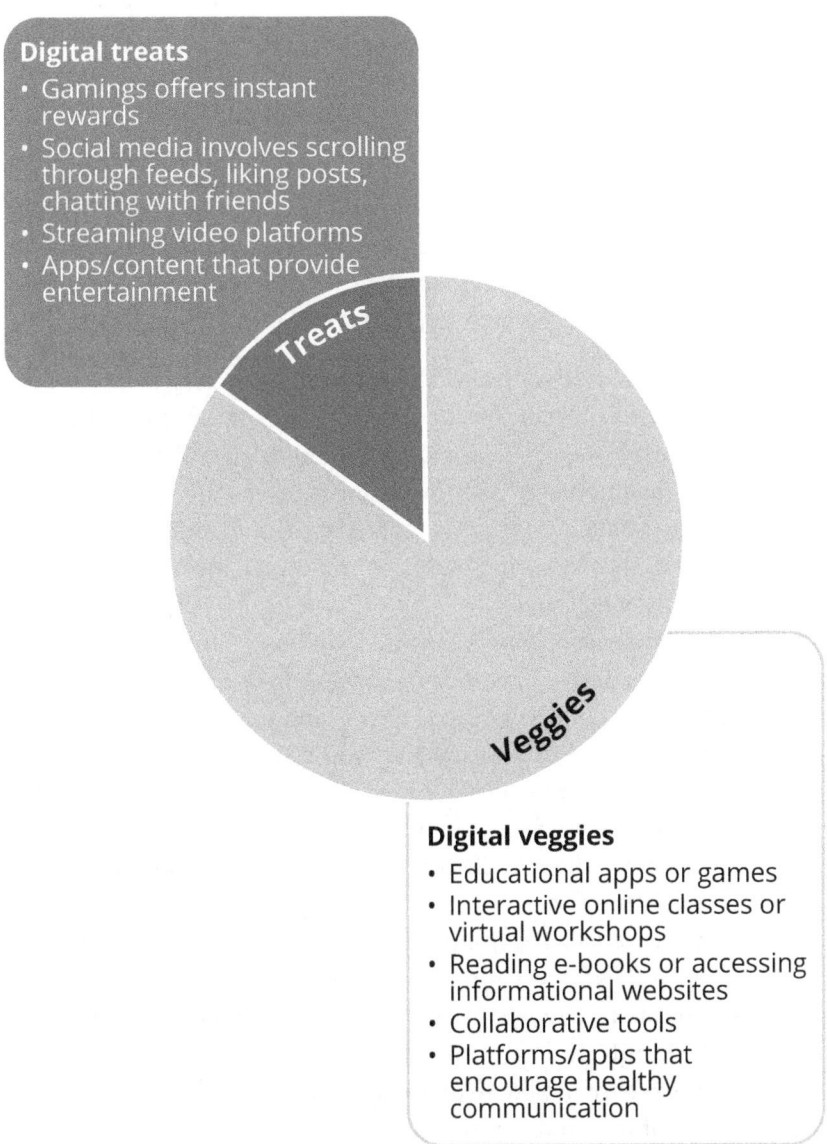

Digital treats
- Gamings offers instant rewards
- Social media involves scrolling through feeds, liking posts, chatting with friends
- Streaming video platforms
- Apps/content that provide entertainment

Treats

Veggies

Digital veggies
- Educational apps or games
- Interactive online classes or virtual workshops
- Reading e-books or accessing informational websites
- Collaborative tools
- Platforms/apps that encourage healthy communication

Figure 16.1 *Examples of a healthy digital lifestyle*

On the other hand, digital treats represent the more enjoyable, but less productive, online activities that provide instant gratification—activities that should be consumed in moderation. Digital treats can be a great way to relax or reward yourself after completing other tasks. They may also provide an opportunity for social connection or to explore fun and creativity through games, apps or other online platforms. While these activities can be fun and entertaining, or even nurture creativity and problem-solving skills when balanced properly, excessive consumption can lead to overstimulation, difficulty focusing and less time spent on productive tasks.

It's important to be clear about what kinds of content are acceptable for your child to access. Give clear explanations for why some types of shows, games or apps are not acceptable. You can do this by:

> *Creating a list* of age-appropriate apps, games, websites or platforms that promote learning or creativity, such as educational apps, creative projects (like video editing) or virtual museum tours. Remember: even sites made 'for kids' can include unsuitable content, so it's best to look at them together, talk about what they're seeing and keep communication open about anything that feels off.

> *Using digital treats sparingly.* If your child has spent time pursuing their hobbies and interests, connecting with family and friends in person, completed their agreed chores and homework and it's not within 90 minutes of bedtime, they could spend a short amount of time watching a favourite show or using an appropriate online game. You want them to spend their time doing all the things that have a positive effect on their life and not allow screen time to push those things out.

> *Encouraging active participation when engaging in digital treats;* for example, if they're watching a video, watch with them, ask them questions about it or encourage them to share their favourite part with the family. If they want to play an online game, play with them or have them play with a sibling or friend. This helps make digital treat time more enriching.

By mapping what a healthy balance looks like between digital veggies and treats, we can help our children (and ourselves!) establish better digital habits and a more balanced lifestyle overall.

Re-enter the 'real world'

Setting boundaries around screen use for the whole family is important to improve our relationship with technology and with each other. It also helps better differentiate between digital and real-world activities—a distinction that has become more blurred as digital devices become more and more embedded in our everyday lives.

It can help to create tech-free zones and times by:

> As mentioned on page 309, designate certain areas of the home as 'screen-free zones', such as the dinner table or bedrooms, to encourage all family members to be present with one another and reduce the temptation to use screens excessively.
> Schedule daily or weekly times when the family engages in non-digital activities, such as walks, cooking together or playing games. Use this time to create space for family bonding, conversation or activities not involving screens.
> When possible, take a family trip focusing on exploration and bonding without the distractions of screens. These experiences help reinforce the value of real-life interactions and experiences.
> Replace online activities with offline activities, such as outdoor play, reading and face-to-face interaction, to help children manage their energy, improve their attention and regulate their emotions.
> Make time for outdoor play, sports or even simple activities like walking, biking or stretching. As we discussed in Chapter 10, physical activity can help to reduce the restlessness caused by excessive screen use, alongside overall brain health and emotional regulation.
> Support their social connections by encouraging offline interactions and social events with peers where screens are not involved, like a day at the beach or park or visiting a museum or theme park. Explain that while socialising online can feel easy, face-to-face interaction builds stronger social and emotional skills.

Build flexibility and adaptability into the routine

While structure is essential, children with ADHD also benefit from some flexibility. There will be days when things don't go according to plan, and that's okay. Allowing some room for adaptability will help your child feel more in control and less resistant to the boundaries you set.

Make exceptions when appropriate. Allow occasional flexibility for special events, like family movie nights or a new video game they're excited to try. Use these moments as rewards for meeting offline goals (e.g., finishing a homework assignment, being active).

For children with ADHD, the key to managing screen time effectively lies in creating structure without rigidity. By setting clear boundaries, promoting quality content, balancing screen and offline activities, and modelling healthy habits, you help your child build a more balanced relationship with technology. These habits will not only improve their ability to focus and regulate their emotions, but also provide them with the skills they need to thrive in an increasingly digital world.

As your children grow and technology continues to evolve, it's important to review the family agreement periodically to ensure it remains relevant.

> ➤ Revisit the rules (see page 307): After a few weeks or months, have a family meeting to discuss how the agreement is working. Make any necessary adjustments based on changes in your child's needs, technology trends or family dynamics.
> ➤ Adapt for teens: As children get older, adjust the rules to give them more independence while ensuring boundaries are maintained.

Be a role model

Switching off from your digital devices is so important so you can recharge and reconnect with one another and the world around you—and it's not just for your child, but for you too. Studies show that parental smartphone use is linked to reduced responsiveness to children's bids for attention, feelings of anger and sadness in children during interactions where parents are on their phones, and lower emotional intelligence in children who receive less meaningful interactions.[10]

As the primary role model in your child's life, you play a crucial part in shaping how your child interacts with technology.[11] Children with ADHD, in particular, can be highly influenced by the behaviours they observe, as they often struggle with impulse control and self-regulation. This makes it even more important for you to set positive examples when it comes to managing digital habits.

Modelling healthy technology use isn't just about limiting screen time, it's about demonstrating intentional, mindful and balanced digital engagement. Try these strategies:

> Communicate openly with your child about your own technology use and how you're managing it. Share the benefits of balance and setting limits.
> Set an example by being mindful of your own technology habits. Use your devices intentionally and adhere to the family contract; for example, by avoiding screen use during family time and setting screen time limits for yourself.
> When using technology, explain your thought process to your child; for example, 'I'm using my phone to check my email for work, and then I'll put it down so I can focus on our game.'
> Make a conscious effort to engage in real-world conversations without distractions. Put your phone away during family time to show relationships come before screens.
> If you're out for a family dinner or other situation where screens are likely to be reached for, discuss with your child non-screen alternatives to bring along (e.g. card game, colouring, travel games).
> Share activities that don't involve screens, whether it's cooking, reading, hiking or playing a board game. Show your child that fun and connection can happen offline too.
> Show your child that technology can be used for good by creating tech-related goals, such as learning a new skill or completing an online course.

By modelling intentional, mindful digital habits, you're teaching your child how to engage with technology in a healthy, balanced way. You're not just setting rules, you're offering your child a blueprint for how to use screens responsibly so they can enjoy all the benefits that technology has to offer, while maintaining their focus, relationships and wellbeing.

Creating a family contract is about fostering a healthy relationship with technology, one that supports learning, connection and personal growth. By working together, setting clear boundaries and modelling positive habits, you'll help your child develop healthier digital habits that last.

Managing potential screen addiction

Addiction can feel like a strong word, especially when used in the context of children, but when we use screens, the same brain chemistry is at play as in other forms of addiction. In particular, dopamine plays a major role as one of our feel-good neurotransmitters. We engage in a behaviour or ingest a substance that raises our dopamine levels, and it makes us feel good. We like it and we want more of it.

We may then chase that experience for that feel-good factor and that's how addiction pathways arise. We're not addicted to playing, we're addicted to the rewards. This effect is, again, strengthened when rewards are random or unpredictable, in which case, we're not even hooked on the reward itself, but the anticipation of it.[12] A notification or a high score in a video game is an intermittent reward that we're constantly anticipating, keeping us in a habitual loop.

Can we blame ourselves (or our children) for constantly checking our phones, using social media or playing games? The truth is, the digital world is designed to be addictive. Most of the apps have been designed purposely to grab our attention and keep us there for as long as possible. Tristan Harris, former design ethicist at Google,[13] outlined the ways in which 'big tech' companies have embedded features in their products specifically designed to spike our dopamine and keep us scrolling, and making them money with every swipe.

Children are often experiencing dopamine spikes through screen use that exceed what is healthy for their still-developing brains.[14] This can cause overstimulation and dysregulation both in the short and long-term as their brains need more and more dopamine to reach the same level of reward. This is particularly true for people with ADHD who struggle to produce and regulate dopamine on their own, and often engage in more dopamine-seeking behaviours than their neurotypical peers.

The more stimulating the experiences your child has, the more they become stimulation dependent (in the same way someone may become drug-dependent), and the more a non-stimulated state seems boring by comparison. Imagine your young person has their adrenaline and dopamine surging from playing a few hours of an immersive video game and then imagine how boring it feels, in comparison, to have to sit in a classroom, do their homework or even talk to people in person.

So, what do you do if you suspect screen use is an issue for your child?

Spot the signs

Signs your child is unable to control their screen use and may be experiencing elements of screen addiction include:

> excessive amount of time spent online and difficulties controlling their screen time independently or adhering to agreed screen time limits
> loss of interest in, or enjoyment of, offline activities they previously found pleasurable (e.g., sport, dating, family time)
> neglecting offline activities that are part of daily living (e.g., personal hygiene, schoolwork, physical interactions with friends and family)
> sleep deprivation/sleep problems
> feeling wired but tired
> increased aggression or emotional distress (in general/when screen time ends).

So many parents in my courses and online community describe highly distressing scenes related to screen addiction with children as young as seven threatening to harm themselves when their gaming devices are removed, or highly charged family conflict when attempting to enforce screen time limits. It's heartbreaking to see your child in pain and distress.

Empathise and be curious

Again, bring it back to the calm, compassionate, connected parenting philosophy. Many of us may think, 'Why are they so emotional about this? It's just a game.' It's important to understand that your child is battling against the pull of digital tools and platforms designed to keep them engaged, and they're experiencing powerful chemical reactions in their brain, making it hard for them to simply switch off.

With this in mind, consider what else might be going on in their lives that powers their unhealthy relationship with technology.

> Are they finding it hard to make friends?
> Are they still developing their social skills?
> Do they need permission to stop using their screens?
> Are they feeling disempowered?
> Do they feel unsure about their strengths or interests?
> Do they need to find some meaning in their lives: a sense of purpose or passion?
> Are they still developing a sense of who they are?

We all use the online world as a means of escape. It's what's going on emotionally for people that makes them susceptible to addiction. Help your young person understand what motivates their screen use and which aspects are most compelling for them, or seek the help of a mental health professional to help you do this.

Help them understand their relationship with technology

It's important to help your child understand their own emotional responses to screen time, such as becoming anxious, irritable or restless, before they reach a heightened state.

Talk to them about how screens make them feel: 'Do you feel calm or overstimulated after playing that game?' Practice relaxation techniques after screen time, such as deep breathing or mindfulness exercises, to help your child transition smoothly to other activities.

Chapter 11 outlines a range of techniques to support emotional and nervous system regulation in your child. Experiment with these and find ones that are helpful in the context of screen use.

Seek professional help

It's important to recognise screen addiction can be a real and serious condition that may require support from a trained professional. Specialised therapy can help your child build a healthier relationship with technology and address any underlying emotional needs or stressors contributing to excessive use.

Teaching digital citizenship

In an ever-more online world, conversations with your child about safe and responsible behaviour in their digital world are critical. For children with ADHD who may have more emotional or impulsive responses, or struggle with understanding boundaries both online and offline, it's even more important to intentionally shape a healthy relationship with technology.

Teaching your child to be a good digital citizen means ensuring they understand online interactions require them to behave with the same respect, empathy and kindness they would offline, in the 'real world'.[15] It requires us to build their capability to contribute to the online world through competent and positive engagement with digital technologies that allow them to learn, create and engage.[16] It also involves clear conversations about how to protect their privacy and ensure the safety of themselves and others.

What does this mean in practice?
Key principles of good digital citizenship include[17]:

> ➤ acting with empathy, respect and kindness in every interaction, both on and offline
> ➤ appreciating cultural differences and respecting diverse perspectives

- engaging thoughtfully when disagreeing, and avoiding name-calling or personal attacks
- telling someone when they feel unsafe, and standing up for others who may be the target of unsafe or disrespectful online behaviour (including reporting it, when needed)
- not posting or sharing content that poses a threat to their safety or others'
- being aware of their feelings and how they're influencing how they're interacting online.

Talking about digital citizenship

Conversations about digital citizenship are important for all children. For children with ADHD, it can be more challenging to explain these abstract concepts in a way they will absorb and take seriously, especially when they're struggling with impulse control and dysregulation.

Communicating key messages in a clear, engaging and relatable way can help understanding. Here's how to make these important conversations stick:

Keep it simple

Children with ADHD often struggle with abstract language and long lectures, so instead of vague warnings like 'Be careful online', offer clear, specific examples they can understand and relate to, such as:

- 'Don't share your full name, school or address online. Pretend you're protecting your secret superhero identity.'
- 'If a message makes you feel weird or upset, always tell me.'

Use short, direct sentences and repeat key messages often — repetition helps information stick.

Make it relevant and personal

Children with ADHD are more likely to pay attention when something feels directly relevant to their lives. Link your conversation to real-life situations they care about; for example:

➤ 'Imagine someone in your game group starts being rude or pressuring you. What could you do?'
➤ 'What would you want your friends to do if someone was being mean in a group chat?'

Use examples from their favourite games, platforms or social media apps to make the conversation feel real, not hypothetical.

Use analogies, metaphors and stories

ADHD brains love stories and visuals. Use metaphors like:

➤ 'The internet is like a big city: some parts are amazing, others are dangerous, and you need to stick to safe streets.'
➤ 'Think of your personal information like your toothbrush — you wouldn't share that, so don't share passwords either.'

Use role-play and interactive learning

Don't just talk — act it out. Role-playing is a powerful ADHD-friendly tool for teaching digital skills:

➤ Practice how to respond if someone is being mean online.
➤ Show your child what to do if they get a suspicious message or link.
➤ Try giving and receiving digital compliments respectfully.
➤ Practise how to leave a group chat politely or block/ report someone.

The more they practice, the more confident and prepared they'll feel in real digital situations.

(continued)

Teach digital responsibility in real-time

Instead of formal 'sit-down talks', use teachable moments as they arise. When your child is using a device:

> ➤ Ask questions like, 'What comments would be kind in this game chat?'
> ➤ If you overhear something online, say, 'How do you think that message made the other person feel?'
> ➤ Praise good digital citizenship in the moment: 'You handled that so respectfully. Great job!'

This helps your child connect learning to action in real life, when it matters most.

Talk about privacy

Describe online privacy as a safety shield that protects them from harm:

> ➤ 'Would you give your house keys to a stranger? Then don't share your passwords.'
> ➤ 'If you wouldn't say it on a loudspeaker at school, don't post it online.'

Teach them to ask:

> ➤ Who will see this?
> ➤ Is it kind?
> ➤ Could it be misunderstood?
> ➤ Would I be okay if a teacher or grandparent saw it?

Simple checklists like this build internal filters that children can use before they post or share.

Empower, don't scare

Fear-based messages can overwhelm or shut children down. Focus on empowerment over fear:

➤ 'You have the power to make good choices online.'
➤ 'If something goes wrong, we'll work through it together.'
➤ 'Mistakes happen. What matters most is learning from them.'

Let them know you're on their team — not just monitoring, but mentoring.

Teaching online safety and digital responsibility to your child isn't about a one-time lecture, it's an ongoing conversation. The more practical, relatable and empowering you make the message, the more likely it is to stick. Your calm guidance and real-time coaching will help your child grow into a confident, respectful and responsible digital citizen, one click at a time.

Help your child navigate the digital world safely

A myriad of online resources exist to provide further information on staying safe online. Here is a list of practical tools and resources to help equip your family to thrive in today's complex digital landscape.

Australian eSafety Commission

The Australian Government–funded eSafety Commission (safety.gov.au) provides a range of information, resources and tools for parents, children and young people to promote safety and responsible conduct online. This includes tailored resources for culturally diverse groups, priority cohorts and translated resources. 🌐

Digital parenting programs

The ADHD Support Australia (adhdsupportaustralia.com.au) online Digital Parenting Program seeks to provide a comprehensive deep-dive into the topics outlined in this chapter, alongside a library of digital resources, coaching and community. ⊕

Parental control and monitoring tools

As mentioned on page 310, tools enabling parents to monitor and control what content their children can access to ensure it's safe and age-appropriate exist. They can also help implement agreed screen time limits and boundaries.

Some examples include Circle Home Plus, Bark and Qustudio. You don't have to navigate the digital world alone. With the right combination of tools, programs and support, you can help your child build healthy digital habits, navigate online spaces safely, and thrive both on and offline. Your calm leadership and the right resources will help your child feel empowered, not overwhelmed by technology.

Chapter Seventeen

Raising capable children: Supporting transitions and independence

Guide gently, support often, and watch your child grow into themselves.

Throughout your child's life they'll face a number of major transitions: new school years, starting high school, moving into post–high school education and eventually into the adult world. These transitions can be tricky for most children, but those with ADHD may find them especially overwhelming due to their challenges with executive function, emotional regulation and adapting to new expectations.

Every major life transition tends to amplify ADHD symptoms due to an increase in executive functioning demands. Whatever the transition, stronger skills in planning, organisation, time management and emotional regulation are required. For children with ADHD these skills are still developing. Often two to three years behind their neurotypical peers socially and emotionally, when the environment places sudden new expectations on them, their ADHD-related challenges can feel more intense and overwhelming. Understanding these times can cause symptom flare-ups, which are not regressions but predictable responses to increased demands, helps you respond to your child with empathy, patience and an appropriate level of support.

The new school year

A new school year introduces new and unfamiliar teachers, changing routines, increased academic expectations and new peers. These shifts can feel disorienting for many children, but your child will require more support and guidance in order for it to go smoothly. See Chapter 14 for more on school support.

Coach-approach strategies:

> *Collaborate:* Work with your child to reflect on which accommodations or routines have worked successfully in previous years. Use open-ended questions such as 'What do you think helped you stay focused last year?' or 'What helpful changes could we make to your study space for this year?'
> *Co-create goals:* Rather than setting goals *for* your child, co-create goals *with* your child; for example, 'What's one thing you want to feel proud of this term?' helps your child decide what's important to them so they can take ownership.
> *Scaffold routine building:* Before school starts, talk to your child about any changes in routine that may happen to help them gradually make that shift. This might include guiding them in setting alarms or organising their school bag, then gradually stepping back and letting them take over these tasks.
> *Coach social confidence:* If your child struggles with social interactions, spend time role-playing common scenarios and helping them come up with possible strategies. Give them opportunities to practise their social skills in real life by enrolling them in activities based on their interests or through playdates or get-togethers. For more social skills strategies see Chapter 15.

High school

Starting high school is a significant developmental leap for your child. Expect:

> - a much larger environment
> - different subject teachers
> - increased commuting by themselves
> - new peers/older students
> - increased academic demands
> - more organisation (e.g., new timetables, navigating different classrooms, assignment due dates).

The level of executive functioning required is a massive step up from their previous school experience. Now is the perfect time for your parent-coach skills to come into their own, and for you to guide your teen to increase their independence and encourage them to become their own advocate.

Coach-approach strategies:

> - *Let them organise themselves:* Empower your teen by guiding them to create their own system for managing homework and activities. Don't tell them what to do; let them work out what works for them. Offer them tools but let them decide which ones they want to use. Try: 'How do you want to keep track of assignments this year?'
> - *Foster self-advocacy:* In high school, your teen will need to effectively communicate their needs to teachers. It's best if you begin guiding them in this practice in smaller ways while they're still at primary school for a more gradual shift. Help them feel more confident about handling these conversations independently by role-playing scenarios with them at home.
> - *Support interests:* Encourage your teen to take part in extracurricular programs aligned with their interests and that assist their skill development, including social skills. Doing an activity because they love it is important, they don't necessarily have to be good at it. Identify what lights them up and support them to find suitable activities. Praise their efforts in trying something new, even if it doesn't go perfectly.

> *Transfer responsibility gradually:* Don't wait until they hit Year 12 to start coaching their independence. Start as soon as possible. Let them take the lead on managing their assessment due dates, catching up on work or checking their emails, with you available as a sounding board, coach and guide.

Post-secondary education

The move into the adult world of university, college or TAFE requires an enormous increase in your young person's level of self-reliance. There's no one to constantly chase them up for missed assignments, classes or turning up on time. The stakes are higher now — they won't be getting detention, but the consequences might be getting kicked out of, or failing, their course.

It's both an exciting and daunting time for any young person, and one where your coach approach is needed more than ever. Just because they've turned 18, doesn't mean they're quite ready to be fully independent. Keep in mind your young person with ADHD is up to two to three years behind socially and emotionally, so may not be quite ready to be fully independent yet. However, by guiding them to build their real-world life and executive function skills gradually, they will confidently move through this stage of their life and eventually be able to navigate this phase independently.

Coach-approach strategies:

> *Guide research:* Guide your young person to research accommodations and support options offered by universities or training institutions. Have them make calls or send emails themselves, with you supporting them in the background.
> *Gradually strengthen executive functioning:* Continue to build your young person's skills in planning, prioritising and following through by chunking tasks and setting regular check-ins. Gradually reduce how often you check in, allowing them to build trust in their own systems.
> *Teach life skills collaboratively:* Your young person needs to build important life skills such as financial literacy, budgeting, meal planning, managing appointments and so on. These skills are

all coachable. Work together to upskill them; for example: 'Let's create a budget. How much do you think you'll need each week?'

> *Promote healthy habits:* As adulthood approaches, your child will benefit from understanding how lifestyle choices can support their physical health, mental wellbeing, and ADHD-related challenges. Instead of prescribing self-care routines, encourage curiosity. Remind them by asking, 'What helps you feel more focused?' or 'What's one thing you could do this week to recharge?'

Driving and increased independence

Having a teen who is ready to learn to drive is a significant and often nerve-wracking transition for parents and teens. Learning to drive and gaining the freedom to go out independently is a milestone which can bring both excitement and a level of increased risk. For young people with ADHD, their challenges with attention, impulsivity and executive function can impact driving safety and decision-making.

Coach-approach strategies:

> *Set boundaries:* Scaffold the *learning to drive process* with clear limits and agreements, such as only driving with a supervising adult at first, avoiding night-time driving or not driving with friends in the car until they gain more experience. Collaborative planning might include agreeing on how many supervised practice hours they'll complete each week or setting rules around phone use in the car.
> *Have open, non-judgemental conversations*: Discuss safety, responsibilities and expectations with your young person (e.g., speeding, texting while driving).
> *Role-play scenarios:* Role-play what your young person will do if they get lost, feel overwhelmed or unsafe, or face peer pressure.
> *Reflect on their readiness:* Encourage them to reflect on how they'll maintain their boundaries with strategies like setting timers for return times or using checklists before leaving the house.

Gradually, with your support in the background, they can build the skills — and the confidence — to navigate the world more independently and responsibly.

Entering the workforce

When your young person transitions into the workforce, this calls for a major mindset shift. You'll now have to step right back and trust in what you've taught them and their ability to go it alone. However, as a young adult with ADHD, they will still need your support sometimes, so aim to become a steady presence in the background, offering guidance when needed.

Coach-approach strategies:

> *Career coaching:* Explore career paths with your young adult, but let them take the lead. Ask questions, such as: 'What kinds of work give you energy?' or 'Who could you talk to for more information about that job?'
> *Build life confidence:* Instead of always trying to solve your young person's problems, ask questions like: 'What's worked in the past?' or 'What could you try next time?' Encourage them to reflect on and learn how to make their own decisions.
> *Encourage ongoing ADHD management:* Your young adult may be utilising therapy, ADHD coaching or medication. Guide them to reflect on what works well for them and when they require additional support, but respect their ownership of the process so they choose their own path.
> *Celebrate progress:* Always acknowledge your young person's growth, including small wins. This helps build their confidence and ability to make independent decisions.

Emotional support

These transitions are likely to trigger some degree of anxiety, self-doubt or emotional overload in your child. Acknowledge your young person's emotions as valid, while gently guiding them to navigate these with growing independence.

Coach-approach strategies:

- ➤ *Listen first:* Resist the temptation to rush in and solve their problems. Step back and act as a calm sounding board, reflecting their feelings back to them: 'It sounds like you're feeling overwhelmed about starting university. Want to talk through what's on your mind?'
- ➤ *Normalise and model resilience:* Sharing stories about your own transition challenges can help your young person know it's normal and okay to struggle, and that transitions to the next stage of life often feel messy.
- ➤ *Co-create coping strategies:* Collaborating with your child to co-create calming strategies was explored in Chapter 11, so your child may already be competent at creating a plan for when they feel anxious or dysregulated, but ask: 'What helps when you're feeling anxious?' Let them decide what works best for them.
- ➤ *Be their cheer squad:* Reminding your young person of their past wins and efforts reassures them that they've got this. Your consistent belief in them helps shape their belief in themselves for the future.

Coach-approach parenting means growing with your child, scaffolding their skills when and where needed, but always with the goal of stepping back so they can take over and become independent. Every transition your child makes is a chance for them to learn, grow and build independent life skills and a confident life.

By coaching instead of controlling, guiding rather than directing, you'll empower your child to step into their future with resilience, self-awareness and confidence.

Part V

Empowering the whole family to thrive

Strong families aren't perfect—they're connected, compassionate and committed to growing together, one imperfect step at a time.

Raising your neurodivergent child calls for more than just strategies, it calls for a strong, connected family foundation. In this final part, we focus on the relationships holding it all together, the culture you co-create within your home, sibling bonds and the 'village' you build around you. Let's explore how to build resilience as a family, nurture harmony among siblings and find the support you need to feel seen, understood and empowered. By grounding these processes in the 6Cs of Connection, Compassion, Curiosity, Calm, Collaboration, and Consistency, it reminds you that thriving isn't just about your child, it's about the wellbeing of the whole family. When families grow together with intention and heart, they can weather any storm—and rise stronger for it.

Chapter Eighteen

Connection dynamics: Building a resilient family together

A resilient family bends without breaking, holds
space for each other's differences, and keeps moving
forward with love—even when it's messy.

Much of what we've explored so far has centred around your relationship
with your child: how to understand their unique needs, support their
development and parent with calm and compassion. In Part II you learned
how you can shape your child's experience of the world and influence
their development.

Family life is rarely experienced in isolated relationships. It's dynamic,
layered and full of moving parts, with each family member's emotions,
needs and responses impacting the whole family. Your family works
as a connected unit: what affects one person affects every person, just
not always in exactly the same way. This idea, known as family systems
theory, helps you understand how neurodivergence shapes your family
dynamics, and vice versa. ADHD is one of many individual different,

but interconnected, experiences, identities and behaviours contributing to overall family relationships and functioning.

You've explored how to show up with calm and compassion for your child, it's now time to zoom out and ask: *What family am I trying to create?* This is where the 6Cs become more than parenting tools, they become your shared compass.

When your whole family has a sense of who you are together — your values, your strengths and what matters most — you give your children a powerful sense of belonging and emotional safety that enhances your connection. It also provides you with more clarity and consistency to lean on when things get hard.

Some questions to ponder (or note down in your parenting journal):

➤ What do we want our family to *feel* like?

➤ What qualities do we want to stand for, even in tough moments?

➤ How do we want to treat each other?

Creating a shared family culture through connection

Building a strong sense of family connection starts with recognising and celebrating the diversity of the individuals within it, alongside establishing shared family values and a culture everyone understands and contributes to.

All families have a unique culture, even if it's never spoken about explicitly. It shows up in the:

➤ way you handle stress
➤ tone of your daily conversations
➤ expectations in your home
➤ way conflict is resolved.

The question isn't *whether* you have a family culture, but whether it's happening by default or by design.

Shared values

Shared values help families anchor themselves in something bigger than individual behaviour. What matters most to you as a family? Is it kindness? Respect? Growth? Courage? Humour?

Sit down as a family (or with your partner, if your child is young) and list four to six values in your parenting journal that you want your family to live by. You might find your answers reflect the 6Cs and sound like:

➤ 'We stay calm when we can.'
➤ 'We speak with compassion.'
➤ 'We work together to solve problems.'
➤ 'We're curious about what's going on beneath the behaviour.'

These become your 'compass' for decision-making and conflict resolution. When things get tough, ask: 'Does this choice support our values?' When everything feels chaotic, values can ground you.

They also help create a shared language siblings can use to support one another, or that your neurodivergent children can use when they feel misunderstood. For example, a family value like 'We all get to take space when we need it' normalises the need to take time to regulate without shame and helps all members of the family set boundaries.

Keeping your family values front and centre

Help your family keep these values front of mind by making them visible in your home and embedding them in your routines and rituals by:

➤ turning it into a fun, collaborative activity by creating a family values poster, a 'team [last name] manifesto', or a short phrase capturing your family's purpose, such as: 'In our family, we try our best, repair when it's messy and love each other'

(continued)

> choosing one value to focus on each week in family meetings

> asking daily/weekly reflection questions like, 'Which C helped us the most today?' or 'Which C felt hardest this week and what could help?'

By weaving the 6Cs into everyday life, you're not just raising emotionally aware children, you're creating a home where *everyone* has room to grow.

Building connection 🙌

Strong family connections aren't built through big holidays or perfect parenting, they're built in the small, everyday moments. Creating consistent, reliable connection points anchors everyone and strengthens relationships over time, especially in families where ADHD may be in the mix and things often feel chaotic and unpredictable. I discussed these ideas on page 106, but to give you a clear idea in *this* chapter, here are a few simple, meaningful ways to build connection with your *whole* family.

Family rituals

Rituals give your child a sense of predictability and belonging. They don't have to be fancy; the key is consistency and togetherness. For example:

> Pancake Sundays or Taco Tuesdays
> tidying up together music
> family motto
> special greetings
> goodnight routines
> weekly 'family meeting' over snacks where everyone shares what went well that week, any challenges they faced, goals for the week ahead or something they're grateful for
> regular walks after dinner (no phones)
> weekly family movie nights.

Little traditions create shared memories and emotional safety, which is especially important when the rest of life feels overwhelming.

One-on-one time

It's important to create one-on-one time for each of your children, even ten minutes a day of your undivided attention can make a huge difference. It doesn't have to be 'quality' time, just *your* time. One-on-one time could look like:

> - letting your child choose how to spend the time (even if it's watching them build Lego or draw)
> - sitting on their bed at night and asking one open-ended question ('What made you laugh today?')
> - going for a drive or walk—no agenda
> - using 'micro-moments' like waiting in line or walking to school to connect.

You'll often find your child will talk most when you're *not* directly asking questions, just being present and available.

Playfulness

Humour and silliness disarm power struggles and help everyone regulate. You don't need to be a clown, just loosen the tension, such as:

> - using a funny accent when giving boring instructions
> - racing to see who can tidy up fastest
> - adding a goofy 'dance break' to get through transitions
> - making up silly nicknames
> - turning chores into games ('Who can match the most socks in two minutes?').

Using humour in your daily life enables everyone to take life a little less seriously. Having a laugh every now and then reduces stress, while deepening your connections.

Resolving conflict

You're human, and it's inevitable you'll lose your temper sometimes—that's okay—the important thing is what you do next.

> ➤ Own your behaviour without blaming theirs: 'I got frustrated and shouted. That's not how I should have handled things.'
> ➤ Model how to apologise: 'I'm sorry I snapped. Can we talk about what happened?'
> ➤ Offer a reconnection ritual: a hug, a code word or just sitting beside them.
> ➤ Ask how they felt and listen without defensiveness.
> ➤ Explain what you'll do differently: 'I'll try to keep calmer in future'.

Whenever you successfully resolve conflicts, it's an opportunity to model emotional maturity and growth, which not only rebuilds trust, but teaches them how to resolve conflicts not just within the family, but in the wider world.

Celebrating differences

Your default position may be to focus on what's going wrong or what's not working. Try flipping your position to notice more of the positives, naming and celebrating each family member's strengths. You'll find everyone's self-esteem, confidence and trust grows when you do. This could be as simple as statements like:

> ➤ 'I saw how hard you worked to focus today even though I know it's tricky for you.'
> ➤ 'You showed real courage by asking for help.'
> ➤ 'I'm proud of how I kept my cool even when things went sideways.'
> ➤ 'Thank you for taking your plates to the kitchen.'

Organise a visual reminder of how much you're all growing and developing by keeping a family wins jar or board to catch and celebrate those moments. Keep it somewhere visible, encouraging everyone to contribute and make it part of your daily life, perhaps making a weekly family ritual to review and celebrate the wins. See Table 18.1 for examples.

Table 18.1 *Examples for a family win board*

Family members	Behaviours that could be celebrated
Children (all)	Stayed at the table for the whole meal.
	Used words instead of shouting when frustrated.
	Got ready for school without reminders.
	Tried again after getting upset; didn't give up.
	Helped a sibling without being asked.
	Used their strategy to stay calm during homework.
	Remembered to pack their bag!
	Did something kind for a friend.
	Told the truth, even when it was hard.
	Let their sibling have a turn without fighting.
	Used kind words during a disagreement.
	Showed patience during a meltdown.
	Gave space when needed.
Parents	Stayed calm during a tough meltdown.
	Took a break instead of yelling.
	Made space for one-on-one time.
	Apologised and repaired after a rough moment.
	Asked for help instead of powering through.
	Said 'yes' to self-care.
	Responded with compassion instead of correction.
	Let go of perfection and embrace 'good enough'.
Other family members (e.g., grandparents, partners)	Backed up the parenting plan with love.
	Showed up to support even when it was hard.
	Offered help in a calm and non-judgemental way.
	Made time for connection with the children.

Leading with compassion ♥

If connection is the heart of your family, compassion is what keeps it beating. Compassion helps you show up with kindness when things are challenging, choose understanding instead of blame, and remind each other that perfection is not a prerequisite for being loved.

We've discussed showing compassion for your child to strengthen your relationship and avoid constant correction and redirection. When this compassion is extended to your whole family — yourself included — you create a consistent safe family culture where people can mess up and try again.

Compassion teaches your children to show grace and compassion for others: their siblings, parents/carers and other relationships in their life. The more your children see compassion in action (toward them, toward others and toward yourself), the more they internalise it — and that becomes part of who they are.

Start normalising compassionate communication at home using strategies like:

➤ scripts for apologies emphasising responsibility and connection
➤ sharing stories where characters repair after mistakes
➤ celebrating acts of kindness and repair in family meetings
➤ modelling forgiving yourself out loud.

Compassion isn't just for your children, it's something we all need, especially when things go wrong. When your partner, co-parent or another caregiver snaps, forgets something important or handles situations differently than you would, it's easy to slip into blame or frustration. But just like our children, the adults in our lives are also navigating stress, exhaustion and sometimes their own unhealed patterns. Extending compassion in these moments doesn't mean excusing unhelpful behaviour, it means making space for understanding, assuming good intentions and remembering we're all doing the best we can with the tools we have.

Compassion is about creating an environment where everyone feels safe to mess up and come back together. When adults in your child's life show each other grace, they model emotional maturity, teamwork and resilience—that's a powerful example for children to grow up with.

Your family won't always get it right—tempers will flare, feelings will get hurt, you'll say things you regret—but in a compassionate family, these blow ups are followed by smoothing things over again and reconnecting. Making up with each other just needs to be sincere. When practised over time, everyone in your family will know how to make things right again *and* feel secure knowing that when things go wrong, they'll be okay again.

Staying curious as a family ⚲

Curiosity is one of the most underused superpowers in family life. When conflict erupts, when someone's behaviour doesn't make sense or when emotions are running high, your first instinct is often to correct, control or shut it down. But what if, instead of reacting, you paused and asked, 'What's really going on here?'

Curiosity allows you to slow down and seek understanding before jumping to conclusions. This open-minded, compassionate inquiry changes everything by softening defensiveness, reducing blame and helping everyone feel more emotionally safe because they're being *understood*, not just managed.

Curiosity teaches your children (and yourself) to approach challenges not as failures but as opportunities to learn about yourself and each other.

A family mantra could be 'curiosity before reacting' and you could make it a family habit to get curious before reacting to situations. It might feel awkward at first but, over time, it teaches your children that they don't have to have all the answers right away. They can slow down, ask questions and seek to understand before reacting.

This mindset doesn't just help your family, it gives your children a tool they'll use in friendships, partnerships, workplaces and communities for the rest of their lives.

Model curiosity

Model curiosity aloud, especially in emotionally charged situations:

> ➤ 'I wonder if you're feeling overwhelmed right now?'

> ➤ 'This seems really hard. What do you think is making it tricky?'

Remember that while your child is emotionally dysregulated, they're unable to use the logical thinking part of their brain, so there's no point asking them questions or trying to get curious with them. Always assist your child to regulate and *then* ask your curious questions:

> ➤ 'You had such a big reaction. What do you think was going on for you?'

These gentle reflections invite conversation instead of shutting it down. They also teach your child that *all behaviour is communication*, and feelings are something we *explore* rather than punish.

Practise curiosity in everyday moments, not just when things are hard. Get interested in what your child or partner is thinking, what lights them up, how they solve problems and what they find challenging. Curiosity is connection in action.

Curiosity prompts

Introduce reflective questions at dinner, in the car or during family meetings:

> ➤ 'What surprised you today?'
> ➤ 'What's something you've been wondering about lately?'
> ➤ 'What did you notice about someone else's feelings today?'
> ➤ 'What's one thing that was hard today, and why do you think it felt hard?'
> ➤ 'What do you need from the rest of us when you're having a tough time?'

These conversations help your child build emotional intelligence and help your family become more attuned to each other's inner worlds. It reduces reactivity and builds empathy because the more you understand, the less you blame.

Creating a calm family ✿

Calm doesn't have to mean silence, stillness or compliance, it isn't about a quiet house or perfectly behaved children. It's about *nervous system regulation*: yours and theirs. (See Chapter 11 for more on this.)

In a family, nervous systems are *contagious*. If one person is dysregulated, it affects the whole household. Think of it like tuning forks: when one rings loudly, the others pick up the vibration. But the good news is, regulation is contagious too. When one person stays grounded, it helps everyone else feel calmer.

Your nervous system is the most powerful influence in the room. You don't have to be perfectly calm all the time (no one is!), but when you practise returning to calm, you model emotional resilience. When you support your children to do the same, you help them feel safe enough to regulate themselves over time.

Showing compassion when you're regulated is way easier, so building in calming rituals, self-awareness and supportive routines creates the space for compassion to happen. If you're dysregulated, your nervous system is more likely to interpret your child's behaviour as threatening, disrespectful or personal. When you pause (even briefly), you create a window to respond with compassion instead of reactivity.

This is how we begin to create a calm family environment—not by controlling emotions but by learning to ride the waves together.

Create a 'family calm plan'

Instead of expecting everyone to regulate on their own, make calm a *team effort*. Sit down as a family and ask:

> ➤ 'What helps each of us feel calm or safe when we're overwhelmed?'
> ➤ 'What do we notice in each other when things are starting to feel "too much"?'
> ➤ 'What signals can we use to take a break *before* things boil over?'

Come up with a:

> *family 'reset word' or phrase* (e.g., 'Koala time!' or 'Cloud break') that acts as an agreed cue to pause. It can be used for everyone to stop and breathe together or simply to signal that the person who said it needs a break. The key is that the whole family respects its meaning.
> *regulation station* stocked with sensory tools, fidgets, noise-cancelling headphones or calming visuals (see page 118).
> *shared ritual,* like a three-breath pause before meals, a calming playlist everyone loves or five minutes of silent drawing after school.

These small habits help shift the tone of your household over time, telling each person in your family: 'It's okay to feel big feelings here. We know how to come back to calm together.'

You'll inevitably have moments where calm flies out of the window and, when it does, model *compassion* through repair. This emotional honesty doesn't make you look weak, it builds trust. It shows your children that calm isn't about perfection, it's about returning to connection when you've gone off-course.

Collaborating as a family ♟

Moving from *control* to *collaboration*, especially in an ADHD household, is a powerful shift for your family. Instead of solving problems *for* your child or issuing top-down commands, you solve things *with* them. That simple change in approach can transform your family dynamic.

Collaboration is about creating a team culture where everyone's voice matters, solutions are built together and responsibility is shared. It's not about giving in or letting your child run the show but about helping your child feel *part of the process*, not just subject to it.

When your child feels ownership, their cooperation improves, their problem-solving skills grow and they start to feel like they *belong* not just in your home but in the flow of how your family functions. Refer back to Chapter 6 where we looked at involving your child in conversations about what's not working and inviting their participation in finding solutions, rather than issuing rules or consequences.

This goes for the whole family. Use family meetings as a structured way to practice collaboration as a family. They don't need to be long-winded or overly formal, just a check-in space to *reconnect, celebrate, solve* and *plan* together.

Family conflict example

Here is a step-by-step example involving siblings disagreeing over chores, showing how the CPS Model can lead to mutual understanding and a workable solution.

It's not fair!

Twelve-year-old Mia (neurotypical) and ten-year-old Max (diagnosed with ADHD) constantly argue about who does more chores. Mia feels like she always ends up cleaning more, while Max avoids or forgets his tasks and then gets let off the hook. Max feels picked on and overwhelmed by expectations. Tensions are high and fights are frequent.

Step 1: Hear each child's concern

The parent brings both children together and calmly says: 'I've noticed chores have been causing a lot of arguments lately, and I want to hear from both of you what's feeling hard about it, so we can figure out a better way together.'

Mia: 'I always end up cleaning more. Max gets distracted and just walks off, and then I have to finish everything. It's not fair.'

Max: 'I don't mean to! I forget or I get stuck. And then everyone gets mad at me, even when I try.'

The parent reflects both sides with empathy: 'Okay, I hear that Mia feels like she's picking up the slack, and Max feels like it's hard to remember or stay on task, even when he's trying. That must feel frustrating for both of you.'

Step 2: Define the adult concern

Now the parent shares the broader concern without blame, staying solution-focused: 'My concern is I want everyone in the family to feel things are fair and that we're all contributing in a way that works for each of us. I also want to make sure no one feels overwhelmed and we don't end up arguing every day.'

Step 3: Invitation to problem-solve together

Parent: 'I wonder if there's a way for us to divide the chores so that Mia doesn't feel like she's doing everything and Max doesn't feel overwhelmed or forgetful. Do either of you have ideas?'

Mia: 'I just want a list or something where we both have our jobs and it's even.'

Max: 'Can I have reminders? And maybe I get shorter chores or ones I don't hate? Like I can vacuum, but I hate folding clothes. It takes forever and I mess it up.'

Parent helps clarify and co-create a plan: 'That sounds reasonable. What if we write out a chore chart together and choose tasks that feel fair? Max, we can include reminders or a visual checklist and shorter tasks you can complete in chunks. Mia, we can check in weekly to make sure the balance still feels fair to you. And if anyone wants to swap chores, we can talk about it rather than arguing.'

Final plan (collaboratively created)

> Each child chooses their preferred chores from a shared list (some flexibility).
> Max gets visual checklists and breaks tasks into steps (e.g., vacuum one room at a time).
> Mia agrees not to take over Max's chores unless they've talked first.
> Family check-in happens once a week to review the chore split and make changes if needed.
> Parent offers gentle support (body doubling, timers) if Max struggles to get started.

Likely outcomes

> Mia feels heard and that her effort is recognised.
> Max feels supported, not blamed or shamed.
> The family shifts from power struggles to shared problem-solving.
> Siblings gain skills in collaboration, negotiation and empathy.
> Equity replaces equality: each child contributes based on what's fair, not identical.

What this teaches

> ADHD isn't an excuse, it's a difference that requires supportive scaffolding.
> Children are more invested in solutions they help create.
> Equity means each child gets what they need to succeed, not the exact same expectations.

Simple family meeting structure (20 to 30 minutes)

Family meetings don't need to be long or formal to make a difference. A simple, consistent structure helps keep everyone engaged, gives each family member a voice and turns problem-solving into a shared effort rather than a source of conflict. These meetings also bring the 6Cs to life by building _connection_, encouraging _communication_ and fostering _collaboration_ as part of everyday family life.

> Check-in: 'How's everyone feeling today?'
> Celebrations and appreciations: 'What's something someone in the family did this week you appreciated?'
> Challenges and solutions: 'Is there anything tricky we need to talk about?'
> Brainstorm ideas: Let everyone contribute to a solution, even wild ideas!
> Plan week ahead: Do a check of the calendar or visual schedules for upcoming events.
> Connection close: End with a game, a joke or a shared treat.

(continued)

> Over time, these meetings reinforce the idea your family is a team, conflict is normal, solutions come from *everyone* and each person has a valuable role to play.

Finding a family rhythm with consistency 👣

Consistency often gets a bad rap in ADHD households because, let's face it, life with neurodivergent children can feel anything but predictable. But consistency doesn't mean rigid schedules or military-style structure. It means creating *reliable patterns* and *emotional steadiness* that help everyone feel safe, supported and less overwhelmed.

In a family context, consistency is about:

> following through on what you say
> holding boundaries with kindness
> creating rhythms your child can rely on
> building a home environment where expectations are clear and fair.

When children know what to expect (and what's expected of them), it reduces anxiety, emotional reactivity and the need for constant correction. It also helps you feel less reactive and more grounded.

Create predictable rhythms

Once you define who you are as a family, start to build in small rituals and routines that reinforce this ethos. This is where consistency comes in, not as rigid rules, but as *predictable rhythms* that help everyone feel safe and grounded.

Creating consistent, predictable routines and rhythms helps normalise the structure children with ADHD need to thrive. Rather than singling them out with rigid rules or extra 'systems', these daily rhythms offer a shared foundation that benefits everyone. Think of them not as strict schedules, but as scaffolding for your family's nervous system.

Predictable routines reduce uncertainty, support smoother transitions and create a sense of safety, especially for your neurodivergent child who struggles with change or feels dysregulated by the unknown. They don't need to be perfect or timed to the minute. What matters most is consistency and clarity—knowing breakfast always comes after waking, that wind-down time happens after dinner or that a visual checklist is always on the fridge. These gentle patterns help 'hold together' the day and make the invisible support your child needs feel natural, shared and sustainable for the whole family.

The goal isn't to become the 'perfect' Brady Bunch family, it's to create a home where each member of your family knows: 'This is who we are. This is how we come back to each other. This is what we do when things go wrong.'

Because when your family is connected via shared values and safe, predictable and consistent rhythms, everyone in your family has a stronger foundation to grow from.

Keep rules simple, clear and family-wide

Inconsistent rules lead to power struggles and frustration. On the flip side, too many rules become overwhelming, especially for ADHD brains. The sweet spot? A few simple, family-wide rules everyone agrees to and understands.

> ➤ 'We speak respectfully to each other, even when we're upset.'
> ➤ 'We take breaks when our bodies or brains need space.'
> ➤ 'We help clean up after ourselves.'
> ➤ 'We ask before taking someone else's things.'

Post them somewhere visible. Go over them in a family meeting and, most importantly, model them yourself.

Consistency in boundaries, rules and routines

Consistency in boundaries and routines isn't just important for your child with ADHD, it's essential for all family members. When expectations are clear, predictable and applied fairly across the household, it creates a sense of emotional safety for everyone. Children will push against limits (that's part of growing up), but they feel more secure when they know where the edges are, and that those edges don't change depending on the day, mood or who they are.

This doesn't mean treating every child exactly the same. Equity matters more than equality—some children will need more reminders, visual supports or co-regulation to meet those expectations. But the rules and values stay the same, and that's what builds trust.

That might sound like:

> ➤ 'In our family, we speak respectfully to each other, even when we're upset.'
> ➤ 'Everyone gets 30 minutes of outside play after school, then we move on to homework or quiet play.'

Consistency is about being reliable, not harsh or inflexible. It means your child knows what to expect and trusts you'll follow through with calm and compassion, not chaos or punishment.

Sometimes consistency sounds like: 'I know the usual rule is chores before playtime, but you've had a tough day. Let's take a break first, then we'll tackle them together.'

The most effective family boundaries are rooted in kindness, not control. When rules and routines are applied with clarity, empathy and flexibility when needed, they become a steady rhythm the whole family can move to, not a battleground.

Consistency isn't about perfection, it's about showing up in the same way, with the same core values, again and again, so your children (ADHD or not) can count on you and grow within a strong, respectful framework.

You're already doing it

The fact that you're reading this book says you're thinking about how to do better, connect more deeply and create a thriving family environment—that *is* the work. You're already living the 6Cs in so many ways, even if you haven't been calling it that.

There'll be hard, disconnected days, and days when you lose your temper or can't stick to your routines. But your ability to *return*—to repair, reconnect and keep showing up—is what makes your family resilient.

You're not just raising your child with ADHD, you're raising your whole family grounded in empathy, safety and strength—that's something to be incredibly proud of.

So when things feel chaotic, come back to this compass:

> ➤ Connection brings us closer. 👐
> ➤ Calm regulates and anchors. 🪷
> ➤ Curiosity helps us understand. 🔍
> ➤ Collaboration strengthens our team. 🤝
> ➤ Compassion softens the hard moments. ♥
> ➤ Consistency builds trust and safety. 🕊

You won't get it right every time, but you'll keep coming back and trying again—and that's what thriving families do.

Chapter Nineteen

Family relationships: Building positive sibling relationships

> Supporting sibling relationships isn't about
> preventing rivalry, it's about creating connection,
> compassion and a bond that lasts a lifetime.

The relationship between siblings can be one of the strongest, most important and meaningful relationships your child will have, but also often the most challenging. When one or more of your children have ADHD, the dynamics between them can become even more complex and intense. A combination of impulsivity, emotional reactivity and differing support needs often leads to conflict.

If you're raising one or more children with ADHD, you've probably already noticed how much emotional energy and time it takes. It's a lot and, therefore, often leaves less in the tank for their siblings—your quieter child, the 'easy' one, the child who doesn't explode or melt down.

This situation can unintentionally make your other child or children feel overlooked, frustrated or unfairly expected to 'cope' or 'understand', leading to resentment, both towards their sibling and you.

You, therefore, need to actively nurture positive sibling relationships as part of your family resilience building plan. It's possible to foster a family environment where your children learn to understand each other's differences, build empathy and form lifelong strong, supportive bonds. Sibling relationships provide a rich opportunity to teach your children compassion, social-emotional skills and resilience. With the right tools, you can reduce conflict and nurture connections between your children, creating a family culture that values teamwork, empathy and emotional safety.

This chapter is for your neurotypical child as well as for you. Your neurotypical child isn't just a bystander, they're part of your family system and, of course, deserve the same support, love and validation as their neurodivergent sibling.

To build a truly resilient family, you need to see each person in the family clearly and meet their needs in the best way possible. Help sibling relationships thrive by fostering an environment where their connection is grounded in empathy, understanding and mutual respect by implementing a few of the practical strategies discussed here.

Your family as a 'system'

In families where neurodivergence is present, it's common for siblings to unconsciously take on specific roles in relation to one another. We've spoken about how children with ADHD can often be made to feel like the 'problem' child, impacting their self-esteem and emotional wellbeing. They may adapt to these feelings of internalised blame by playing other roles, such as 'the joker' (using humour or entertainment to ease tension) or 'the overachiever' (overcompensating to prove their value within the family).

For neurotypical siblings, they may take on the role of 'the peacemaker', the 'responsible one', or the 'invisible child' whose needs are less important to express in the context of a sibling who may find some things harder than they do or require extra time and attention.

Commonly identified impacts on siblings include:

➤ Parentification. Your neurotypical child often becomes parentified, taking on adult-like responsibilities far beyond their years. This can happen when parents, overwhelmed by the demands of managing ADHD, unintentionally rely on their more regulated child to keep the peace, care for their sibling or suppress their own needs, leading to emotional strain and a loss of their own childhood.

➤ People-pleasing. Siblings of children with ADHD may also become people-pleasers, trying to be the 'good' child to reduce chaos at home or to avoid adding to their parents' stress. Some do this out of a sense of survivor guilt (feeling they must compensate for their sibling's struggles) or to earn love and approval by being low-maintenance.

➤ Seeking connection. Some may go the opposite way, acting out or creating their own crises in an unconscious bid to reclaim attention, recognition or a sense of significance in the family dynamic.

While these coping strategies are understandable, it's critical to avoid casting individual family members in rigid roles. Traditional applications of family systems theory may unfairly cast neurodivergent children as the family member whose behaviour 'causes' tension or needs intervention.

Instead, a neuro-affirming approach encourages parents to create a safe space for each child to develop and express their own unique identity, needs and voice. All children (regardless of diagnoses) have needs and deserve space for emotional expression, identity exploration and autonomy. When your child's unique strengths are affirmed and their identity allowed to evolve over time, siblings can play an active and reciprocal role in each others' wellbeing and in developing their true self.

Let's explore some practical strategies to support a functioning family system.

Acknowledge and validate feelings

By acknowledging the challenges existing in your home, and validating *all* your children's feelings without making them feel any shame for expressing them, your children will feel heard and understood.

Your child with ADHD often has additional support needs that take up more of your time and attention. Don't make the mistake of getting so caught up in them that you pay less attention to your neurotypical child thinking that, because they *can* cope with less attention, they like it. Even if they *understand* it, your neurotypical child may well be feeling overlooked or less important, resentful, pressured to be the 'easy' child or confused or hurt by their sibling's behaviour. They may also feel a certain amount of guilt for having these understandable feelings

It's so important to let them talk about their experiences without judgement, without trying to fix it and without making them responsible for your emotions or their sibling's needs. If your child expresses frustration about their ADHD sibling's behaviour, don't dismiss it or minimise their feelings with 'you should be more understanding' or 'they can't help it'.

Validate their experience and acknowledge their feelings, then gently help them understand their sibling's challenges without forcing them to feel empathy before they're ready. You might try saying:

> 'I see how frustrating this is. Your feelings matter too.'
> 'I know I've been spending a lot of time helping your brother, and that might feel unfair.'
> 'You're allowed to be upset. This is hard for all of us sometimes.'

It's okay to acknowledge that parenting with ADHD can be unpredictable, emotionally exhausting and can shift the balance of attention in a family, and that it can hurt your other children.

Help them understand

One of the best things you can do to reduce frustration and promote compassion between siblings is help neurotypical siblings understand what ADHD is (and isn't) in developmentally appropriate ways. Knowledge empowers siblings to feel less confused about their ADHD sibling's behaviour, and helps them develop patience and empathy. The goal isn't to force empathy, it's to build understanding.

Reading books or stories that help your child understand ADHD is a great strategy to help explain difficult concepts and understanding through perspective-taking.

> Explain behaviours in simple terms yourself by saying something like:
>   - 'His brain works fast. Sometimes that makes it hard for him to wait his turn.'
>   - 'Your sister's brain works a little differently. Sometimes that means she reacts fast or forgets what she's supposed to do.'
>   - 'It's not that he doesn't care, it's that his brain makes some things harder and he's learning, just like you are.'

Have age-appropriate conversations and ask reflective questions to help siblings develop empathy for their sibling, while learning how to handle challenging situations, such as:

> 'How do you think your brother felt when that happened?'
> 'What do you think would've helped in that moment?'
> 'What would you want someone to do if you were in her shoes?'

Set clear family rules and expectations

Consistency and structure benefit everyone, not just children with ADHD. Create simple, family routines and expectations all siblings understand. When each child knows what's expected, and the same rules apply with clear boundaries, sibling conflict tends to decrease.

Let your children voice concerns and come up with shared solutions during family meetings where you establish your rules, routines and boundaries. This is a bit like many children do when they start a new school year and they collaboratively agree on a set of rules that benefit everyone. This will build ownership and cooperation among your children. During your family meeting:

> make kindness and respect non-negotiable
> set ground rules such as no name-calling, hitting or hurtful language
> use visual cue cards or reminders, if needed
> reinforce the concept everyone is responsible for how they treat others, even when big emotions are present.

Be mindful not to let your household structure centre solely around your child with ADHD. Structure should support everyone's wellbeing, including your neurotypical children who also need calm, predictability and emotional space.

Promote equity

Children often measure fairness in terms of equality (i.e., with getting exactly the same), but with ADHD in the mix, equal treatment isn't always possible or even fair since each child needs different kinds of support. Instead, focus on meeting each child's individual needs and regularly pointing out their unique strengths.

Explain often that fairness means giving each person what they need, not treating everyone exactly the same, and everybody's needs are different. Use simple examples, such as: 'Your brother needs reminders to stay on task. You might need help when you're upset. Both are important.'

Avoid labels and comparisons

Celebrate each of your children's unique personalities and strengths and avoid making comparisons or labelling any of your children. Never use language that pits siblings against each other such as:

> ➤ 'Why can't you be more like your sister?'
> ➤ 'He's the quiet one. You're the difficult one.'

These phrases may seem harmless enough or may just 'slip out' in a heated moment, but they will fuel resentment and shape sibling identities in unhelpful ways. Instead, celebrate each child's unique strengths and personality without making anyone the 'easy one' or the 'problem child'.

Teach conflict skills

Sibling rivalry and jealousy are natural parts of family life, but when one child has ADHD, the dynamics can easily become more intense. Your neurotypical child may feel frustrated by the attention their sibling gets or resent the extra support and flexibility they receive. Your child with ADHD, on the other hand, may struggle with rejection sensitivity, impulsivity or feelings of failure compared to their sibling.

Rather than trying to eliminate conflict altogether (which is unrealistic!), your goal is to reduce resentment, create fairness and foster empathy and emotional skills that help your children develop healthy, respectful relationships for life.

When conflict starts, try coaching instead of correcting:

> Help each child name their feelings: 'You felt angry because ...'
> Teach 'I feel' statements: 'I feel left out when ...'
> Model repair: 'What could you do to make things right?'

Your children are always watching you, so model good conflict resolution where you handle your own frustrations with empathy, take responsibility for mistakes and speak respectfully even during conflicts. In this way, you're teaching them how to do the same with each other.

Create connection rituals

Siblings need time to connect not just time to stop fighting. Build in small rituals that foster bonding, such as:

> bedtime compliments ('Say one nice thing about each other')
> sibling 'buddy time' with a shared activity
> weekly family games or joint projects (e.g., baking, puzzles, Lego).

You're helping them build memories that say: 'We're on the same team.'

Encourage teamwork

Use language that reinforces collaboration instead of competition:

> 'We're all on the same team.'
> 'Let's solve this together.'
> 'I love how you helped your sister with that—that's real teamwork!'

Set up opportunities for cooperation by:

> building something together
> cooking a meal together
> working toward a shared goal or challenge.

These moments reinforce connection through shared success.

Help anticipate challenges

Spend time helping your neurotypical child anticipate challenges and role-playing calm responses with them, so you empower them with how to handle what can be challenging situations effectively.

Start conversations with reflective questions such as:

> 'What could you do if your brother interrupts again?'
> 'How might you respond if your sister gets upset at dinner?'

Catch and celebrate the good stuff

Make sure all your children feel seen, valued and appreciated, not just for their achievements, but for who they are. Point out their strengths as often as possible:

> 'You're so thoughtful.'
> 'You have such a creative imagination.'
> 'I love how patient you were today.'

Always be on the lookout for moments of kindness, cooperation or emotional maturity from all your children—and name them out loud.

> 'I saw how you helped your brother when he was upset. You were so kind.'
> 'You gave your sister space when she needed it. You showed real empathy.'

Similarly to the family win board I talked about in Chapter 18, you could also start a 'kindness jar' or sticker chart that visually reinforces your appreciation of these moments.

It's as important for your children to have solid relationships with each other as it is for you to have solid relationships with each of them. The sibling relationship is one that lasts a lifetime and, under usual circumstances, is one that will outlive you or your partner, so it's a relationship that should be nurtured carefully. It doesn't need to be perfect—it can be messy, argumentative and emotional while still being deeply meaningful.

By validating each child's experience, fostering empathy and guiding them through conflict with compassion, you're not just intervening in sibling conflicts, you're raising emotionally intelligent humans who understand how to connect, repair and care for one another—and that's a lifelong gift you can bestow upon them.

Chapter Twenty

Finding your village: Building your ADHD support network

Thriving isn't a solo journey. When you build the right team around you, both you and your child can rise.

They say it takes a village to raise a child—and that's for a *neurotypical* child! These days, many parents don't have the luxury of extended family nearby or a close-knit community. If you do, count yourself lucky to have one or both of those, you've already got a great foundation, and even better if those in your 'village' understand ADHD.

But for many, parenting feels isolating, and raising a neurodivergent child is not something you should have to do alone. ADHD touches every part of your child's life and supporting them requires more than love and patience. It takes knowledge, strategies, resilience and a strong support system.

Your village may include extended family, friends and neighbours, but it also needs to include a trusted team of professionals who understand your child's needs and support *you* along the way.

This chapter is your roadmap to building that village.

Prioritise with the Parenting Hierarchy of Needs

When everything feels urgent, it's hard to know where to begin or what's worth your time, energy and money. Let's be honest: therapies and supports can be costly, so it's essential to focus on what will make the biggest difference first.

That's exactly why I created ADHD Support Australia—to help parents cut through the overwhelm and find the right support at the right time.

The Parenting Hierarchy of Needs framework (introduced in Chapter 4 and shown in Figure 20.1) offers a clear path forward. It starts with your child's most foundational needs and helps you prioritise what comes next. It's not just about understanding your child, it's about knowing when and where to seek help so you can move forward with more clarity and confidence.

Start at the base: Biological stability

At the very base of the Parenting Hierarchy of Needs is biological stability, and this is where your village begins. No parenting strategy will work if your child is overtired, hungry, overwhelmed or physically unwell.

Support at this level might include working with a nutritionist who understands the ADHD-gut connection (Chapter 8), improving sleep hygiene (Chapter 9) or learning how blood sugar affects mood and focus (Chapter 8). It may also mean leaning on your partner or extended family to help with routines (Chapter 7), meals or physical activity (Chapter 10).

You're not failing if you can't do it all alone. You're wise to seek out support to help your child build a strong foundation. These foundations aren't just for your child, they matter just as much for you and the rest of your family too.

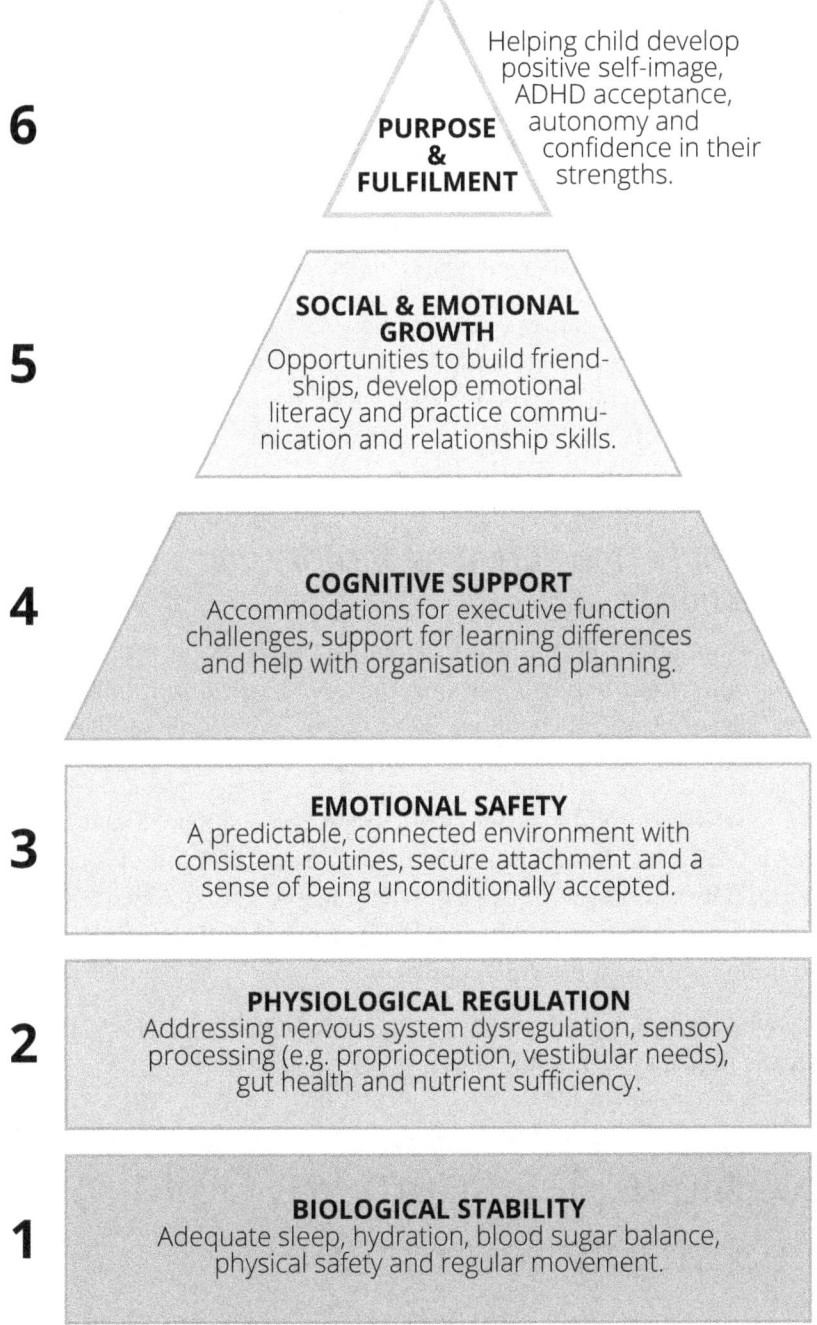

6 PURPOSE & FULFILMENT — Helping child develop positive self-image, ADHD acceptance, autonomy and confidence in their strengths.

5 SOCIAL & EMOTIONAL GROWTH — Opportunities to build friendships, develop emotional literacy and practice communication and relationship skills.

4 COGNITIVE SUPPORT — Accommodations for executive function challenges, support for learning differences and help with organisation and planning.

3 EMOTIONAL SAFETY — A predictable, connected environment with consistent routines, secure attachment and a sense of being unconditionally accepted.

2 PHYSIOLOGICAL REGULATION — Addressing nervous system dysregulation, sensory processing (e.g. proprioception, vestibular needs), gut health and nutrient sufficiency.

1 BIOLOGICAL STABILITY — Adequate sleep, hydration, blood sugar balance, physical safety and regular movement.

Figure 20.1 *The Parenting Hierarchy of Needs*

Physiological regulation: Calming the nervous system 🪷

As you move up the Parenting Hierarchy of Needs, the next focus is physiological regulation: understanding and supporting your child's nervous system (Chapter 11). This is where occupational therapists and integrative practitioners can be key allies, especially if your child experiences sensory challenges, emotional reactivity or gut-related issues.

These professionals can provide practical tools to help your child feel more calm and comfortable in daily life. Don't underestimate the power of connecting with others who've walked a similar path. ADHD-informed educators, parent support groups and fellow parents can offer both empathy and valuable lived experience.

Emotional safety: Creating security and connection 🙌

At the emotional safety level, the focus is on creating a predictable, connected environment with secure attachment, consistent routines and a deep sense of being unconditionally accepted. As explored in Chapter 11, your child needs to feel safe, loved and valued for who they are.

This is where calm, compassionate parenting (Chapter 5), along with clear routines and boundaries (Chapter 6), truly come into play. You'll find guidance throughout this book, and also through ADHD-specific parenting programs, coaching or ADHD-aware therapists who can help you build the right support structures.

Trusted friends, supportive partners and family members who 'get it' are also key in helping your child feel accepted, just as they are.

Cognitive development: Building on a strong foundation

Once your child's foundational needs (biological stability, physiological regulation and emotional safety) are met, you can more effectively support their cognitive development. This includes skills like planning, memory, focus and learning strategies.

Many parents understandably want to start here, but as you've seen throughout this book, my philosophy is to build from the ground up. If your child is overtired, dysregulated or dealing with something like constipation, cognitive strategies won't stick. You need to address those basics first.

At this stage, your village might expand to include educational psychologists, executive function coaches or specialist tutors who understand how your child learns best and can help you advocate for their needs at school (Chapter 14).

Social and emotional development: Connecting with the world 🙌

With cognitive support in place, your child is better equipped to thrive socially and emotionally. They need safe, supportive spaces to practise friendship, build emotional literacy and strengthen communication skills, whether through social skills groups, programs like PEERS or inclusive community activities (Chapter 15).

This stage isn't just about teaching your child how to engage with the world, it's also about helping the world understand, include and accept your child for who they are.

Purpose and fulfilment: Helping your child thrive

At the top of the hierarchy lies purpose and fulfilment. This is where your focus shifts to nurturing your child's autonomy, confidence and sense of self-worth. It's about helping them see that ADHD isn't something to be 'fixed', but a part of who they are, with unique strengths and gifts to celebrate.

Support at this level may come from mentors, ADHD coaches or role models with lived experience. But it also comes from you holding a vision of success on your child's terms, and guiding them to develop the strategies and life skills that help them thrive.

As you move through the hierarchy, your village will evolve, but your role as the architect of that support network remains constant. By starting with strong foundations and building upward, you create the conditions for your child to truly flourish. You don't have to do it alone, the right team helps carry the load and uplifts both you and your child.

Why building a support team matters

As we explored in Chapter 3, ADHD often comes with co-occurring conditions, and one professional alone usually can't cover everything your child might need. That's why building a strong, well-rounded support team is so important. The right team helps ensure your child is accurately diagnosed, taking into account both co-occurring conditions and those that can mimic ADHD, so nothing vital is missed.

Back in Chapter 2, we looked at which professionals can diagnose ADHD and prescribe medication. Now, let's take a closer look at those key clinicians.

Paediatricians

Paediatricians are often the first stop when concerns about your child's attention, behaviour or emotions arise. A general paediatrician can diagnose ADHD, prescribe medication and refer you to allied health professionals.

Developmental paediatricians have extra training in neurodevelopmental conditions such as ADHD, autism and intellectual disability, making them a great option if your child has complex or co-occurring needs.

Some families seek *integrative paediatricians* who combine standard medical care with lifestyle and natural approaches. These practitioners explore root causes like gut health, nutrient deficiencies, sleep or environmental triggers (like mould or toxins), alongside traditional treatments like medication. Their approach particularly appeals to families seeking gentler, root-cause-focused care.

Paediatricians typically take a detailed developmental and family history, review school reports and ask for ADHD rating scales to be completed. After diagnosis, they provide formal reports and guide treatment, often starting and monitoring medication, with regular check-ins every few months, especially during big transitions.

Child and adolescent psychiatrists

Child and adolescent psychiatrists are medical doctors who specialise in diagnosing and treating mental health and neurodevelopmental conditions like ADHD, especially when symptoms are complex or accompanied by anxiety, depression, trauma or severe behavioural issues.

While paediatricians can diagnose and support children with ADHD, psychiatrists are often the next step if your child hasn't responded well to treatment or is experiencing significant emotional or behavioural challenges.

Psychiatrists take a holistic view, looking at mental health, family history, school reports and structured assessments. They provide formal reports and can prescribe and manage complex medication plans, especially when multiple conditions are present or stimulants aren't well tolerated.

You might be referred to a psychiatrist if your child's distress is escalating, their school can't is severe or paediatric support hasn't been enough. They often work alongside other professionals and check in regularly to monitor symptoms and treatment.

Who's who in your allied health team

Beyond doctors, allied health professionals offer specialised support across many areas of your child's development. These university-qualified experts, such as occupational therapists, psychologists and speech pathologists, help with everything from emotional regulation and sensory needs to language, motor skills and learning.

Each professional brings a unique piece of the puzzle, helping you get a fuller picture of your child's strengths and challenges. When the right professionals work together (and with you), you're more likely to see meaningful, lasting progress.

The next section breaks down the most common allied health professionals you might work with. You won't need them all, but knowing who does what helps you choose wisely when issues arise.

Psychologists

Psychologists support your child's emotional wellbeing, behaviour, learning and development, and they're often central to an ADHD support team. Some offer assessments, others provide therapy and many do both. But not all psychologists are the right fit for neurodivergent kids, so it's important to find one experienced in ADHD who uses evidence-based, respectful neuro-affirming approaches.

There are different types of psychologists, each with their own area of focus.

Clinical psychologist
Best for: Emotional regulation, anxiety, depression, trauma, behaviour issues and family support.

Clinical psychologists are trained to assess and treat mental health concerns. They can help your child navigate big feelings, overwhelming moments, low self-esteem or reactive behaviour using therapies like cognitive behavioural therapy (CBT) or dialectical behaviour therapy (DBT; see page 374 for more on this). They may also contribute to an

ADHD diagnosis and write reports needed for medication, school accommodations or NDIS, often working alongside a paediatrician or psychiatrist.

Developmental psychologist

Best for: Diagnosing ADHD, autism, intellectual disability and guiding early intervention.

Developmental psychologists specialise in how children grow and develop emotionally, socially and cognitively. They're especially helpful if your child is under six or has a complex mix of behaviours you're trying to make sense of. With a broad lens, they can spot overlapping conditions and steer you toward the right early supports.

Educational psychologist

Best for: Learning challenges, school behaviour, assessments and classroom strategies.

Educational psychologists focus on how your child learns and functions at school. They assess for issues such as dyslexia, dysgraphia or executive function struggles, and create reports that guide school supports, learning plans and exam accommodations. If school is a struggle, they're a key part of the team.

Neuropsychologist

Best for: Clarifying complex or overlapping challenges and understanding how your child's brain works.

Neuropsychologists conduct detailed assessments to uncover how your child thinks, learns and processes information. They help differentiate ADHD from autism, learning issues, anxiety or intellectual disability. Their reports are often used for NDIS, school supports or long-term planning, especially when previous assessments haven't provided clear answers.

Which one should you choose?

You don't need to see every type of psychologist; many have experience across multiple areas. The most important thing is to find someone who understands ADHD and neurodivergence, communicates well and is open to working with your wider team.

Start by identifying your child's most pressing need, whether that's emotional, academic or diagnostic clarity. Your GP or paediatrician can help guide you to the right starting point. A good psychologist can often address several areas or collaborate with others when needed.

Above all, choose someone who can support both your child and you as a parent, helping you understand, connect with and advocate for your neurodivergent child.

Explaining psychological therapies

Children with ADHD often face big emotions, frustration, rejection sensitivity and impulsivity. These challenges may be intensified by anxiety, learning issues or past trauma. While therapy doesn't 'fix' ADHD, evidence-based approaches can help children (and parents) build emotional awareness, learn calming strategies and feel more in control.

Cognitive behavioural therapy (CBT)

CBT helps children notice unhelpful thoughts, work through big emotions, and learn more supportive ways of responding. It's most effective for children aged seven and older with ADHD and co-occurring anxiety, anger or low self-esteem. ADHD-friendly CBT uses visuals, repetition and games to boost engagement. While it doesn't reduce core symptoms like distractibility, it can improve emotional regulation, coping and daily functioning, especially when paired with parent support or medication.

Dialectical behaviour therapy (DBT)

Originally designed for intense emotions and impulse control issues, DBT is a strong fit for children and teens with ADHD who are explosive, reactive or rejection sensitive. It teaches emotional regulation, distress tolerance, mindfulness and social skills. When parents learn how to use these tools, DBT can help reduce meltdowns, impulsivity and pushback that happens when a child feels overwhelmed.

Acceptance and commitment therapy (ACT)

ACT helps children accept tough thoughts and feelings without getting stuck. It's great for impulsivity, emotional intensity, low motivation and self-criticism, especially in neurodivergent teens. ACT builds mindfulness, flexibility and values-based action and forms the basis of programs like NeuroACT. Early research shows it can improve emotional regulation and behaviour in young people with ADHD.

Family therapy

ADHD can impact the whole family, not just your child. Family therapy helps improve communication, reduce conflict, and support emotional connection. It's especially helpful when siblings feel left out, resentful or act out in response to the extra attention their ADHD sibling receives. Strengthening family dynamics benefits everyone.

Psychotherapy

Psychotherapy supports your child's mental health, emotions and behaviour through talk-based approaches like CBT, DBT, ACT, play therapy and more. Delivered by psychologists, counsellors or social workers, it provides a safe space to explore feelings, build insight and learn coping tools. It's especially helpful when your child's ADHD is paired with anxiety, low self-esteem or social and mood challenges.

Equine therapy

Equine-assisted therapy uses guided interactions with horses to build emotional regulation, confidence, focus and communication. It's especially helpful for children with ADHD[1] who struggle in traditional therapy settings or with verbal expression. Horses respond to non-verbal cues, helping children develop self-awareness, impulse control and patience. While it's not a replacement for traditional therapy, equine therapy can be a valuable complement, particularly for children who thrive outdoors, in movement-based settings or around animals. Always choose a certified, neurodivergence-informed provider.

Trauma-informed therapy and eye movement desensitisation and reprocessing (EMDR)

Children with ADHD often face repeated rejection or failure, which can lead to chronic stress or trauma responses. If your child is reactive, fearful or has experienced trauma, a trauma-informed psychologist or counsellor can help.

EMDR is one approach that helps children process emotional experiences and reduce anxiety. While not specific to ADHD, trauma-informed care can be a game-changer for children stuck in cycles of meltdowns or shutdowns.

Somatic therapy

Somatic therapy recognises that stress, trauma and emotional dysregulation are often stored in the nervous system, not just in the mind. For children with ADHD, who are frequently hypersensitive, reactive or emotionally intense, somatic therapy can help restore balance from the bottom up. Rather than starting with thoughts, somatic therapy begins with the body, helping children notice and regulate their internal states so they can move toward safety, calm and connection.

A somatic psychotherapist works with children using body-based tools to regulate their physiology, including:

> *breathwork* to reduce arousal and bring awareness to the present moment
> *grounding techniques* like pushing against a wall, holding heavy items or using textured or temperature-based sensory tools
> *bilateral stimulation* (e.g., tapping, rocking, movement) to help integrate emotional responses
> *co-regulation practices*, where the therapist models calm, connected presence to help the child feel safe enough to shift their state
> *body-based storytelling, movement games, or mindfulness* adapted for younger children.

This approach is ideal for kids who are often dysregulated, shut down, avoidant or not responsive to talk therapy. It's especially helpful for those with sensory issues or trauma histories.

Somatic therapy builds a child's capacity for self-regulation and resilience, helping them feel calm and connected so they can better engage in learning, therapy and relationships. It complements traditional therapies by helping kids *feel* safe before they're asked to *talk* through challenges.

When to seek therapy

You might consider therapy if your child is overwhelmed by emotions, avoiding school, struggling with friendships or dealing with anxiety or depression. For teens, it can also support motivation, identity, executive function and self-advocacy.

Therapy is usually conducted weekly or fortnightly but varies based on your child's needs and family capacity. Some children need more frequent support during stressful times, while others do well with monthly check-ins once progress is made. The best outcomes happen when parents stay involved and therapists collaborate with schools and other professionals.

Choosing the 'perfect' therapist isn't the goal. Starting with someone who understands ADHD and connects well with your child is what matters most.

Supporting co-occurring chronic illness

If your child also lives with chronic health issues, such as gut problems, fatigue, pain, POTS, Ehlers-Danlos Syndrome or immune challenges, it's vital to work with a therapist who understands the mind-body connection. Sadly, many neurodivergent children (especially girls) are dismissed or told their symptoms are 'just anxiety', which can delay care and cause harm.

Look for a trauma-informed therapist who takes their physical symptoms seriously, collaborates with your medical team, and integrates pacing, somatic tools and emotional support. Your child deserves to be believed, validated and treated as a whole person, not divided into mental vs physical health.

Supporting gender exploration

If your child or teen is exploring their gender, it's essential to find a therapist who offers a safe, affirming space—someone who listens without judgement, pressure or assumptions. Many neurodivergent children, including those with ADHD, think differently about identity, including gender. What they need most is time, curiosity and compassion as they make sense of who they are.

Look for a therapist who is gender-affirming but not directive—someone who prioritises emotional wellbeing, encourages self-reflection and supports your child's unique journey. Your role is to stay connected, listen with empathy and remind them they're loved just as they are.

Speech pathologists

Speech pathologists (or 'speechies') help children understand and use language, process verbal information and communicate socially. For children who struggle with listening, following instructions, expressing themselves clearly or making friends, a speech pathologist can be a wise choice.

Children with ADHD often experience challenges in receptive language (understanding what others say), expressive language (finding the right words to say), and pragmatic language (knowing how to use language in social settings). These difficulties can easily be misinterpreted as inattention, oppositional behaviour or poor listening. A speech pathologist who specialises in ADHD, who understands how attention, working memory and impulsivity impact language and communication, can improve social functioning, emotional regulation and classroom behaviour.[2] They may also work on auditory memory, sequencing or word retrieval, all common weak spots in ADHD.

Consider a speechie if your child often says 'What?', misses parts of conversations, has trouble expressing themselves or struggles socially. Targeted support can improve not just communication but also self-esteem, emotional regulation and peer relationships.

Occupational therapists (OTs)

OTs help children develop the practical, physical, emotional and sensory skills they need to succeed in daily life, like sitting still in class, tying shoelaces, managing emotions or tolerating noisy environments. For children with ADHD, OTs can be especially helpful with sensory regulation, fine and gross motor skills, executive functioning, emotional control, routines and organisation.

They might help improve handwriting, build tolerance to textures or sounds, create visual schedules, or teach self-regulation through play.

Consider an OT if your child struggles with sensory sensitivity, coordination (fine or gross motor skills), can't sit still to complete tasks or has difficulty managing transitions. OTs often work with children from preschool age through to adolescence, and they're particularly helpful during key developmental transitions, such as starting school or entering high school.

Audiologists

Audiologists assess hearing and how the brain processes sound. While they're known for diagnosing hearing loss, they also identify auditory processing disorder, which often mimics or co-exists with ADHD.

Children with auditory processing disorder may appear to 'tune out', frequently ask 'What?' or struggle to follow verbal instructions, especially in noisy environments like classrooms. These challenges can look a lot like inattention, but they're about how the brain processes sound. An audiologist will determine whether your child's listening difficulties are due to auditory processing disorder or hearing loss, ensuring you're not missing an important piece of the puzzle.

If your child is easily distracted by noise, misses parts of conversations or struggles with auditory memory or sequencing, consider an audiology assessment (usually accurate from age seven).

Dietitians

A dietitian is a university-trained health professional who specialises in nutrition and its impact on physical, mental and behavioural health. Dietitians can play an important role in supporting brain function, emotional regulation, energy levels and even sleep, particularly when diet, gut health or fussy eating are part of the picture. Dietitians tailor strategies to your child's unique needs, preferences, sensitivities and any co-occurring health issues (see Chapter 8 for more on supporting your child's diet).

Dietitians can help with blood sugar regulation, food sensitivities, nutrient deficiencies, gut-brain health and elimination diets. They also support families with children who are picky eaters, avoid certain food groups, or experience sensory sensitivities around food—challenges that are common in children with ADHD. A dietitian who specialises in neurodivergence will also understand the role of dopamine, inflammation and the gut microbiome, and may recommend dietary changes or supplements that support cognitive and emotional function.

Naturopaths

A naturopath is a practitioner trained in natural and holistic healthcare, focusing on identifying and addressing the root causes of symptoms rather than just managing them. A naturopath provides support across multiple areas: nutrition, gut health, sleep, stress, detoxification, immune health and environmental sensitivities. Naturopaths take a whole-child approach, looking at how physical, emotional, dietary and lifestyle factors interact to influence behaviour, mood and attention. While they don't diagnose ADHD, many are experienced in working alongside families who are either exploring alternatives to medication or want to complement mainstream care with natural strategies.

A neurodivergence-informed naturopath might explore food intolerances, inflammation, gut health, blood sugar imbalances or micronutrient deficiencies using tools like dietary tweaks, supplements, herbs and functional testing.

If your child is highly sensitive, has multiple health or behavioural concerns, or if you're looking for a gentler, more individualised approach alongside therapy or medication, a naturopath can be a valuable part of your team.

Exercise physiologist

An exercise physiologist is a university-qualified allied health professional who specialises in using movement and exercise to support physical, mental and neurological health. For children with ADHD, especially those who also have hypermobility syndrome, exercise physiologists can design safe, tailored movement programs supporting core strength, motor coordination, posture, stamina and emotional regulation. Hypermobility often brings fatigue, joint instability and poor muscle tone, which can contribute to clumsiness, low endurance or even anxiety about physical activity.

An exercise physiologist can help your child develop confidence through movement that feels good, not overwhelming. Sessions might include balance work, strength training, cardio and body awareness activities that improve both physical wellbeing and cognitive focus. Research shows regular, structured physical activity can improve attention, executive function and mood in children with ADHD (see Chapter 10).

Chiropractic and osteopathic care

Chiropractors and osteopaths focus on body alignment, muscle tension and nervous system balance.

While these therapies don't treat ADHD directly, some families include them to support sleep, reduce physical tension and support nervous system regulation, especially in children with sensory sensitivities or retained reflexes.

Chiropractors use gentle spinal adjustments, while osteopaths often take a more whole-body, hands-on approach using soft tissue techniques, cranial osteopathy and movement-based support. Some parents report improvements in calmness, focus and self-regulation after consistent sessions, although research is still emerging.

Choose qualified, experienced practitioners who work respectfully with neurodivergent children. If your child is highly sensitive to touch or movement, go slowly—and always follow your gut about what feels right for your child's body and boundaries.

Vision therapy and behavioural optometry

Some children with ADHD-like symptoms actually have undiagnosed vision challenges, such as tracking issues, poor eye teaming or visual processing delays, that can make reading and focus much harder. Behavioural optometrists assess these subtle issues, which are often missed in regular eye exams.

These challenges can make it hard for a child to maintain focus, follow text or stay engaged with schoolwork, leading to behaviours that look like inattention, frustration or 'daydreaming'.

Vision therapy uses structured eye exercises to strengthen visual skills, and while research is still growing, it can help reduce eye strain, improve reading and support learning in kids with coexisting visual problems. Consider an assessment if your child avoids reading, skips lines, rubs their eyes or seems visually overwhelmed despite perfect eyesight.

Creative and body-based therapies

Creative and body-based therapies, such as art therapy, music therapy, play therapy and dance/movement therapy, offer children with ADHD a safe, nonverbal way to express emotions, process experiences and develop self-regulation. These therapies are especially beneficial for children who struggle to articulate their feelings in words or who become overwhelmed by traditional talk-based approaches.

Through drawing, drumming, movement or storytelling, children explore big emotions, build social understanding and connect more deeply with their bodies. These therapies are typically child-led and strengths-based, helping kids feel empowered and understood. While research is still emerging, creative therapies can reduce stress, improve self-esteem and support emotional growth in children with ADHD and trauma histories.[3] If your child is often shut down, anxious, highly dysregulated or just more expressive through movement or creativity, these therapies can be a wonderful support.

Other supports

Beyond allied health professionals, there are many other tools and services that can make a big difference to your child's life. From the right tutor or executive function coach to movement-based programs, mindfulness or assistive tech, sometimes it's these less traditional supports that help unlock your child's strengths. In this section, we'll explore complementary options that can boost learning, confidence and emotional wellbeing and support your whole family to thrive.

ADHD coaching

ADHD coaching is a practical, goal-oriented, real-world support to help individuals with ADHD develop the skills, strategies and habits they need to navigate everyday life more effectively. For teens and older children, coaching focuses on building executive functioning skills like planning, organisation, time management and task initiation. It can also help with motivation, self-confidence and emotional resilience. While ADHD coaching is not therapy, it complements therapeutic work by offering actionable tools in a supportive and collaborative way.

Parent ADHD coaching helps caregivers better understand the ADHD brain, reduce power struggles, build connection and parent more effectively. Parents learn how to create structure, support emotional regulation and shift their mindset from 'won't' to 'can't yet'. Coaching improves self-awareness, follow-through and functional outcomes, particularly when coaching is consistent, strengths-based and tailored to the individual.

Executive function coaching

Executive function coaching is similar to ADHD coaching, but specifically targets executive skills like time management, organisation, planning and follow-through. It's ideal for older children and teens who are capable but overwhelmed, perhaps missing deadlines, losing track of tasks or struggling to stay organised. It's usually provided by psychologists, ADHD coaches or specialist educators.

Academic tutors and learning supports

Academic tutors can be an important part of your child's support team, not just to help with what they struggle with, but to nurture their confidence, independence and strengths. Those trained in neurodivergence know how to break tasks down, use visual tools and support executive functioning like planning and organisation. They can assist with literacy, numeracy and homework to take pressure off you at home and explicitly teach study skills, such as how to revise, structure an essay or study in ways that work for their ADHD brain.

Great tutors can pre-teach content so your child feels prepared and confident in class, improving both their engagement and results. But it's not just for areas of difficulty — tutoring can also extend your child's areas of strength and, when tailored to your child's needs, it becomes a confidence-building part of their learning journey.

Ask your child's tutor to work collaboratively with their school and allied health professionals to ensure support is consistent across settings where necessary.

Don't forget the school team

Your child's teachers, school counsellors, learning support staff and leadership are key players in their daily life. These professionals see your child in one of the most demanding environments of the day, and when they're informed, empathetic and proactive, they can become valuable allies who can adjust classroom strategies, reduce stressors and highlight strengths.

School counsellors can offer emotional support, build social-emotional skills and be a safe point of contact when things get tough.

These professionals spend over six hours a day with your child, so when school and home work together, the impact is amplified and your child feels more understood, supported and capable. (See Chapter 14 for tips on navigating school.)

Behavioural parent training (BPT)

BPT is one of the most evidence-based supports for children with ADHD. Instead of focusing on the child, it empowers parents with tools to improve behaviour, strengthen connection and reduce stress, many of which we've covered in this book.

ADHD-specific parenting programs teach strategies in practical, supportive ways. BPT is particularly helpful for reducing intense or challenging behaviours and preventing escalation into more serious difficulties later in adolescence. Research shows BPT not only helps families navigate stressful moments more calmly, but also boosts parent confidence—reducing overwhelm and improving day-to-day connection at home.[4] It's often recommended before or alongside medication, especially for younger children, because when parents feel equipped, everyone benefits.

Movement-based programs

Regular physical activity isn't just good for physical health, it's also an effective way to regulate the nervous system. Movement helps release excess energy, increase dopamine and serotonin, and improve focus, mood and emotional control. Activities like martial arts, yoga, circus arts, dance, rock climbing or trampolining help children develop body awareness, self-regulation, confidence and perseverance, all within a structured, engaging setting.

Unlike team sports, which can sometimes feel overwhelming, these non-competitive options allow children the chance to progress at their own pace while building routine, discipline and resilience. Rhythm, repetition and coordination are naturally regulating for the ADHD nervous system. Find something your child enjoys and doesn't feel pressured to perform in so they'll stick with it. (See Chapter 10 for more on the benefits of exercise.)

Mindfulness practices for neurodivergent children

Traditional meditation might feel impossible for your child with ADHD but mindfulness can be incredibly effective when it's adapted to their needs.

It's not about sitting still, but about tuning into the present through movement, breath, sound or sensation. Programs integrating movement-based mindfulness, storytelling, visuals or playful breathing exercises can help children develop greater emotional awareness, self-regulation and stress tolerance.

Research shows mindfulness boosts attention and emotional regulation and reduces impulsivity when programs are tailored appropriately for neurodivergent brains.[5] It's about helping your child build a calm, connected relationship with their body and mind, one small moment at a time. (See Chapter 11 for more.)

Assistive technology

Technology can be a support when used intentionally. Tools like visual timers, reminder apps, audiobooks, speech-to-text software or organisational apps can reduce friction and support independence. These are especially helpful for visual learners or children who struggle with executive functioning.

Where to start

With so many options, it's easy to feel like you need to do *everything at once* to give your child the best chance. But trying to juggle too many interventions can overwhelm both you and your child.

Use your Parenting Hierarchy of Needs (page 60) as a compass. Start with strong foundations: emotional safety, routines and connection. Ask yourself: *What's the biggest current challenge in daily life?* That's your starting point.

> ➤ Focus on one or two priorities, not everything at once.
> ➤ Start with what matters most right now, not what's easiest to access.
> ➤ Get referrals from neurodivergent-informed professionals or communities.
> ➤ Keep a shared goal sheet to track what each provider is working on.
> ➤ Reassess every six to 12 months as needs evolve.
> ➤ Small, intentional steps lead to lasting progress.

Choosing the right professional or therapy

When deciding who to work with, ask yourself:

> ➤ Do they have ADHD and neurodivergence experience?
> ➤ Are they trauma-informed and neuro-affirming?
> ➤ Do they involve you as the parent?
> ➤ Are they flexible and focused on your goals, not just their protocol?
> ➤ Will they collaborate with your broader team?
> ➤ Most importantly, does your child feel safe and comfortable with them?

The right fit matters more than the title.

Get your team working together

Progress isn't just about what you do, it's about how well your team works together. When therapists, teachers and professionals communicate and align on shared goals, things move forward more smoothly.

Encourage collaboration by:

> ➤ asking providers to share reports, attend informal planning chats or align on priorities
> ➤ keeping everyone updated on what others are working on
> ➤ focusing on shared goals like improving school participation, emotional regulation or independence.

You're the hub of the wheel, and by staying clear on your priorities and fostering connection between your supports, you become not just your child's advocate, but their project manager, coach and calm centre. Progress doesn't come from doing everything, it comes from doing the right things, together.

Sometimes professionals don't collaborate as you would wish. When this happens, trust your instinct and lived experience and prioritise those who work collaboratively and respectfully, advocating for what you *know* works for your child.

Your extended village

Not all support comes with a therapy plan or professional title. Some of the most meaningful help comes from your informal village: the friend who checks in after a hard day, the parent in a Facebook group who just *gets it*, the coach who patiently builds your child's confidence on the soccer field. These everyday heroes offer understanding, relief and connection, often when you need it most.

ADHD parenting communities, online support groups and neurodivergent-affirming Facebook groups can be lifelines. They offer resources, therapist recommendations, hard-won wisdom and the priceless comfort of 'me too'.

Sometimes, a well-timed meme or meltdown story in the car park is just what you need to keep going.

Extended family, neighbours, godparents or family friends can offer practical help: school pickups, meals or a breather when you're running on empty. Mentors, sports coaches, music teachers and scout leaders often form strong bonds with children outside of therapy or school, helping them build confidence, belonging and self-worth.

And let's not forget the emotional support for *you*. Whether it's a WhatsApp group chat with mums, a partner who's learning alongside you or a friend who listens without judgement, your support network matters just as much as your child's. ADHD is a marathon, not a sprint, and having people around you who understand, uplift and show up makes all the difference.

Pulling it all together

Raising any child doesn't come with an instruction manual, but raising a child with a variety of challenges often calls for a roadmap. Hopefully this chapter has helped provide you with that roadmap.

From psychologists and OTs to speech pathologists, tutors, coaches, family and friends, your support team can be as diverse and dynamic as your child. Every member of your village (professional or personal) adds a layer of strength, insight and care that helps your child move closer to their full potential.

You won't need every support all at once, and you don't have to figure it all out today. Start with what matters most right now. Trust your instincts and know it's okay to ask for help. What you're building isn't just a therapy plan, it's a community—one rooted in understanding, connection and love. Keep going. You're your child's greatest advocate and with the right support around you, there's every reason to believe things can, and will, get better.

Join the ADHD Support Australia Facebook Group at facebook.com/ADHDSupportAustralia. ⊕

Conclusion — Staying on the rollercoaster: How to keep going

Keep showing up. It's consistency, not perfection, that counts.

There's a moment all parents reach, often alone in the dark, after the house finally goes quiet, when you wonder how much longer you can do this. Even when you think you've done everything you can, you'll still experience moments where you feel trapped in an endless cycle of emotional highs and lows with no sign of balance. Some moments everything feels thrilling—your child makes progress, you feel connected, you navigate a tough situation with grace. And then, out of nowhere, everything swings the other way—there's a meltdown at bedtime, a school email you weren't expecting or a moment where you lose your cool. That's the emotional rollercoaster we call parenting!

Parenting a neurodivergent child brings unique challenges. It doesn't follow the usual path and you'll often feel you or your child are misunderstood by others in your world who don't quite grasp what you're going through. This can leave you feeling isolated and second-guessing your choices. You're trying to calm your child's nervous system and yours, responding to invisible triggers, navigating systems that weren't built for your child and trying to hold your family together in the process. It's a big ask and it's easy to feel overwhelmed, burnt out or as though you're not doing enough.

If you were feeling exhausted, discouraged or uncertain before you started this book—and maybe still are—you would not be alone. The parenting journey you've been on has required more patience, more emotional energy and more resilience than most other parents—I know that better than most.

But now you've made it to the conclusion of this book, I trust you're feeling more empowered, optimistic and inspired to move forward with confidence on your parenting journey. Don't be concerned that it's too late or feel any sense of guilt because you've done things differently up to this point. We're all learning, evolving and growing every day—none of us is perfect and it's only once we know better that we're able to do better.

You may be in the process of reading this book cover to cover before making any changes, or you may have jumped into the parts you felt were priority areas for you, or you might have taken steps as you've been reading. You may have already known some of what I've written here, or you may have had a complete mindset shift and many 'a-ha!' moments throughout. Either way, I hope what you've discovered here will translate into achievable, actionable steps you can implement carefully over time to obtain the results you want.

Now it's time to take action. You've gained knowledge and, hopefully, some inspiration, but if you don't take action and make changes, all the knowledge in the world isn't going to alter your reality. I get it—it's daunting and it takes courage. But just start.

Start with remembering your 'why'.

Your 'why' is your parenting *north star*. It's the deeper reason behind the way you want to parent, the relationship you want to have with your child and the long-term foundation you're building, even if you can't see the full picture yet.

Your 'why' doesn't have to be profound; it just has to be true for you.

Use your parenting journal to come up with your 'why' using this simple prompt:

I choose to parent with [your chosen value] because I want [desired outcome for your child/family/self].

Your 'why' might be:

> 'I want my child to feel safe being exactly who they are.'
> 'I never felt emotionally safe growing up, and I want to break that cycle.'
> 'I believe connection builds cooperation more than control ever will.'
> 'My child deserves to be understood, not punished for having a different brain.'
> 'I choose to parent with curiosity because I want my child to feel seen, not judged.'
> 'I choose connection because I believe relationships matter more than routines.'

Once you've decided on your 'why', write it down and put it somewhere you'll see it often: on a sticky note, a poster, in your planner, on your phone lock screen etc.

Once you're clear on your 'why', revisit the Parental Hierarchy of Needs (Chapter 5).

Remember you need to work from the bottom up:

> *Biological stability:* Is my child physically and emotionally safe right now? Are they tired, hungry or thirsty?
> *Physiological regulation:* Is my child (or me!) too dysregulated to function?
> *Emotional safety:* Have I connected with my child as a *person*, not just a behaviour? Is this a predictable environment where my child feels unconditionally accepted? Are we using routines and expectations that support us?

- ➤ *Cognitive support:* Is my child supported in all the ways that they need?
- ➤ *Social and emotional growth:* What opportunities does my child have for building friendships, developing emotional literacy, and practising communication and relationship skills?
- ➤ *Purpose and fulfilment:* What am I working toward? What kind of family are we trying to be?

This model reminds you that trying to fix a routine when everyone is dysregulated or expecting problem-solving when you're disconnected won't work. You have to meet needs in the right order.

Once these basic needs are being met, start with one or two priority challenges at a time to avoid more overwhelm. Don't make the mistake of trying to do it all at once. Don't be impatient. Take your time to put one foot firmly in front of the other and try to nail each step before taking the next.

You'll soon find yourself reaching a place where you feel like you're beginning to make noticeable progress. The improvements will encourage you to keep going with the small but steady changes you're making. You don't have to do everything perfectly, just keep moving forward and showing up. Every time you choose connection over compliance, compassion over criticism, consistency over chaos it adds up. It shapes your child's nervous system, their sense of safety and your family's long-term wellbeing. The small changes are what matters and that's what creates massive change over time.

It's easy to forget what happened last week, last month or last year, so a great idea is to track your progress. Instead of looking for big milestones or noticeable symptom reduction, try tracking the smaller breakthroughs to see how far you've come. You may say, 'My child is still having meltdowns; nothing's changed' but how many meltdowns, how severe are they, how long do they last—has this changed over time? It's sometimes only when we look back with clear insight, we see the progress being made. This could look like:

- ➤ how quickly your child recovers from hard moments
- ➤ whether they're more open to repair after conflict
- ➤ how long it takes *you* to recover emotionally
- ➤ how your mindset has shifted since you started this journey.

You'll find a baseline tracker on my website at adhdsupportaustralia .com.au to help with this ⊕, or make notes in your parenting journal.

Parenting your child will still come with emotional ups and downs. You'll still have moments of uncertainty, frustration and exhaustion. You'll still face setbacks and have days when it feels like you're taking two steps forward and one step back. Your parenting journey will test you, stretch you and perhaps, at times, unravel you. Don't ever think you're failing. You're evolving, and no matter how much they push you or how long it takes, so is your child. The difference now is that you're not riding blind. You now know where to place your focus and what matters most.

Throughout this book, you've expanded your understanding of ADHD, and explored practical parenting tools, mindsets shifts and the importance of nervous system regulation for you and your child. You've explored everything to ensure you can build a strong foundation for your child from nutrition and sleep to screen and social wellness, school advocacy, raising self-esteem, improving family relationships and finding your wider support network.

You're now equipped with a new way of responding to your child (and to yourself) guided by my Calm, Connected, Compassionate Parenting Philosophy and the 6Cs: Connection, Compassion, Curiosity, Calm, Consistency and Collaboration. These pillars are anchor points for your unpredictable journey. When things feel chaotic (or you're not sure what to do next) just come back to them.

Create a quick reflective practice to use during overwhelming moments:

> ➤ Stop. Breathe.
> ➤ Ask: What's my job right now? (Hint: It's probably not to fix everything.)
> ➤ Choose one C to focus on in this moment.
> ➤ Offer that to yourself first, then to your child.
> ➤ Reset when needed. There's no limit to how often you can begin again.

Regularly ask these questions to ground yourself.

- 🫁 *Connection*: Have I connected with my child today outside of managing them?
- ❤️ *Compassion*: Can I soften how I speak to myself or to them right now?
- 🔍 *Curiosity*: What might be going on underneath this behaviour— for them or for me?
- 🌀 *Calm*: What can I do to regulate myself before reacting?
- 👤 *Collaboration*: Can I involve my child in solving this instead of imposing a fix?
- 🔄 *Consistency*: What routine can I return to right now to feel safe again?

This isn't about perfect parenting, it's about steady, values-based parenting and showing up (even shakily) aligned with what you believe.

Often, the stress points in your day or week are predictable. Get curious. Become a reflective detective and ask:

- ➤ What moments consistently trigger meltdowns, conflict or shutdowns?
- ➤ What's happening around those moments—before and after?
- ➤ What's worked (even a little bit) in the past to soften them?
- ➤ What could we try adding, removing or adjusting next time?

When you do this, you can create a plan that reduces chaos and helps you feel more confident.

When reaching for these tools starts to become a habit, even slowly or imperfectly, then you're moving in the right direction. Any new way of thinking or responding takes effort. It feels so hard and awkward at first that you just want to slip back into your default way of dealing with things. So have compassion for yourself; you're learning new habits. They take time, but once they become a habit, they become easier.

Remind yourself that progress is never linear and resilience is built not by avoiding struggles, but by learning how to keep moving through them with love. You may not always see the results immediately but the work you're doing matters. You may not always feel confident, calm or know the answers, but you're capable and committed and you're doing your best—and that's what matters. Once you see your child responding positively and your daily life becoming easier, you'll want to continue on this road.

One of the central tenets of this book is nervous system regulation—including yours. You can't pour from an empty cup, so ensure you've taken on board all you read in Chapter 7 and you're making room to create your own solid foundations from which to parent. When your child is intense, unpredictable or in crisis mode, your nervous system is always scanning for the next explosion. You may find yourself tense even when things are calm because part of you is always braced for what could go wrong. This chronic emotional vigilance is exhausting and, over time, it wears down your ability to respond with patience, compassion and clarity.

Learning to protect your emotional energy isn't selfish, it's *essential*. It's how you stay in the parenting game for the long haul as a grounded, compassionate presence your child can depend on. You can even apply your 6Cs to yourself in the hard moments and ask yourself questions like:

- 🙌 *Connection:* Have I connected with anyone who supports me this week?
- ♥ *Compassion:* Can I offer myself the same kindness I give my child?
- 🔍 *Curiosity:* What might I be feeling underneath this irritation or fatigue?
- 🧘 *Calm:* What helps me feel calm, and when did I last do that?
- 👥 *Collaboration:* Who could I ask for help right now, even in a small way?
- 🕯 *Consistency:* Am I pushing too hard to maintain routines when I'm depleted?

You're a human parenting under pressure, and you deserve the same care, flexibility and understanding you give your child. You're allowed to take breaks, to need time, to fall apart and come back together. Your journey isn't a sprint, it's a long, twisty, high-stakes marathon, and if you're going to stay the course, you need to refill your own cup regularly. Protecting your emotional energy isn't stepping away from your family, it's stepping up for them from a place that's sustainable.

You'll have setbacks. There'll be mornings starting with conflict and nights ending in tears. Don't see those as failures, see them as part of the learning curve, part of what it means to raise a child who experiences the world differently. That rollercoaster won't vanish, but now, perhaps the highs and lows aren't quite as overwhelming as they once were. If you're starting to notice changes, however small, if you're approaching your child with more compassion, curiosity and calm, you've already made real progress.

Always, always celebrate the tiniest of wins you experience because every step forward counts. No matter how small it may seem, it's progress — a step in the right direction. Don't compare yourself, or your child, to others — your journey is your own. It's not a race, it's about the personal bests for you, your child and your family. That's all that matters.

It's easier to celebrate the visible wins, like when your child sleeps through the night, gets a great report from school or is ready for school on time, but there's another success you often don't give yourself credit for. That success is the quiet, everyday courage you show in *continuing* to keep trying to do what's best after a hard day, every time you choose connection over control, every time you regulate instead of react — these are all moments of success that are worth celebrating. You might not feel like you're achieving much, but to keep moving forward, even when it's hard, is an achievement.

Use your parenting journal to create a small daily or weekly ritual to honour your efforts. Jot down one thing you did well each day or answer a journal prompt such as 'One thing I'm proud of this week is ...' Or invent a mantra for yourself such as 'I'm doing my best and that's all I can do'. Celebrating your efforts — even when the results aren't always visible — goes a long way to keeping your heart in the game and your spirits lifted.

This book has created a clear map for you to follow so, little by little, your life *can* become more manageable. The rollercoaster can begin to even out. You'll find more calm in your home, and feel closer and more connected to your child. Your child will begin to feel safer, more understood and more able to thrive in their own unique way.

The thread that weaves through all of it is your unique child. There's no cookie-cutter solution and no perfect parent. There's just the next right step, taken with care, love and as much consistency as you can manage.

A calmer life, a happier, more confident child and stronger family relationships are possible. There's no quick fix, but there is a way forward and your roadmap is in the pages of this book.

If this has reminded you of anything, let it be this: *you're still here,* still learning, still loving, still trying and showing up for your child.

You're not alone; you're doing your best—and you've come further than you think.

You've got this!

All the best

Vivian

Acknowledgements

To my younger daughter: Your courage, resilience and unique way of seeing the world have been my greatest teachers. The experiences we've shared in our mother -daughter journey have shaped the heart and purpose of this book. It is because of our journey together that this work could take shape and now offer support to others. In writing it, I've gained new understanding that will continue to enrich our relationship and help shape a future filled with greater connection, compassion and growth.

To my older daughter, who gathered my scattered thoughts and helped shape them into the structure of this book, and who has walked beside me through all the seasons of our family's journey. Your compassion, insight, and quiet strength have taught me as much as anything I've written here. You've been both my sounding board and my encouragement, and I am so grateful for the depth of understanding you bring to our lives.

To my husband, whose steadfast support and willingness to carry everything else gave me the time and space to write—but more than that, whose love, patience, and belief in me have been the steady heart of our family. You have walked this journey with me every step of the way, holding us all together with strength, kindness and unwavering care. I could not imagine doing life—or this work—without you.

To my cat, Misty, my constant companion for twenty remarkable years—always by my side through long days and late nights, reminding me to pause, breathe, and simply *be*. You've been a quiet source of comfort and calm, and a part of our family's story in your own gentle way—just as our beloved Brandy was in her time.

I could not have done this without any of you. Thank you, my family, for your patience, understanding and love.

Resources

> ADHD Support Australia (adhdsupportaustralia.com.au) provides a wide range of resources for parents, teens and adults with ADHD. Online support includes Parenting Children with ADHD, Parent Coaching, the Digital Parenting Program, PEERS® Certified Provider for Teens & Young Adults, and NeuroACT Stress Management for teens or adults. They also offer expert online talks (with a large back catalogue for Patreon members), a supportive Facebook community (facebook.com/groups/ADHDSupportAustralia), and a Directory of Professionals, Services & Resources.

> Australian Government, *Disability Discrimination Act* 1992, Australian Government, legislation.gov.au/C2004A04426/2018-04-12/text
> Australian Government, Disability Standards for Education 2005, Australian Government, education.gov.au/disability-standards-education-2005
> Australian Government, eSafety Commission, Australian Government, esafety.gov.au

- Delahooke, M 2020, *Beyond Behaviours: Using brain science and compassion to understand and solve children's behavioural challenges*, John Murray Learning.
- Ede, G 2024, *Change Your Diet, Change Your Mind: A powerful plan to improve mood, overcome anxiety and protect memory for a lifetime of optimal mental health*, Yellow Kite.
- Dr Sarah Wilkes-Gillan, Occupational therapist and researcher specialising in social communication support for neurodivergent children. Some of the social skills strategies for younger children in Chapter 15 were kindly contributed by Dr Wilkes-Gillan. She has also presented as a guest expert for ADHD Support Australia. Find out more: drsarahwilkesgillan.com.au
- Greene, RW 2021, *The Explosive Child: A new approach for understanding and parenting easily frustrated, chronically inflexible children*, 6th edn, HarperCollins US.
- Kaplan, BJ & Rucklidge, JJ 2021, *The better brain: Overcome anxiety, combat depression, and reduce ADHD and stress with nutrition.* HarperCollins.
- Palmer, C 2022, *Brain Energy: A revolutionary breakthrough in understanding mental health—and improving treatment for anxiety, depression, OCD, PTSD, and more*, BenBella Books.
- Tsabary, S 2018, *The Awakened Family*, Yellow Kite.

References

Chapter 1

1. Verheul, I, Rietdijk, W, Block, J, Franken, I & Larsson, H 2016, 'The association between attention-deficit/hyperactivity (ADHD) symptoms and self-employment', *European Journal of Epidemiology*, vol. 31, pp. 793–801.
2. Lerner, DA, Verheul, I & Thurik, R 2019, 'Entrepreneurship and attention deficit hyperactivity disorder: a review and research agenda', *Journal of Business Venturing Insights*, vol. 11, p. e00127.
3. Edwards, N 2013, 'The Voice judge Will.i.am tells of his battle with ADHD', *Mirror*, 28 April.
4. Chillemi, K 2025, *Using the brain science of ADHD as a guide for neuro-affirming practice*, Australian Academic Press.
5. Brooks, R & Goldstein, S 2002, *Raising resilient children: Fostering strength, hope, and optimism in your child*, McGraw-Hill.

Chapter 2

1. American Psychiatric Association 2022, *Diagnostic and statistical manual of mental disorders: DSM-5-TR*, 5th edn, American Psychiatric Publishing.
2. Martin, J 2024, 'Why are females less likely to be diagnosed with ADHD in childhood than males?', *The Lancet Psychiatry*, vol. 11, no 4, pp. 303–10.
3. Choi, J 2015, 'The gender imbalance in ADHD', *Australian Medical Student Journal*, https://www.amsj.org/archives/4536

Chapter 3

1. Biederman, J, Faraone, SV, Spencer, TJ, Mick, E, Monuteaux, MC & Aleardi M 2005, 'Functional impairments in adults with self-reports of diagnosed ADHD: A controlled study of 1001 adults in the community', *Journal of Clinical Psychiatry*, vol. 67, no. 4, pp. 524–40.
2. Kessler, RC, Adler, L, Barkley, R, Biederman, J, Conners, CK, Demler, O, et al. 2006, 'The prevalence and correlates of adult ADHD in the United States', *American Journal of Psychiatry*, vol. 163, no. 4, pp. 716–23.

3. Meinzer, MC, Lewinsohn, PM, Pettit, JW, Seeley, JR, Gau, JM, Chronis-Tuscano, A, et al. 2014, 'Longitudinal associations between ADHD symptoms and depressive symptoms across adolescence', *Journal of Youth & Adolescence*, vol. 30, no. 6, pp. 546–53.
4. Jarrett, MA & Ollendick, TH 2008, 'A conceptual review of comorbidity in children with attention-deficit/hyperactivity disorder and anxiety', *Clinical Psychology Review*, vol. 28, no. 7, pp. 1266–80.
5. Csecs, JLL, Iodice, V, Rae, CL, Brooke, A, Simmons, R, Quadt, L, et al. 2022, 'Joint hypermobility links neurodivergence to dysautonomia and pain', *Psychological Therapy & Psychosomatics*, vol. 12.
6. Sigra, S, Hesselmark, E, Bejerot, S 2018, 'Treatment of PANDAS and PANS: a systematic review', *Neuroscience Biobehaviour Review*, vol. 86, pp. 51–65.

Chapter 4

1. Castellanos, FX & Proal, E 2012, 'Large-scale brain systems in ADHD: beyond the prefrontal–striatal model', *Trends in Cognitive Sciences*, vol. 16, no. 1, pp. 17–26.
2. Faraone, SV & Larsson, H 2019, 'Genetics of attention deficit hyperactivity disorder', *Molecular Psychiatry*, vol. 24, no. 4, pp. 562–75.
3. Rucklidge, JJ & Johnstone, J 2010, 'Nutritional supplements reduce aggression in children with attention-deficit/hyperactivity disorder (ADHD): a randomized controlled trial', *Journal of Child Psychology & Psychiatry*, vol. 51, no. 3, pp. 276–284.
4. Kara, T, Önalan, E, Şen, H, et al. 2020, 'Comparison of the fecal microbiota of children with ADHD and healthy controls', *The Turkish Journal of Pediatrics*, vol. 62, no. 5, pp. 771–9.
5. Cortese, S, Faraone, SV, Konofal, E & Lecendreux, M 2009, 'Sleep in children with attention-deficit/hyperactivity disorder: meta-analysis of subjective and objective studies', *Journal of the American Academy of Child and Adolescent Psychiatry*, vol. 48, no. 9, pp. 894–908.
6. Hale, L, Berger, LM, LeBourgeois, MK & Brooks-Gunn, J 2011, 'Social and demographic predictors of preschoolers' bedtime routines', *Journal of Developmental & Behavioral Pediatrics*, vol. 32, no. 3, pp. 165–73.

Chapter 6

1. Langberg, JM, Epstein, JN, Urbanowicz, CM, Simon, JO, Graham, AJ 2008, 'Efficacy of an organization skills intervention to improve the academic functioning of students with attention-deficit/hyperactivity disorder', *School Psychology Quarterly*, vol. 23 no. 3 pp. 407–17.
2. DuPaul, GJ & Stoner, G 2014, *ADHD in the schools: Assessment and intervention strategies*, 3rd edn, The Guilford Press.

Chapter 7

1. Calderone, A, Latella, D, Impellizzeri, F, de Pasquale, P, Famà, F, Quartarone, A, et al. 2024, 'Neurobiological changes induced by mindfulness and meditation: a systematic review', *Biomedicines*, vol. 12, no. 11, p. 2613.
2. Baikie, KA 2005, 'Emotional and physical benefits of expressive writing', *Advances in Psychiatric Treatment*, vol. 11, no. 5, pp. 338–46.

3. Pennebaker, JW & Beall, SK 1986, 'Confronting a traumatic event: Toward an understanding of inhibition and disease', *Journal of Abnormal Psychology*, vol. 95, no. 3, pp. 274–81.

Chapter 8

1. Abhishek, F 2024, 'Dietary interventions and supplements for managing attention-deficit/hyperactivity disorder (ADHD): A systematic review of efficacy and recommendations', *Cureus*, vol. 16, no. 9, p. e69804.
2. Adams, JB, Audhya, T, McDonough-Means, S, Rubin, RA, Quig, D, Geis, E, et al. 2011, 'Nutritional and metabolic status of children with autism vs. neurotypical children, and the association with autism severity', *Nutrition & Metabolism*, col. 8, no. 34.
3. Meyer, H 2024, 'The potential impact of brain glucose levels on the manifestation of ADHD symptoms', The A.D.D. Resource Centre, https://www.addrc.org/the-potential-impact-of-brain-glucose-levels-on-the-manifestation-of-adhd-symptoms/
4. Zhou, F 2016, 'Dietary, nutrient patterns and blood essential elements in Chinese children with ADHD', *Nutrients*, vol. 8, no. 6, p. 352.
5. Bloch, MH & Qawasmi, A 2011, 'Omega-3 fatty acid supplementation for the treatment of children with attention-deficit/hyperactivity disorder symptomatology: systematic review and meta-analysis', *Neuropsychopharmacology*, vol. 36, no. 6, pp. 1587–95.
6. Konigs, A 2016, 'Critical appraisal of omega-3 fatty acids in attention-deficit/hyperactivity disorder treatment', *Neuropsychiatric Disease & Treatment*, vol. 12, pp. 1869–82.
7. Calder, P 2017, 'Omega-3 fatty acids and inflammatory processes: from molecules to man', *Biochemical Society Transactions*, vol. 45, no. 5, pp. 1105–15.
8. ADHD Evidence Project 2025, 'Meta-analysis reports mild association between junk food and ADHD in children and adolescents', ADHD Evidence Project, https://www.adhdevidence.org/blog/meta-analysis-reports-mild-association-between-junk-food-and-adhd-in-children-and-adolescents
9. Roberts, JR, Dawley, EH & Reigart, JR 2018, 'Children's low-level pesticide exposure and associations with autism and ADHD: a review', *Pediatric Research*, vol. 85, pp. 234–41.
10. Allen, DH, Van Nunen, S, Loblay, R, Clarke, L & Swain, A 1984, 'Adverse reactions to foods', *The Medical Journal of Australia*, vol. 141, no. SP5, pp. S38–42.
11. Konstantynowicz, J 2012, 'A potential pathogenic role of oxalate in autism', *European Journal of Paediatric Neurology*, vol. 16, no. 5, pp. 485–91.
12. Gaur, S 2022, 'The association between ADHD and celiac disease in children', *Children*, vol. 9, no. 6, p. 81.
13. McCann, D 2007, 'Food additives and hyperactive behaviour in 3-year-old and 8/9-year-old children in the community: a randomised, double-blinded, placebo-controlled trial', *The Lancet*, vol. 370, no. 9598, pp. 1560–7.
14. Pinto, S 2022, 'Eating patterns and dietary interventions in ADHD: a narrative review', *Nutrients*, vol. 14, no. 20.
15. Brenner, A 1977, 'A study of the efficacy of the Feingold diet on hyperkinetic children. Some favorable personal observations', *Clinical Pediatrics (Philadelphia)*, vol. 16, no. 7, pp. 652–6.

16. Schab, DW & Trinh, N-HT 2024, 'Do artificial food colors promote hyperactivity in children with hyperactive syndromes? A meta-analysis of double-blind placebo-controlled trials', *Journal of Developmental Behavioral Pediatrics*, vol. 35, no. 6, pp. 423–34.

17. Hontelez, S 2021, 'Correlation between brain function and ADHD symptom changes in children with ADHD following a few-foods diet: an open-label intervention trial', *Scientific Reports*, vol. 11, no. 22205.

18. Rios-Hernandez, A 2017, 'The Mediterranean diet and ADHD in children and adolescents', *Pediatrics*, vol. 139, no. 2, p. e20162027.

19. Rucklidge, JJ & Kaplan, BJ 2014, 'Broad-spectrum micronutrient treatment for attention-deficit/hyperactivity disorder: rationale and evidence to date', *CNS Drugs*, vol. 28, no. 9, pp. 775–85.

20. Camilleri, E 2024, 'A brief overview of the medicinal and nutraceutical importance of Inonotus obliquus (chaga) mushrooms', *Heliyon*, 2024, vol. 10, no. 15, p. e35638.

21. Van Paassen, J 2024, 'The cognitive-enhancing effects of lion's mane in a rodent model of attention-deficit hyperactivity disorder (ADHD): A research protocol', *Undergraduate Research in Natural and Clinical Science and Technology (URNCST) Journal*, vol. 8, no. 11, pp. 1–6.

22. Trebaticka, J 2006, 'Treatment of ADHD with French maritime pine bark extract, Pycnogenol', *European Child & Adolescent Psychiatry*, vol. 15, no. 6, pp. 329–35.

23. Baziar, S 2019, 'Crocus sativus L. versus Methylphenidate in treatment of children with attention-deficit/hyperactivity disorder: A randomized, double-blind pilot study', *Journal of Child & Adolescent Psychopharmacology*, vol. 9, no. 3.

24. McElhanon, BO, McCracken, C, Karpen, S, Sharp, WG, et al. 2014, 'Gastro-intestinal symptoms and autism spectrum disorder: A potential link', *Pediatrics*, vol. 133, no. 5, pp. 872–83.

25. Aarts, E, Ederveen, THA, Naaijen, JN, Zwiers, MP, Boekhorst, J, Timmerman, HM, et al. 2017, 'Gut microbiome in ADHD and its relation to neural reward anticipation', *PLoS One*, vol. 12, no. 9, p. e0183509.

26. Critchfield, JW, van Hemert, S, Ash, M, Mulder, L & Ashwood, P 2011, 'The potential role of probiotics in the management of childhood autism spectrum disorders, *Gastroenterology Research & Practice*, vol. 2011, p. 161358.

27. Bundgaard-Nielsen, C, Lauritsen, MB, Knudsen, JK, Rold, LS, Larsen, MH, Hindersson, P, et al. 2023, 'Children and adolescents with attention deficit hyperactivity disorder and autism spectrum disorder share distinct microbiota compositions', *Gut Microbes*, vol. 15, no. 1, p. 2211923.

28. Elmehy, DA, Elmansory, BM, Gamea, GA, Abdelhai, DI, Abd-Elsalam, SM, Salamah AM, et al. 2023, 'Parasitic infections as potential risk factors for attention deficit hyperactivity disorder (ADHD) in children', *Journal of Parasitic Diseases*, vol. 47, no. 1, pp. 82–92.

29. Wang, LJ, Li, S-C, Yeh, Y-M, Lee, S-Y, Kuo, H-C, Yang, C-Y 2023, 'Gut mycobiome dysbiosis and its impact on intestinal permeability in attention-deficit/hyperactivity disorder', *The Journal of Child Psychology & Psychiatry*, vol. 64, no. 9, pp. 1280–91.

30. Allahyari, P, Torki, SA, Kavkani, BA, Mahmoudi, Z, Sadat, M, Hoseini, M, et al. 2024, 'A systematic review of the beneficial effects of prebiotics, probiotics, and synbiotics on ADHD', *Neuropsychopharmacology Reports*, vol. 44, no. 2, pp. 300–7.

31. Gokcen, C, Kocak, N, Pekgor, A 2011, 'Methylenetetrahydrofolate reductase gene polymorphisms in children with attention deficit hyperactivity disorder', *International Journal of Medical Science*, vol. 8, no. 7, pp. 523–8.

32. Gu, Q, Liu, J, Zhang, X, Huang, A, Yu, X, Wu, K, et al. 2025, 'Association between heavy metals exposure and risk of attention deficit hyperactivity disorder (ADHD) in children: a systematic review and meta-analysis', *European Child & Adolescent Psychiatry*, vol. 34, no. 3, pp. 921–41.

Chapter 9

1. Scott, N, Blair, PS, Emond, AM, Fleming, PJ, Humphreys, JS, Henderson, J, et al. 2013, 'Sleep patterns in children with ADHD: a population-based cohort study from birth to 11 years', *Journal of Sleep Research*, vol. 22, no. 2m pp. 121–8.

2. Krause, AJ, Simon, EB, Mander, BA, Greer, SM, Saletin, JM, Goldstein-Piekarski, AN, et al. 2017, 'The sleep-deprived human brain', *Nature Reviews Neuroscience*, vol. 18, no. 7, pp. 404–18.

3. Beebe, DW 2011, 'Cognitive, behavioral, and functional consequences of inadequate sleep in children and adolescents', *Pediatric Clinics of North America*, vol. 58, no. 3, pp. 649–65.

4. Balbo, M, Leproult, R & Van Cauter, E 2010, 'Impact of sleep and its disturbances on hypothalamo-pituitary-adrenal axis activity', *International Journal of Endocrinology*, vol. 2010, p. 759234.

5. McCaffery, JM 2016, 'Partial sleep deprivation impacts impulsive action but not impulsive decision-making', *Physiology & Behaviour*, vol. 164, pp. 214–19.

6. Yoo, S-S, Gujar, N, Hu, P, Jolesz, FA & Walker, MP 2007, 'The human emotional brain without sleep—a prefrontal amygdala disconnect', *Current Biology*, vol. 17, no. 20, pp. R877–R878.

7. Goldstein, AN & Walker, MP 2014, 'The role of sleep in emotional brain function', *Annual Review of Clinical Psychology*, vol. 10. pp. 679–708.

8. Palmer, CA & Alfano, CA 2017, 'Sleep and emotion regulation: An organizing, integrative review', *Sleep Medicine Reviews*, vol. 31, pp. 6–16.

9. Goldstein, AN & Walker, MP 2017, 'The role of sleep in emotional brain function', *Annual Review of Clinical Psychology*, vol. 5, no. 1, pp. 1–17.

10. Kopasz, M, Loessl, B, Hornyak, M, Riemann, D, Nissen, C, Piosczyk, H & Voderholzer, U 2010, 'Sleep and memory in healthy children and adolescents—a critical review', *Sleep Medicine Reviews*, vol. 14, no. 3, pp. 167–77.

11. Ruby, NF, Brennan, TJ & Heller, HC 2008, 'Circadian rhythms and mood: Insights from animal models', *Current Opinion in Psychiatry*, vol. 21, no. 1, pp. 59–64.

12. Karatsoreos, IN, Bhagat, S, Bloss, EB, Morrison, JH & McEwen, BS 2011, 'Disruption of circadian clocks has ramifications for metabolism, brain, and behavior', *Proceedings of the National Academy of Sciences*, vol. 108, no. 4, pp. 1657–62.

13. Scott, AJ, Webb, TL, Martyn-St James, M, Rowse, G & Weich, S 2021, 'Improving sleep quality leads to better mental health: A meta-analysis of randomised controlled trials', *Sleep Medicine Reviews*, vol. 60, p. 101556.

14. Lovato, N & Gradisar, M 2014, 'A meta-analysis and model of the relationship between sleep and depression in adolescents: Recommendations for prevention and intervention', *Sleep Health*, vol. 1, no. 1, pp. 3–10.

15. Tsereteli, N, Vallat, R, Fernandez-Tajes, J, Delahanty, LM, Ordovas, JM, Drew, DA, et al. 2022, 'Impact of insufficient sleep on dysregulated blood glucose control under standardised meal conditions', *Diabetologia*, vol. 65, no. 2, pp. 356–65.

16. Van Cauter, E, Spiegel, K, Tasali, E & Leproult, R 2008, 'Metabolic consequences of sleep and sleep loss', *Sleep Medicine*, vol. 9, Suppl 1, pp. S23–S28.

17. Shentu, W, Kong, Q, Zhang, Y, Li, W, Chen, Q, Yan, S, et al. 2025, 'Functional abnormalities of the glymphatic system in cognitive disorders', *Neural Regeneration Research*, vol. 20, no. 12, pp. 3420–47.

18. Ma, J, Chen, M, Liu, GH, Gao, M, Chen, N-H, Toh, CH, et al. 2025, 'Effects of sleep on the glymphatic functioning and multimodal human brain network affecting memory in older adults', *Molecular Psychiatry*, vol. 30, pp. 1717–29.

19. Brown, TM, Brainard, GC, Cajochen, C, Czeisler, CA, Hanifin, JP, Lockley, SW, et al. 2022, 'Recommendations for daytime, evening, and nighttime indoor light exposure to best support physiology, sleep, and wakefulness in healthy adults', *PloS Biology*, vol. 20, no. 3, p. e3001571.

20. Gooley, JJ, Chamberlain, K, Smith, KA, Khalsa, SB, Rajaratnam, SM, Van Reen, E, et al. 2011, 'Exposure to room light before bedtime suppresses melatonin onset and shortens melatonin duration in humans', *Journal of Clinical Endocrinology & Metabolism*, vol. 96, no. 3, pp. E463–472.

21. Wehr, TA 1991, 'The durations of human melatonin secretion and sleep respond to changes in daylength (photoperiod)', *Journal of Clinical Endocrinology & Metabolism*, vol. 73, no. 6, pp. 1276–80.

22. Del Campo, N, Chamberlain, SR, Sahakian, BJ & Robbins, TW 2011, 'The roles of dopamine and noradrenaline in the pathophysiology and treatment of attention-deficit/hyperactivity disorder', *Biological Psychiatry*, vol. 69, no. 12, pp. e145–e157.

23. Hamblin, MR 2016, 'Mechanisms and applications of the anti-inflammatory effects of photobiomodulation', *AIMS Biophysics*, vol. 3, no. 3, pp. 337–61.

24. Berson, DM, Dunn, FA & Takao, M 2002, 'Phototransduction by retinal ganglion cells that set the circadian clock', *Science*, vol. 295, no. 5557, pp. 1070–3.

25. Halgamuge, MN 2013, 'Behavioral changes in honeybees vs. humans following low exposure to microwave radiation', *Electromagnetic Biology & Medicine*, vol. 32, no. 2, pp. 207–29.

26. Bortkiewicz, A 2019, 'Health effects of radiofrequency electromagnetic fields (RF EMF)', *Industrial Health*, vol. 57, no. 4, pp. 403–5.

27. Bijlsma, N, Conduit, R, Kennedy, G & Cohen, M 2024, 'Does radiofrequency radiation impact sleep? A double-blind, randomised, placebo-controlled, crossover pilot study', *Frontiers in Public Health*, vol. 12.

28. Ivanov, I, Miraglia, B, Prodanova, D & Newcorn, JH 2024, 'Sleep disordered breathing and risk for ADHD: Review of supportive evidence and proposed underlying mechanisms', *Journal of Attention Disorders*, vol. 28, no. 5, pp. 686–98.

Chapter 10

1. Chan, YS, Jang, JT & Ho, CS 2022, 'Effects of physical exercise on children with attention deficit hyperactivity disorder', *Biomedical Journal*, vol. 45, no. 2, pp. 265–70.

2. Ratey, JJ & Loehr, JE 2011, 'The positive impact of physical activity on cognition during adulthood: a review of underlying mechanisms, evidence and recommendations', *Reviews in the Neuroscience*, vol. 22, no. 2, pp. 171–85.

3. Sun, Q, Yu, M & Zhou, X 2022, 'Effects of physical exercise on attention deficit and other major symptoms in children with ADHD: A meta-analysis', *Psychiatry Research*, vol. 311, p. 114509.

4. Pontifex, MB, Saliba, BJ, Raine, LB, Picchietti, DL & Hillman, CH 2012, 'Exercise improves behavioral, neurocognitive, and scholastic performance in children with ADHD', *Journal of Pediatrics*, vol. 162, no. 3, pp. 543–51.

5. Hoza, B, Smith, AL, Shoulberg, EK & Linnea, K 2014, 'A randomized trial examining the effects of aerobic physical activity on attention-deficit/hyperactivity disorder symptoms in young children', *Journal of Abnormal Child Psychology*, vol. 43, pp. 655–67.

6. Cerillo-Urbina, A, Garcia-Hermoso, A, Sanchez-Lopes, M & Pardo-Guijarro, MJ 2014, 'The effects of physical exercise in children with attention deficit hyperactivity disorder: a systematic review and meta-analysis of randomized control trials: Exercise and attention deficit hyperactivity disorder', *Child Care Health & Development*, vol. 41, no. 6.

7. Engemann, K, Pedersen, CB, Arge, L & Tsirogiannis, C 2019, 'Residential green space in childhood is associated with lower risk of psychiatric disorders from adolescence into adulthood', *Proceedings of the National Academy of Sciences*, vol. 116, no. 11, p. 201807504.

8. Ratey, JJ & Loehr, JE 2011, 'The positive impact of physical activity on cognition during adulthood: a review of underlying mechanisms, evidence and recommendations', *Reviews in the Neurosciences*, vol. 22, no. 2, pp. 171–85.

9. Chan, YS, Jang, JT & Ho, CS 2021, 'Effects of physical exercise on children with attention deficit hyperactivity disorder', *Biomedical Journal*, vol. 45, no. 2, pp. 265–70.

10. Chang, YK, Liu, S, Yu, HH & Lee, YH 2012, 'Effect of acute exercise on executive function in children with attention deficit hyperactivity disorder', *Archives of Clinical Neuropsychology*, vol. 27, no. 2, pp. 225–37.

11. Hoza, B, Martin, CP, Pirog, A & Shoulberg, EK 2015, 'Using physical activity to manage ADHD symptoms: The state of the evidence', *Current Psychiatry Reports*, vol. 18, no. 12, p. 113.

12. Chaddock, L, Erickson, KI, Prakash, RS, Kim, JS, Voss, MW, VanPatter, M, et al. 2010, 'A neuroimaging investigation of the association between aerobic fitness, hippocampal volume, and memory performance in preadolescent children', *Brain Research*, vol. 1358, pp. 172–83.

13. Larun, L, Nordheim, LV, Ekeland, E, Hagen, KB & Heian, F 2006, 'Exercise in prevention and treatment of anxiety and depression among children and young people', *Cochrane Database of Systematic Reviews*, vol. 3, p. CD004691.

14. Ekeland, E, Heian, F, Hagen, KB, Abbott, J & Nordheim, L 2004, 'Exercise to improve self-esteem in children and young people', *Cochrane Database of Systematic Reviews*, vol. 2004, no. 1, p. CD003683.

15. Kadri, A, Slimani, M, Bragazzi, NL, Tod, D & Azaiez, F 2019, 'Effect of Taekwondo practice on cognitive function in adolescents with attention deficit hyperactivity disorder', *International Journal of Research in Public Health*, vol. 16, no. 2, p. 204.

16. Feng, L, Ren, Y, Cheng, J & Wang, Y 2021, 'Balance training as an adjunct to methylphenidate: A randomized controlled pilot study of behavioral improvement among children with ADHD in China', *Frontiers in Psychiatry*, vol. 11, p. 552174.

Chapter 12

1. Orth, U & Robins, RW 2014, 'The development of self-esteem', *Current Directions in Psychological Science*, vol. 23, no. 5, pp. 381–7.

2. Sowislo, JF & Orth, U 2013, 'Does low self-esteem predict depression and anxiety? A meta-analysis of longitudinal studies' *Psychological Bulletin*, vol. 139, no. 1, pp. 213–40.

3. Mann, M, Hosman, CM, Schaalma, HP & de Vries, NK 2004, 'Self-esteem in a broad-spectrum approach for mental health promotion', *Health Education Research*, vol. 19, no. 4, pp. 357–72.

4. Barkley, RA 2013, *Taking Charge of ADHD: The complete authoritative guide for parents*, Guilford Press.

5. ibid.

6. Shaw, P 2007, 'Attention-deficit/hyperactivity disorder is characterized by a delay in cortical maturation', *Proceedings of the National Academy of Sciences (US)*, vol. 104, no. 49, pp. 19649–54.

7. ibid.

8. White, EM, DeBoer, MD & Scharf, RJ 2019, 'Associations between household chores and childhood self-competency', *Journal of Developmental & Behavioural Pediatrics*, vol. 40, no. 3, pp. 176–82.

9. Katzenmajer-Pump, L 2021, 'Low level of perfectionism as a possible risk factor for suicide in adolescents with attention-deficit/hyperactivity disorder', *Frontiers in Psychiatry*, vol. 12.

10. Eccles, JS & Barber, BL 1999, 'Student council, volunteering, basketball, or marching band: What kind of extracurricular involvement matters?', *Journal of Adolescent Research*, vol. 14, no. 1, pp. 10–43.

11. Deci, EL & Ryan, RM 2000, 'The "what" and "why" of goal pursuits: Human needs and the self-determination of behavior', *Psychological Inquiry*, vol. 11, no. 4, pp. 227–68.

Chapter 13

1. AADPA n.d., 'Australian evidence-based clinical practice guideline for attention deficit hyperactivity disorder (ADHD)', AADPA, https://adhdguideline.aadpa.com.au/

2. Mechler, K 2023, 'Evidence-based pharmacological treatment options for ADHD in children and adolescents', *Pharmacology & Therapuetics*, vol. 230, p. 107940. (https://pubmed.ncbi.nlm.nih.gov/34174276/)

3. Off-label means a doctor is prescribing a drug in a way that differs from its official approval, such as for a different age, condition or dosage, based on their clinical judgement and experience.

Chapter 14

1. Korpershoek, H, Canrinus, ET, Fokkens-Bruinsma & de Boer, H 2019, 'The relationships between school belonging and students' motivational, social-emotional, behavioural, and academic outcomes in secondary education: a meta-analytic review', *Research Papers in Education*, vol. 35, no. 6, pp. 641–80.
2. Allen, KA, Slaten, CD, Arslan, G, Roffey, S, Craig, H & Vella-Brodrick, DA 2021, 'School Belonging: The importance of student and teacher relationships', In: Kern, ML, Wehmeyer, ML, eds, *The Palgrave Handbook of Positive Education*, Palgrave Macmillan.

Chapter 15

1. Dunbar, RM 2025, 'Why friendship and loneliness affect our health', *Annual New York Academy of Sciences*, vol. 1545, no. 1, pp. 52–65.

Chapter 16

1. Stiglic, N & Viner, RM 2019, 'Effects of screentime on the health and well-being of children and adolescents: a systematic review of reviews', *BMJ Open*, vol. 9, p. e023191.
2. Nikkelen, SW, Valkenburg, PM, Huizinga, M & Bushman, BJ 2014, 'Media use and ADHD-related behaviors in children and adolescents: A meta-analysis', *Developmental Psychology*, vol. 50, no. 9, pp. 2228–41.
3. Andreassen, CS, Billieux, J, Griffiths, MD, Kuss DJ, Demetrovics, Z, Mazzoni E, et al. 2016, 'The relationship between addictive use of social media and video games and symptoms of psychiatric disorders: A large-scale cross-sectional study', *Psychology of Addictive Behaviours*, vol. 30, no. 2, pp. 252–62.
4. Swing, EL, Gentile, DA, Anderson, CA & Walsh, DA 2010, 'Television and video game exposure and the development of attention problems', *Pediatrics*, vol. 126, no. 2, pp. 214–21.
5. Koepp, MJ, Gunn, RN, Lawrence, AD, Cunningham, VJ, Dagher, A, Jones, T, et al. 1998, 'Evidence for striatal dopamine release during a video game', *Nature*, vol. 393, no. 6682, pp. 266–8.
6. Lima Santos, JP, Soehner, AM, Biernesser, CL, Ladouceur, CD, Versace, A 2025, 'Role of sleep and white matter in the link between screen time and depression in childhood and early adolescence', *JAMA Pediatrics*, vol. 179, no. 9, pp. 1000–8.
7. Huang, C 2017, 'Time spent on social network sites and psychological well-being: a meta-analysis', *Cyberpsychology, Behaviour & Social Networking*, vol. 20, no. 6, pp. 346–54.
8. Magee, CA, Lee, JK & Vella, SA 2014, 'Bidirectional relationships between sleep duration and screen time in early childhood', *JAMA Pediatrics*, vol. 168, no. 5, pp. 465–70.
9. Ferrari, GLM, Pires, C, Sole, D, Matsudo, V, Katzmarzyk, PT & Fisberg, M 2019, 'Factors associated with objectively measured total sedentary time and screen time in children aged 9-11 years', *Journal of Pediatrics (Rio de Janeiro)*, vol. 95, no. 1, pp. 94–105.

10. Selak, MD, Merkaš, M & Žulec Ivanković, A 2025, 'Effects of parents' smartphone use on children's emotions, behavior, and subjective well-being', *European Journal of Investigation in Health, Psychology and Education*, vol. 15, no. 1, p. 8.

11. Hamm, K 2023, ' Study finds parents' phone use in front of their kids can harm emotional intelligence', *Science + Technology*, https://news.ucsb.edu/2023/020867/screen-time-concerns

12. Clark, L, 2023, 'Engineered highs: Reward variability and frequency as potential prerequisites of behavioural addiction', *Addictive Behaviours*, vol. 140, p. 107626.

13. The Social Dilemma n.d., Homepage, The Social Dilemma, https://thesocialdilemma.com/

14. Hong, SB, Zalesky, A, Cocchi, L, Fornito, A, Choi, EJ, Kim, HH, et al. 2013, 'Decreased functional brain connectivity in adolescents with internet addiction', *PLoS One*, vol. 8, no. 2, p. e57831.

15. Royal Holloway, University of London, n.d., 'Digital Citizenship, University of London, https://libguides.rhul.ac.uk/DigitalCitizenship

16. Council of Europe n.d., Digital citizenship education, Council of Europe, https://www.coe.int/en/web/education/digital-citizenship-education#{%22271421625%22:[0]

17. Royal Holloway, University of London, n.d., 'Embracing digital civility', University of London, https://libguides.rhul.ac.uk/ld.php?content_id=35147696

Chapter 20

1. Helmer, A 2024, 'Equine Assisted Occupational Therapy for Children with ADHD (Astride): Protocol development and preliminary study', *Clinical Neuropsychiatry*, vol. 21, no. 1, pp. 88–98.

2. Korrel, H, Mueller, KL, Silk, T, Anderson, V & Sciberras, E 2017, 'Research review: Language problems in children with attention-deficit hyperactivity disorder—a systematic meta-analytic review', *Journal of Child Psychology & Psychiatry*, vol. 58, no. 6, pp. 640–54.

3. Bromann Bukhave, E, Creek, J, Linstad, AK & Frandsen, TF 2025, 'The effects of crafts-based interventions on mental health and well-being: A systematic review', *Australian Occupational Therapy Journal*, vol. 72, no. 1, p. e70001.

4. Doffer, D, Dekkers, T, Hornstra, R, Van der Oord, S, Luman, M, Leijten, P, et al. 2022, 'Sustained improvements by behavioural parent training for children with attention-deficit/hyperactivity disorder: A meta-analysis into longer-term child and parental outcomes', PsyArXiv Preprints, https://osf.io/preprints/psyarxiv/cymva_v1.

5. van de Weijer-Bergsma, E, Formsma, AR, de Bruin, EI & Bogels, SM 2012, 'The effectiveness of mindfulness training on behavioral problems and attentional functioning in adolescents with ADHD', *Journal of Child & Family Studies*, vol. 21, no. 5, pp. 775–87.

Index